REVISITING WALDO'S
ADMINISTRATIVE STATE

Other Titles in the Series

REVISITING WALDO'S ADMINISTRATIVE STATE

Constancy and Change in Public Administration

DAVID H. ROSENBLOOM
and HOWARD E. McCURDY, *Editors*

GEORGETOWN UNIVERSITY PRESS
Washington, D.C.

As of January 1, 2007, 13-digit ISBN numbers will replace the current
10-digit system.
Paperback: 978-1-58901-093-2
Cloth: 978-1-58901-092-5

Georgetown University Press, Washington, D.C.

Library of Congress Cataloging-in-Publication Data

Revisiting Waldo's administrative state : constancy and
change in public administration / David H. Rosenbloom and
Howard E. McCurdy, editors.
    p. cm. — (Public management and change series)
  Includes bibliographical references and index.
  ISBN-13: 978-1-58901-092-5 (cloth : alk. paper)
  ISBN-10: 1-58901-092-2 (cloth : alk. paper)
  ISBN-13: 978-1-58901-093-2 (pbk. : alk. paper)
  ISBN-10: 1-58901-093-0 (pbk. : alk. paper)
1. Waldo, Dwight. Administrative state. 2. Public administration.
3. Organizational change—United States. 4. United States—
Politics and government. I. Rosenbloom, David H. II. McCurdy,
Howard E. III. Public management and change.
  JF1351.R4645 2006
  351.73—dc22   2005027245

This book is printed on acid-free paper meeting the requirements of
the American National Standard for Permanence in Paper for Printed
Library Materials.

13 12 11 10 09 08 07 06   9 8 7 6 5 4 3 2
First printing

Printed in the United States of America

Contents

List of Tables
and Figures

Tables

Figures

Preface

Dwight Waldo's *The Administrative State: A Study of the Political Theory of American Public Administration* (1948) established that public administrative theory is also unavoidably political theory. This insight—obvious to us now—fundamentally changed the study of public administration, presumably forever. Henceforth scholars would analyze the political dimensions of public administrative theories, practices, and reforms. Exploring the politics of administration remains a constant element in the field, even as public administrative theory and practices have changed dramatically. But what has remained constant and what has changed in the political theory of American public administration since *The Administrative State* first appeared? This is the question addressed by *Revisiting Waldo's Administrative State: Constancy and Change in Public Administration.* The editors and seven public administration scholars provide their collective answers with a particular focus on the philosophical, political, ideological, and constitutional underpinnings of the public administrative reform movement that began to sweep the United States in the 1990s.

Our collective effort was made easier by Waldo's updating of his book in 1984, which took the form of a fifty-six-page introduction preceding a reprinting of the 1948 text (Dwight Waldo, *The Administrative State: A Study of the Political Theory of American Public Administration*, 2nd ed. [New York: Holmes & Meier, 1984]). The first edition was issued by the Ronald Press of New York, 1948. All references in this volume are to the second edition unless otherwise noted; the text of the first edition appears essentially unchanged in the second edition, which remains in print. Following Waldo's subtitle, our book forms a study of the political theory of American public administration. While not diminishing the importance of traditional administrative concerns such as cost-effectiveness, the ensuing chapters address one of Waldo's "big questions"—the reconcilability of the U.S. political and administrative systems.

Revisiting Waldo's Administrative State: Constancy and Change in Public Administration contains eleven chapters. They follow the structure of Waldo's first and second editions. The introduction summarizes Waldo's book and explains why *The Administrative State* became so influential and one of the most widely read books in the field. The next two chapters deal with the material and ideological background of modern public administration, a subject that formed the focus of part I of Waldo's original work. These are followed by three chapters covering what Waldo in part II of his book characterized as "problems of political philosophy." The titles of these chapters parallel those used by Waldo. Next are four chapters that closely analyze particular challenges inherent in contemporary administrative reform: understanding the "thinning" or hollowing of administrative institutions; securing human capital for administrative institutions, in this case maintaining the U.S. all-volunteer army; managing the complex relations among public agencies and the private organizations on which public administrators depend for the performance of government work; and developing the capacity to deal with "wicked" policy problems having both ominous consequences and no apparent civilized solutions. These chapters parallel part III of Waldo's book, which critiques special problems arising from the manner in which the then-dominant approaches to public administrative theory treated principles, organization, science, and administrative values. The final chapter shares its title with Waldo's conclusion, "Notes on the Present Tendencies." It weaves together the book's main ideas in assessing the forces shaping the future directions of public administrative thought.

During a lunch at a professional meeting of the National Academy of Public Administration in the early 1990s, one of this book's editors (Rosenbloom) asked Waldo (essentially), "*The Administrative State* was such a devastating attack on the mainstream of the field. How did people treat you when you came to professional meetings like this after the book first appeared?" Waldo replied (exactly), "Nobody spoke to me before 1953." He was serious. Eventually, of course, almost everybody in the field wanted to talk to him.

The editors and authors of this book hope readers will talk to them. Our collective purpose is to advance public administrative thought by gaining a better understanding of public administration's big ideas and questions, how they come to the fore, and what their impact on further theoretical development and practice may be. We share Waldo's belief that public administration needs to be well understood because it plays such a major role in the future of civilization.

Acknowledgments

Revisiting Waldo's Administrative State grew out of a symposium on "The Administrative State Reconsidered," hosted by American University's School of Public Affairs in 2003 to honor the fifty-fifth anniversary of Dwight Waldo's classic work. The symposium could not have been held without the enthusiasm and support of American University's provost at the time, Cornelius Kerwin, and the dean of the School of Public Affairs, William LeoGrande. We thank them for making the entire endeavor possible and contributing greatly to its overall quality. We also thank the people who joined us as authors of this book, John Cadigan, Robert Durant, Patricia Ingraham, Donald Kettl, Norma Riccucci, Barbara Romzek, and Larry Terry, for their participation in the symposium and willingness to revise and carefully craft their papers into the following chapters. We are grateful to everyone else who attended and participated in the symposium, though they are too numerous to name here. Special thanks go to Kimberly Martin and other members of the school staff who completed the often invisible work that allowed the symposium to occur. Professor Suzanne Piotrowski of Rutgers University–Newark helped to keep things running smoothly and to facilitate valuable participation by the symposium's attendees. The book benefited substantially from the very helpful suggestions of anonymous readers for Georgetown University Press, as well as those of its public policy series editor, Professor Beryl Radin. The book is dedicated to the late Dwight Waldo, who made so many things possible for so many of us in the field of public administration.

I

Introduction:
Dwight Waldo's *The Administrative State*

DAVID H. ROSENBLOOM
and HOWARD E. McCURDY

The 2005 American Political Science Association national meeting in Washington, D.C., featured a debate pitting Dwight Waldo's *The Administrative State* against Herbert Simon's *Administrative Behavior*, with the protagonists for each having to argue that theirs was the best book on U.S. public administration written during the twentieth century. Even the protagonist for Simon submitted that Waldo's book had gained "iconic status."[1] Not bad for a book that started out as a 552-page political science dissertation at Yale University in 1942 under the title *Theoretical Aspects of the American Literature of Public Administration*. Subsequently condensed, it was published as *The Administrative State: A Study of the Political Theory of American Public Administration* in 1948. A second edition appeared in 1984. The text of the second volume remained identical to the original but was accompanied by Waldo's new 56-page introduction, which viewed the ideas presented in "retrospect and prospect."[2] The second edition remains in print and continues to influence the way people think and write about public administration.

THE RISE OF THE ADMINISTRATIVE STATE

What accounts for the longevity and impact of *The Administrative State*? Timing is one factor. The book helped mark the end of an intellectual movement that contributed substantially to the shape of U.S. federal administration in the 1930s and 1940s. Generally called the

period of public administration "orthodoxy," the leaders of that movement enjoyed sufficient legitimacy, respect, expertise, and influence to
be called upon to redesign the presidency and the executive branch in
1937.[3]

In this case, however, timing was not everything. The orthodoxy's
intellectual foundations had been seriously compromised prior to the
appearance of Waldo's book in 1948. In prior decades, proponents of
the "human relations approach" demonstrated that by failing to take
account of employees' humanity, the orthodoxy's mechanistic approach to the design of organizations and work processes did not yield
the highest levels of productivity.[4] In 1936, E. Pendleton Herring's
book on *Public Administration and the Public Interest* effectively demolished a major tenet of the orthodoxy—that public administration
could be wholly separate from politics, in the sense of both policy and
partisanship.[5] In 1946, Simon issued a devastating attack on the orthodoxy's claim that its prescriptions rested on scientific principles.[6]
Rather, Simon demonstrated, the principles were more like sets of contradictory proverbs. Others built on these criticisms, and it is safe to
say that by the early 1950s, the orthodoxy had lost virtually all of its
intellectual credibility.[7] This probably would have happened even in
the absence of Waldo's *The Administrative State.*

Waldo's critique of the orthodoxy went deeper than the others, to
the heart of what a field of inquiry such as public administration must
aspire to be. His analysis of orthodox writers yielded four main conclusions. First, notwithstanding the orthodoxy's claim to have discovered
neutral scientific principles for designing administrative structures, orthodox prescriptions contained a distinct political theory. *The Administrative State* delivered, as its subtitle read, "a study of the political
theory of American public administration." In 1948, the idea that public administrative doctrine was also political theory came as a revela-
tion. It opened up an entirely new way of looking at the study and
practice of public administration.

Second, Waldo convincingly argued that orthodox principles were a
product of material and ideological conditions rather than immutable
science. Regarding material conditions, the principles had developed
concurrent with the transformation of the United States from an agrar-
ian to an industrial society dominated by a business culture. The rise of
modern corporations, urbanization, specialization, and the national
experience with prosperity, depression, and wars contributed to the
orthodox worldview. Waldo listed "our constitutional system" among
the material conditions affecting the ways that administrative theorists
framed their thinking and prescriptions.[8] The obvious lesson is that as

material conditions change, including constitutional law, the principles of public administration will change as well. Again, this insight seems obvious today, but it was prescient in 1948, well before the United States became postindustrial and its public administration began to be "reinvented" in consonance.

Ideological conditions also framed the orthodox public administration movement. Waldo listed the mission of America to spread an idealized vision of democracy, the idea of a higher fundamental law, the doctrine of progress, faith in science, and the gospel of efficiency. The "dominant ideas" shaping orthodox public administration created conflicts that its leaders struggled to resolve.[9] Most challenging was the effort to blend democracy with progress and efficiency, and neutral science with the principles of a higher moral law. There is probably no better way to understand the conundrums the ideological framework presented to the orthodoxy than to quote Luther Gulick, a leading orthodox thinker in the 1930s. Gulick wrote, "We are in the end compelled to mitigate the pure concept of efficiency in the light of the value scale of politics and the social order. There are, for example, highly inefficient arrangements like citizen boards and small local governments which may be necessary in a democracy as educational devices." He went on to say, "It does not seem to the writer, however, that these interferences with efficiency in any way eliminate efficiency as the fundamental value upon which the science of administration may be erected." In Gulick's words, the ideological framework served "to condition and complicate, but not to change the single ultimate test of value in administration."[10]

Waldo's third main conclusion was perhaps the most damaging of all. The political theory embedded in orthodox administrative thinking was at odds with U.S. political culture and constitutional design. As just noted, democratic institutions and grassroots public participation in government were viewed as "interferences" with sound administration. In particular, the long-standing constitutional commitment to the separation of powers confounded orthodox principles. It interfered with the hierarchical unity of command necessary for efficiency and the clear lines of responsibility required for direct accountability. Separation of powers also created difficulties in maintaining a separation of administration from politics because Congress continued to exercise tremendous constitutional authority over the creation, organization, powers, processes, funding, staffing, and location of administrative agencies. In their ideal world, the proponents of orthodoxy would have centralized control of federal administration almost exclusively in the president and his closest aides.[11]

Finally, by unmasking the orthodoxy's nondemocratic, centralizing political theory, Waldo put the question of whether there could be a democratic theory of public administration squarely before the field. In terms of setting an intellectual agenda, this is the main contribution of *The Administrative State*. The rich literature on the relationship of bureaucracy and democracy, representative bureaucracy, participatory bureaucracy, grassroots administration, and related topics that developed after 1948 owes much of its intellectual origins to Waldo's work. It is reasonable to surmise that *The Administrative State* also had an impact on practice. By the 1950s, Waldo was widely recognized as a major public administration thinker. From the late 1960s, if not earlier, through the 1970s, he was generally considered the leading academic in the field. (Simon had turned his attention to artificial intelligence and other areas by the time he received his Nobel Prize in 1978.) By delegitimizing the orthodoxy—especially its preference for efficiency over democracy—Waldo gave academic credence to reforms promoting an infusion of democratic values and processes into actual public administration. Freedom of information, open meetings, public participation, and representative bureaucracy were not intended to make public administration more efficient in the orthodox sense but were adopted anyway.[12]

THE DESIGN OF *THE ADMINISTRATIVE STATE*

These four contributions are woven throughout *The Administrative State*. Waldo was a theorist, and his writing was sometimes elliptical. He preferred to lay out all of his arguments and points rather than hammer them home; it is therefore helpful to present an overall summary of the structure and contents of Waldo's book.

Part I of the original edition deals with the rise of public administration. Chapter 1 explains how "the material and ideological background" conditioned the development of the orthodox movement and its core ideas. Chapter 2 deepens the analysis by taking "a closer view [of] the movements, the men and the motifs." Here Waldo notes that the "public administration movement" was well defined by "a core of consistency, of assumptions, of motives, of logic" that gave it a distinctive "ethos."[13] It becomes clear that the term "administrative state" carries a specific normative connotation. It represents the triumph of the progressive movement's ideal of a planned and administered society making heavy use of business methods. Unlike "bureaucracy," the term was not pejorative, though some groups, such as taxpayer organizations, may have favored a smaller, less expensive government. Bureaucracy was fair game for criticism, but the administrative state itself was viewed as a progressive development.

Chapter 3 addresses "scientific management and public administration." The scientific management movement had appeared at the beginning of the twentieth century largely through studies of American factory work. Its leading proponent was Frederick Taylor, whose famous *Principles of Scientific Management* was published in 1911.[14] Waldo notes that the scientific management movement developed separately from public administration but that in "some areas" the two had become "overlapping or indistinguishable."[15] The chapter looks broadly at the role "positivism" plays in the cognitive approaches of scientific management and public management. Waldo notes the manner in which scientific management had made experts in public administration more self-consciously scientific. Among the consequences were a transition in personnel administration from emphasizing "equality" and "moral fitness" to focusing on scientifically determining the "one best way" and "one best man" to perform jobs.[16] Public administration also developed a preference for hierarchical centralization.

By the end of part I, Waldo leaves no doubt that the orthodoxy is value laden, not based on neutral principles, as its leaders claimed. In part II, he examines how the orthodoxy's values and theories bear on "five problems in political philosophy."[17] These are addressed under the following chapter titles: "The Good Life," "The Criteria of Action," "Who Should Rule?" "The Separation of Powers," and "Centralization versus Decentralization." Quoting their own words, Waldo demonstrates the manner in which orthodox writers had taken positions on (1) the purpose of the state (i.e., the good life), (2) the ways in which information should be gathered and decisions made, (3) the personal qualities and formal roles public administrators should have, (4) the distribution of powers within government, and (5) the advantages of centralization relative to decentralization.

Part II of *The Administrative State* changed the intellectual landscape of public administration, perhaps forever, in a number of ways. Most important, Waldo showed that the orthodoxy contained a distinct political philosophy. In addition, his analysis makes it very difficult to believe that any comprehensive theory or approach to public administration can avoid an embedded political philosophy. Finally, although there were inconsistencies and dissents among orthodox writers, Waldo illustrates that, on balance, the orthodoxy's political philosophy was incompatible with U.S. democratic constitutionalism. Stripped to its core, the administrative state promoted by the orthodoxy movement put "the democratic philosophy . . . in the travail of being 're-thought' to accommodate the concept of management and democratic institutions in the throes of change to accommodate the fact of management."[18]

The orthodoxy's "good life" was an idealized vision of a well-planned, industrial, urban society. Its criteria for formulating public policies and developing administrative methods were distinctly (though faultily) scientific. Believing that scientific methods would produce technically objective solutions to public problems, the orthodoxy insisted that government agencies be staffed with experts committed to objective standards. Mass democracy would be managed by administrative experts and through devices such as the election of representatives rather than directed through citizen participation. Noting the degree to which legislators remained preoccupied with political concerns, as well as the necessity for administrators to interpret statutes, the orthodoxy favored a very strong, centralized executive branch. In asserting that the federal executive branch was almost solely the domain of the president (i.e., the chief executive), the orthodoxy put itself at odds with the constitutional separation of powers and the nineteenth-century U.S. political tradition of legislative supremacy. Further, administration would be informed by business methods, even though business firms were not informed by constitutional values, procedures, and structure. Orthodox leaders were so sure that big government managed according to their principles would be safe for the "common man" that they did not even see a need to consult the public. "Democracy," Gulick explained, "is a way of government in which the common man is the final judge of what is good for him." In the very next sentence, however, Gulick arrogates that final judgment to orthodox administrative principles: "Efficiency is one of the things that is good for him because it makes life richer and safer."[19]

Orthodox thinkers promoting these preferences thought they were being utterly pragmatic, confining themselves entirely to the uncontroversial virtues of efficiency. Yet efficiency and the pragmatism from which it arises constitute a political philosophy in the sense that their advocates are forced to take positions on core issues of political theory. In Waldo's view, orthodox reformers were engaged in a form of political discourse using an idiom that suggested that they were not.

Part III, the final section of *The Administrative State*, contains insights on administrative issues current to that period. In it, Waldo critiques the orthodoxy's principles, theory of organization, putative scientific method, and understanding of the values of economy and efficiency. In chapter 9, he asks, "In what sense can principles of [orthodox] administration be said to 'exist,' be 'true' or 'valid'?" He concludes that these principles can claim neither the sanction of higher law nor that of scientific validity. To the extent that orthodox principles were based on "moral necessity," they were difficult to defend as universal and given for all time. As for science, "it must be reported," Waldo wrote, "that with few exceptions the notions of science and scientific method held by the [orthodox] writers are unable to withstand critical examination." Waldo concluded the chapter with a seemingly innocuous statement that put him at odds with a large number of his contemporaries, especially Simon, and future scholars of public administration: "Many administrative matters simply are not, by their nature, amenable to the methods of physical science."[20]

Chapter 10, on "Economy and Efficiency," presents a devastating critique of the orthodoxy's treatment of efficiency as a central value. Waldo claims that "the 'pure concept of efficiency,' proposed by Gulick as the basic 'good' of administrative study, is a *mirage.*" He asks, "Is not efficiency for efficiency's sake meaningless? *Is efficiency not necessarily measured in terms of other values?*" Confronting the entire orthodox tradition head on, Waldo asserts, "I hold that efficiency cannot *itself* be a value." "Things are not simply 'efficient' or 'inefficient,'" he insists. "They are efficient or inefficient for given purposes." Moreover, "efficiency for one purpose may mean inefficiency for another." This position necessarily also ignores or secularizes the "moral significance" that Protestants had vested in efficiency. "The tenet of efficiency is an article in the faith of 'muscular Christianity,'" Waldo correctly notes in observing the theological roots of modern capitalism and organization.[21]

As noted earlier, the orthodox movement was under substantial intellectual attack before the publication of *The Administrative State.* Waldo's final chapter, "Notes on the Present Tendencies," considers the intellectual developments and historical conditions challenging the orthodox tenets. He concluded that "the apparent likelihood of a disintegration of the old outlook and the synthesis of a new must be recognized."[22]

Waldo's conclusion was only partly correct. Orthodox public administration disintegrated as a movement and body of thought. Its elaborate principles have not occupied a central role in master of public administration programs since the 1950s. However, the orthodoxy contained commonsense notions that continue to inform much public administration practice. Neither did a new synthesis emerge, as Waldo suggested, although one may be slowly developing. The new public management (NPM) and reinventing government movements, which began in the 1980s and 1990s, show strong signs of forging a dominant paradigm around the premise that "the role of government is to steer, not to man the oars."[23] Accordingly, the chief function of public agencies is to coordinate the delivery of public services by other organizations rather than to provide them directly.

After the orthodoxy's fall, academic public administration became heterodox. It embraced case studies, behavioralism, democratic theory, best practices, phenomenology, and postmodernism, among other intellectual currents. In practice, U.S. public administration more self-consciously attended to democratic-constitutional values. Congress and the federal courts forced congressional supervision, transparency, representativeness, public participation, and the protection of individual constitutional rights into administrative practice.[24] Before the NPM and reinventing movements developed, the public administration that was taught and practiced could simply be called "postorthodox"— more of a reference to what is was not than to what it had become. Today, it would not be too much to call that phase "Waldonian," although "conventional public administration" would also be an apt term.

RECONSIDERING *THE ADMINISTRATIVE STATE*

Waldo considered much of the introduction to the second edition of *The Administrative State* to be a continuation of his "Notes on the Present Tendencies." The current volume is written in the same vein. Its chapters follow the pattern of *The Administrative State* and consider what has changed significantly and what has not in public administrative thought and practice. These chapters duplicate Waldo's analysis by examining the manner in which the theories and prescriptions of modern public administration address important issues of political philosophy. The chapters also examine the degree to which new preferences erode the capabilities of governmental institutions, itself a philosophic concern. The authors are particularly interested in the impact of recent NPM and reinventing government reforms, including the extent to which they may weaken public administration and produce "thin" administrative institutions in which public officials no longer possess the capacity to respond to the challenges of twenty-first-century public affairs.

Chapter 2, "The Material Background," picks up where Waldo began, with the transforming events promoting the current wave of administrative reform. Whereas earlier reformers were concerned with "hard" activities, such as building dams, bridges, and other infrastructure, contemporary reformers often confront "softer" and more elusive tasks, such as protecting the environment, public health, and workers' safety along with implementing a host of social programs and regulations. The changing mix of governmental activities has affected the tools utilized by reformers, who are now obliged to rely more on process alterations, such as privatization, than on traditional modifications in organizational structure and procedure. Hard activities are much more amenable to assessment using the efficiency criterion than are the softer ones, which require fairness, equity, trust, and other properties on which human relations depend. The latter properties, in turn, can be closely associated with political theory.

Administrative reform is frequently advanced as a matter of "good management." Yet in Waldo's analysis, reform also flows from differing conceptions of the role of the state in pursuing "the good life," that is, visions of the ideal civilization, its core values, and favored processes. Chapter 3, "The Cultural and Ideological Background," demonstrates the manner in which shifting preferences regarding the purpose of the state have given rise to different administrative processes. Whereas Waldo examined the early public administration movement alone, this chapter traces the evolution of political preferences and administrative arrangements throughout U.S. history beginning with concerns over national security and economic development and extending through the broadening of suffrage. The chapter suggests that the quest for universal principles and a value-neutral public administration constitute an ideology of pragmatism, seemingly neutral to its proponents but nonetheless in conflict with competing preferences.

Chapter 4, "The Criteria of Action," revisits public administration's approach to knowing and deciding. Both modern and traditional administrative prescriptions implicitly contain causal statements. A particular administrative reform (X) is designed to promote a desired outcome (Y). The process for knowing whether X will actually produce Y is of the utmost importance. Can public officials and the public trust the claims proffered by experts regarding the likely success of their prescriptions? Despite their general respect for scientific inquiry, advocates of administrative reform tend to derive principles from common experience rather than through systematic experimentation. Disparaging this tendency, Simon argued that no true science of administration could ever be derived from practice. Waldo concurrently observed that administrative choices were "suffused with questions of value."[25] As a consequence of what might be described as the preference for methodological pluralism, the most powerful administrative reforms of the past few decades have disparate and inherently contestable methodological roots. This further elevates the influence of values in designing and adopting reforms.

Chapter 5 returns to the matter of "Who Should Rule?" Like those reforms rising from the orthodox movement, contemporary proposals for administrative reform contain embedded images of the "good administrator." The orthodoxy could not succeed without politically neutral, expert public administrators. Waldo discredited the notion that putatively neutral expertise granted orthodox practitioners the right to rule. The NPM envisions a public administrative service in which administrators simultaneously pursue the conflicting goals of entrepreneurial leadership and continuing neutrality. Other trends further inflame and fracture expectations: disagreements about the proper scope of government, the belief that business executives know best how to run government, and the notion that public administrators should be considered "agents" subject to direction and regulation by politically appointed and elected officials. Unable to integrate these conflicting visions or sort them out by administrative rank and function, contemporary reformers look toward "performance" and the achievement of "results" as the chief criteria for legitimizing administrative decisions and actions.

Chapter 6, "The Separation of Powers," shows that contemporary reformers, like orthodox writers, are stymied by the chief characteristic of American constitutional government. Advocates of the orthodox point of view were never able to find a successful formula for blending what they consider the two functions of government—politics and administration—into the three-branch constitutional division of functions and authority. Theories and recommendations that would place the president solely in charge of the executive branch were anathema to members of Congress. Alternatively, prescriptions for congressional involvement in federal administrative matters foundered on the need to separate politics from administration. Orthodox writers did not envision an expansive role for the federal judiciary in administration, and for the most part, they paid limited attention to the courts.

Contemporary reformers face an even more difficult separation of powers problem because Congress and the federal courts now play much larger institutional roles in federal administration than they did during the orthodoxy's peak influence in the late 1930s. Administration cannot be insulated from legislative and judicial authority. In the Madisonian system, each branch is supposed to have a different vision of what constitutes appropriate administration, and today they do. Today's reformers, like the proponents of orthodox arrangements before them, face major challenges in developing substantial reforms that promote administrative effectiveness without detracting from the vibrancy of the separation of powers and other constitutional arrangements.

The next four chapters examine special issues associated with modern reform, as Waldo did in the final section of his book, which he titled "Some Fundamental Concepts: A Critique."[26] As part of the cross-national movement toward administrative reform, governments around the globe have sought to downsize, privatize, and contract out their work. This is a principal feature of steering rather than rowing. The desire of reformers to dismantle conventional administration in favor of executive empowerment and market-driven mechanisms arose from declining confidence in the capacity of government to carry out the purposes of the modern state. Chapter 7, "The Thinning of Administrative Institutions," argues that such dismantling leads to weaker rather than stronger administrative capacity. Administrative agencies and institutions undergo "thinning," which inevitably feeds the loss of confidence that first precipitated the reforms.

Thinning raises a problem that often afflicts reforms: unintended consequences. Reformers and scholars are often better at diagnosing administrative ills than at fully anticipating how prescriptions for redressing them will work in practice. Unintended consequences may be beneficial, neutral, or harmful. Their presence casts doubt upon reform diagnostics and prescriptions—and therefore the expertise of reformers. In terms of thinning, short-term cost-effectiveness weakens long-term capacity.

Concern over who should rule is strongly influenced by current efforts to make government agencies compete more fully in the marketplace. From a traditional point of view, working for government constitutes a public service for which the state need not provide market-based compensation. Modern reform efforts seek to reverse this approach, making public agencies compete with business firms and other nongovernmental organizations. "Competitive sourcing" requires public administrators to compete for the funding to deliver services as well as to secure the personnel who can accomplish their missions cost-effectively. Agencies that cannot compete effectively for human capital are likely to undergo thinning. As their capacity for performing government functions declines, the more they must outsource. Moreover, the competition for human capital may affect agencies' personnel systems and organizational cultures in unintended, perhaps unpredictable ways. A personnel system that is market driven, by definition, has to embrace what the market dictates.

Chapter 8, "Competition for Human Capital," further illuminates issues associated with who should rule, thinning, and unintended consequences. The U.S. experience with recruitment and retention of personnel for the all volunteer army, which is analyzed in chapter 8, shows how the competition for human capital can affect even hierarchical and relatively closed organizations with venerable institutionalized traditions. The military's efforts to recruit personnel for difficult, dangerous, and undercompensated work led to unforeseen changes in soldiers' seniority, motivation, commitment, and social needs. These changes in turn affect military culture and capacity. It is highly likely that competition for human capital by civilian agencies also has significant impacts on their organizational cultures and capabilities.

Waldo frequently referred to the contribution of business practices to orthodox thinking. Establishing appropriate relationships between business and government has been a central issue throughout the history of U.S. public administration. Ideas about these relationships are expressions of temporal preferences rather than reflections of any eternal truths. Contemporary reformers prefer that administrative agencies rely heavily on business for the conduct of governmental functions. Chapter 9, "Business and Government," analyzes the wide range of contracting and privatization practices currently in use in the United States and the issues surrounding them. It notes how enthusiasm for privatizing has accumulated more rapidly than practical understanding of its effects. A rather doctrinaire notion that relying on the private sector to deliver government services inevitably improves cost-effectiveness is giving way to a realization that privatization imposes administrative adjustments of an unforeseen nature.

Waldo showed how public administration doctrine arose from many currents and thoughts. How predicable is public administration's future? Chapter 10 examines the challenges likely to spur a new round of administrative change, especially "wicked" policy problems such as global warming and population aging. Experts cannot even agree on the facts affecting such problems, much less on how to proceed. Wicked policy problems require administrative approaches that reconceptualize purpose, reconnect with citizens, and redefine administrative rationality. These are traits not emphasized in orthodox and conventional administration and for which today's reformers offer paradoxical advice. Effecting such traits requires a high level of citizen trust that, in turn, necessitates administrative capacity building, transparency of processes, and cultural sensitivity. Yet contemporary reformers deemphasize and marginalize such requirements. By ignoring Waldo's advice to embed technical efficiency within a larger "framework of consciously held [democratic] values," modern reformers put the emerging "neo-administrative state" at risk relative to the wicked problems that will inevitably confront public officials.[27]

Contemporary public administrative thought and practice do not lend themselves to an encompassing synthesis or a single point of view. As an academic field, public administration is often said to be in crisis due to its intellectual, conceptual, and methodological heterodoxy. Stereotypes of bureaucracy notwithstanding, public administrative practices also vary a great deal. The concluding chapter, "Additional Notes on the Present Tendencies," highlights and weaves together key observations in this book, especially those likely to affect future practices and thought. Not surprisingly, the authors agree with Waldo's concluding thoughts that the enterprise of public administration remains daunting and that to succeed through each generation "administrative thought must establish a working relationship with every major province in the realm of human learning."[28] The future of civilization depends on that success.[29]

NOTES

1. See www.h-net.org/%7Epubadmin/newsletters/s05htm#editorial (accessed July 25, 2005). The original edition of *The Administrative State* appeared in 1948; Simon's book appeared the same year, although it carried a 1947 copyright. Dwight Waldo, *The Administrative State: A Study of the Political Theory of American Public Administration*, 2nd ed. (New York: Holmes & Meier, 1984); Herbert A. Simon, *Administrative Behavior: A Study of Decision-Making Processes in Administrative Organization* (New York: Macmillan, 1948).

2. Waldo, *Administrative State*, ix.

3. U.S. President's Committee on Administrative Management, *Report of the Committee with Studies of Administrative Management in the Federal Government* (Washington, DC: U.S. Government Printing Office, 1937).

4. See George Homans, "The Western Electric Researches," in *Readings on Modern Organization*, ed. Amitai Etzioni (Englewood Cliffs, NJ: Prentice Hall, 1969), 99–114.

5. E. Pendleton Herring, *Public Administration and the Public Interest* (New York: McGraw-Hill, 1936).

6. Herbert Simon, "The Proverbs of Administration," *Public Administration Review* 6 (Winter 1946): 53–67.

7. Especially important were Robert Dahl, "The Science of Public Administration: Three Problems," *Public Administration Review* (Winter 1947): 1–11; and Norton Long, "Power and Administration," *Public Administration Review* (Autumn 1949): 257–64.

8. Waldo, *Administrative State*, 11.

9. Ibid., 15.

10. Gulick quoted in ibid., 192.

11. This was the advice of the President's Committee on Administrative Management.

12. Chapters 7 and 11 of Waldo's summary reflections on public administration in *The Enterprise of Public Administration* (Novato, CA: Chandler & Sharp, 1980) indicate strong support for democratizing public administration.

13. Waldo, *Administrative State*, 24.

14. Frederick W. Taylor, *The Principles of Scientific Management* (1911; repr., New York: Harper & Row, 1967).

15. Waldo, *Administrative State*, 49.

16. Ibid., 58.

17. Ibid., 67.

18. Ibid., 99.

19. Luther Gulick, "Notes on the Theory of Organization," in *Papers on the Science of Administration*, repr. ed., ed. Luther Gulick and L. Urwick (New York: Augustus M. Kelley, 1969), 11.

20. Ibid., 155, 156, 168, 178.

21. Ibid., 187, 193 (emphasis ours).

22. Ibid., 202–3.

23. E. S. Savas, *Privatization: The Key to Better Government* (Chatham, NJ: Chatham House, 1987), 290.

24. David Rosenbloom, "Retrofitting the Administrative State to the Constitution: Congress and the Judiciary's Twentieth-Century Progress," *Public Administration Review* 60 (January/February 2000): 39–46.

25. Waldo, *Administrative State*, 171.

26. Ibid., 153.

27. Ibid., 194.

28. Ibid., 203.

29. Waldo, *Enterprise of Public Administration*, 189.

2

The Material Background

DONALD F. KETTL

It was the best of times, it was the worst of times, it was the age of wisdom, it was the age of foolishness, it was the epoch of belief, it was the epoch of incredulity, it was the season of Light, it was the season of Darkness, it was the spring of hope, it was the winter of despair, we had everything before us, we had nothing before us, we were all going direct to Heaven, we were all going direct the other way—in short, the period was so far like the present period, that some of its noisiest authorities insisted on its being received, for good or for evil, in the superlative degree of comparison only.

—Charles Dickens, *A Tale of Two Cities*

Dwight Waldo wrote *The Administrative State* at a unique Dickensian moment in American public administration. In many ways, it was the best of times. The book, a condensed version of his Yale doctoral dissertation in political theory, appeared in 1948, just as public administration reached its high-water mark. Its best minds had gone to Washington, D.C., to put their theory to work in winning the war. Waldo was one of them. In 1942, he had the chance to take a job teaching political theory at a top-rated university but decided against it. He explained, in the introduction to the 1984 edition of his book, that he had expected to be called up soon for military service, so he went to Washington to take an interim job in one of the new war agencies. The draft passed him over—in fact, he explains, he "was rejected on presentation"—and spent four years supporting the war effort as a public

15

administrator. That experience turned his head from political theory to public administration, but he always approached public administration as a political theorist. "Without the training in political theory I could not have filled the niche I found in public administration," he explained.[1]

The practical experience Waldo acquired during the war strongly influenced his subsequent work, including the labors that led to the publication of *The Administrative State* in 1948. It reinforced his belief, expressed in the opening chapter of the book, that the theories constituting American public administration had evolved from a particular set of "unique economic, social, governmental, and ideological facts." On the historical or material side, those included the closing of the frontier, the advent of specialization, the onset of urbanization, the continuation of the industrial revolution, the appearance of large corporations, and acceptance of what Waldo termed "our business civilization." Most important, the experience of World War II and the growth of the social welfare state (Waldo called it the "Great Society") had shaped administrative theory. "On the one hand the unreality or inconsequentiality of a substantial part of the prewar literature was made manifest; but on the other hand the importance of the enterprise of public administration, the need for more knowledge and greater mastery, were underscored."[2]

Waldo and his fellow Washington warriors emerged from their experience with an uncommon focus on the public interest and a renewed commitment to strengthening the ability of public administration to achieve it. They were confident of their ability to reshape government and improve its function, and from their confidence came President Truman's decision to enlist Herbert Hoover and his fellow commissioners in a blue-ribbon commission dedicated to make government more efficient. Never before had public administration risen to such a level of respect. Never was its work taken more seriously.

At the same time, however, it was the worst of times. A year after Waldo published his book, Norton Long famously aimed a powerful attack below public administration's waterline. Long argued that administration was far less about structure and process than about power: who has it and how it is used.[3] The shift embodied an important critique with which, in many ways, the field is still struggling. Herbert Simon added that decision making, not organizational structure, was the central problem of administration.[4] The shift from bureaucracy to power and decisions—from structure to people, how they accumulated power and how they used it—was a stunning strike on public administration and the ideas that had driven it for two generations. A year before Waldo's book appeared, Robert A. Dahl put the point even more bluntly. Public administration, he wrote, was not yet—and would never become—a genuine science.[5]

Waldo argued, loudly and strongly, that the field's critics were missing the point. He acknowledged the telling arguments that the critics made, and he certainly agreed that public administration had a long way to go in solving the problems that Long, Simon, Dahl, and others raised. But, he argued, even more fundamentally, that the problem involved far more about the nature of science than the problems with public administration. He saw science as a method. Indeed, he argued, "it is not 'scientific' to try to force upon a subject matter a method not suitable to it." Rather, "the nature of the subject matter must define the method. Many administrative matters simply are not, by their nature, amenable to the methods of physical science."[6] Waldo believed that the measured application of common sense, and a careful effort to derive broader propositions from the lessons we learn, could indeed advance our understanding of the field—and the field's ability to contribute to a better society.

If the battles over the field's core issues were fierce and contentious, two features did indeed make it the best of times. Even if they disagreed over the answers, the rival communities at least agreed on the basic questions. First, they agreed on the need to reconcile efficiency with democracy, on the relationship (if not the dichotomy) between politics and administration, on the need for more rigor in the field's approach to public affairs, and on the central importance of bureaucracy in a democracy. Second, they knew that there was a very strong chance that policymakers would pay attention to the answers of the public administration community. Not only did the Hoover Commission find many of its recommendations embraced by public officials, but the second Hoover Commission made broader proposals during the Eisenhower years, and "little Hoover commissions" sprang up around the country. The work was an enduring endorsement of the notion that bureaucracy and its study mattered—and that better bureaucracy could produce a more efficient and effective government.

People believed in government. They believed that bureaucracy was a crucial part of government. They believed that better bureaucracy could produce better government, and they believed that academic researchers could help produce better bureaucracy. Indeed, great thinkers such as Waldo saw a higher power in this mission. The enduring search for fundamental principles in public administration, he wrote, was grounded in "cosmic constitutionalism," flowing from the philosophies of St. Thomas Aquinas, Cicero, and Plato.[7] Waldo came to public administration through political theory, so higher philosophy soaked into his analysis far more than for most writers of his day. But it was impossible to escape the sense of mission that drove postwar public administration. It was indeed the best of times.

THE WORST OF TIMES

By contrast, public administrationists in the early twenty-first century found themselves in the worst of times. There was little agreement about the core questions and even less commitment to paying careful attention to the work of the public administration community. The field found itself fragmented among separate approaches that often communicated little, including public administration, bureaucracy, and public management. Public administration, which stood among the four fields at the founding of the American Political Science Association, found itself at the discipline's fringes. And when reformers sought a new effort to improve the efficiency and effectiveness of bureaucracy, they turned to *Reinventing Government*, written by journalist David Osborne and city manager Ted Gaebler.[8] The Clinton administration launched its own version of the Hoover Commission, the National Performance Review (NPR), which derived its work only slightly from academic research and not at all from public administration. One senior administration official, when asked which academics the NPR relied on for insights replied, "Well, really—none."[9]

For their part, most members of the public administration community rose up against the NPR. David H. Rosenbloom, then editor of *Public Administration Review*, advised reformers, "Don't forget the politics!"[10] Ronald C. Moe warned that the NPR threatened serious damage to American democracy because it sought to uproot administration's links to constitutional practice and administrative law.[11] H. George Frederickson contended that the NPR borrowed too heavily from private-sector reforms and that reformers forgot the *public* foundations of public administration.[12]

People continued to believe in the need for efficiency, but they believed less in government and its ability to achieve it. They increasingly believed that bureaucracy was an impediment to effective government, and many conservatives made the case against most government and its machinery. Public officials rarely looked to the public administration community for sustained analysis of public problems, and public administration rarely looked to God, Aquinas, Cicero, or Plato for guidance, as Waldo did. Meanwhile, new challenges from public policy schools arose. Leaders of those schools sought to push public administration aside as the dominant intellectual force in shaping public discourse about government and its programs. *Implementation*, the classic work by Jeffrey L. Pressman and Aaron Wildavsky, carried the subtitle that helped drive public administration from center stage, reading in part, "How Great Expectations in Washington Are Dashed in Oakland; Or, Why It's Amazing that Federal Programs Work At All."[13] It was hard to escape the sense that public administration—and the broader debate about the great ideas at the core of Waldo's *Administrative State*—had fallen on hard times. Waldo had seen it coming. He wrote that public administration was verging on going "too far in rejecting principles and embracing an uncritical empiricism," and questioned whether the search for "sophistication has become cynicism."[14] It was indeed the worst of times.

From a broader perspective, two larger material facts bridge the substantial gap between Waldo's hopefulness and the struggles of those studying the subject sixty years later. First, those people attentive to the work of government and its practitioners remain inveterate reformers. They rarely express content with government and its performance for long and, no matter how much they dislike government, they cannot do without it. Waldo reminds us that "from the time of the Civil War to the present there has been a 'reform' movement and a reform literature."[15] Second, at the core of this ongoing reform movement has been a constant effort to link, much better and far more effectively, the nature of governmental administration to the jobs government seeks to do. Waldo's impassioned argument that "the nature of the subject matter must define the method" reinforces this second point.

Together, the impetus for reform and the grounding of reform in context shaped some of Waldo's most important contributions to public administration. They also frame the continuing challenge of public administration. The field is about providing answers to the continuing challenge of solving the new demands for reform while remaining strongly rooted in the lasting principles of democratic government, the ideas of Aquinas, Cicero, and Plato. The field is about probing the paradox in the opening of *A Tale of Two Cities*—"we had everything before us, we had nothing before us, we were all going direct to Heaven, we were all going direct the other way"—improving the pursuit of the public interest and avoiding a descent in the other direction.

THE CONTEXT OF GOVERNMENT ACTION

Waldo's book appeared amid one of the most important transformations of American government and American public administration. How government did what it did—indeed, even *what* government did—fundamentally changed in the decades surrounding World War

II. Waldo charted the major developments in the first edition of his book and expanded that list in the second edition.

World War II and Reconstruction

The wartime experience made clear the inadequacy of "a substantial portion of the prewar literature"—the classical or orthodox approach to public administration.[16] At the same time, the arrival of the modern state created a need for doctrines that accounted for the presence of a large, permanent administrative apparatus.

Defense Policy and the Rise of Globalization

The United States found itself with a permanent military machine in a world swept by the end of colonial rule and the hopeful rise of the United Nations. At the core, Waldo saw these as problems of administration for which existing theory had few answers.

The Great Society

As the nation's ambitions grew, so too did the demand for skilled administrators. The social movements of the 1960s fueled innovation and enthusiasm and created a vast new realm for probing the workings of the administrative state.

Science and Technology

From the 1940s through the 1970s, Waldo observed, confidence in "the scientific-technical" grew. Waldo believed that the 1960s, marked by the landing of a man on the moon, marked the peak of the movement. On one hand, he was right. Technology became firmly rooted. On the other hand, he guessed wrong that the speed of advance had slowed. He could scarcely have imagined the implications of the information revolution and the way that information technology would shrink the world. Nor did he imagine the impact that both information technology and the rapid flow of information would transform public administration.

Downhill from Confidence and Affluence

Waldo did presciently capture the "events and conditions that created doubt and pessimism" in government during the postwar years.[17] U.S.

involvement in Vietnam fueled a sense of impotence and alienation. The Great Society promised more than it could deliver. Watergate dashed confidence in public life, and international affairs proved dramatically unstable. The "new initiatives and countermovements" that swept through society flowed through the field of public administration as well—in some cases pushing public administration aside to make room for new approaches such as policy analysis.[18]

In preparing the second edition of his work, Waldo worried a great deal about these changes and about how the academic world responded to them. As always, he fretted about the larger implications for the political theory and the pursuit of the public good:

> The implications of these developments for the political theory of a constitutional-democratic government are many. What is the status of the "truths" discovered by science-technology vis-à-vis the "truths" of constitutional principle or democratic will? Does the presumption/hypothesis that "management is management" wherever it exists deny a claim to government uniqueness: and if it does, does it matter? Do programs in policy analysis or "policy science" collide with constitutional-democratic principle, implying that "public servants" are really "public masters": making policy instead of executing it, even if "impartially" through their expertise and indirectly through their advice in "speaking truth to power"?[19]

Context matters, and context changed dramatically during the period between the commencement of Waldo's dissertation and the issuance of the second edition of his book in 1984. It shifted just as dramatically in the next twenty years. Consider two shifts in particular: the nature of government's tools and the nature of what government tried to do.

Changes in Government's Tools. World War II marked a turning point in the tools of government. Faced with the daunting challenge of arming the military to fight a two-front war, American governmental leaders dramatically increased defense spending. Even after accounting for wartime inflation, defense spending increased fifty-fold from 1940 to 1945. Government officials faced the test of figuring out how best to expand government spending so substantially. Should the government build its own weapons or rely on private contractors? For both policy and pragmatic reasons, the decision was to rely on contractors. It would simply have been impossible to gear up a government-based manufacturing system in time to fight the war. So government officials made the only reasonable choice: they expanded government programs by relying on nongovernmental partners. Everything from the construction of tanks to the development of the nuclear weapons program occurred through contractors. In some cases, the government built and owned the factories but hired contractors to run them.

For public administration, this proved a radical shift. Although traditional public administration held the pursuit of the public interest most dearly, its theoretical foundations grew out of the private sector's scientific management approach, especially the work of Frederick W. Taylor.[20] Classic administration theory was production oriented. It sought to determine how most efficiently to transform inputs into outputs. Public administration embraced this pursuit of efficiency. As Waldo wrote in the introduction to his second edition, "the problems and issues to which efficiency was addressed are with us still."[21] And central to the pursuit of efficiency was the puzzle of how best to structure organizations and their work flow.

The challenge behind the rush to produce war materiel rested within the realization that the actual work was being done outside of the government agencies that managed and paid for the programs. This provided the bright dawn of what various authors have called "government by proxy" and "indirect government"—the pursuit of public goals through nonpublic agencies.[22] Such proxy programs had been growing in importance for some time, but World War II marked a vast expansion of the use of such tools and the point beyond which there was no return. Government agencies structured to manage programs directly—to transform inputs such as money into outputs such as bridges and social payments—suddenly had to cope with the new challenge of managing *other* nongovernmental agencies that actually produced the outputs.

At the least, this was a *different* challenge from what government agencies traditionally had done. It required the sophisticated application of tools, such as contract management, to ensure that the government and its taxpayers got their money's worth. At the most, it was a significantly *harder* challenge, because government agencies were not organized to work indirectly. And it was a huge challenge for public administration, rooted as it was so deeply in the production approach of Taylorism. The organizational environment became more complex, the political stakeholders became more numerous, and the relationships (administrative and political) became more intricate. Public administration was already beset by analysts such as Herbert Simon, who argued that organizational structure was the wrong unit of analysis, and Robert Dahl, who argued that politics mattered more. The field's luminaries found themselves locked in fierce battle with these advocates. But all the while, termites were eating away at the strategic foundation on which, for three generations, the field had been built. Waldo sensed the slippage and reached into the even deeper concept of the public interest in an effort to right the field.

His *Administrative State* appeared at the precise moment that an "administrative state" emerged as a clear and permanent fixture in American politics. But the nature of that state—and the transformations that occurred in the decades after Waldo wrote his classic—posed huge challenges for which the field was ill prepared.

Changes in Government's Strategies. At the same time that government's tools changed, so too did its policy strategies. The government found itself transformed and invigorated by the needs of millions of returning soldiers and civilians leaving wartime factories. The GI Bill funded college tuitions and home mortgages; colleges swelled and housing developments expanded. Economic growth helped pay for new cars, which needed new roads. Government spending for these programs rose rapidly. But just as important, government's ambitions shifted dramatically.

In the 1960s, the balance of government shifted from "hard" to "soft" spending, especially at the federal level.[23] The urban renewal of the 1950s, dedicated to tearing down slums, changed to Model Cities, which focused on rebuilding the social fabric of urban neighborhoods. The federal government committed itself to ending poverty. It expanded Social Security and launched Medicare and Medicaid. It committed to a long-term program to clean the environment, and it launched a new phase of social regulation to make food and products safer. Put together, these new and expanded programs marked a dramatic shift in *what* government did, from a focus on building or delivering physical services (bridges, roads, dams, fire protection, parks) to a focus on providing softer, process-based, quality-of-life services (health care, environmental quality, reduction of poverty).

The shift was neither sudden nor complete. The federal government, of course, continued to pursue hard spending, especially through large military and space programs. The rise of soft programs was gradual, starting in the mid-1960s and expanding through the 1970s. But the impact over time was dramatic. As figure 2.1 shows, national defense—the prototypical hard policy—grew to almost 90 percent of all government spending at the end of World War II. (With demobilization, it dropped quickly but swelled again with the war in Korea.) But in the decades that followed, defense spending fell as a share of all federal outlays. More subtly, the "all other" category—traditional government programs

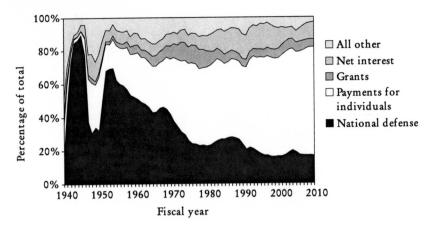

FIGURE 2.1 **Composition of Federal Outlays: 1940–2010**

Note: Data for fiscal years 2005–2010 are estimates.
Source: U.S. Office of Management and Budget, Budget of the United States Government, Fiscal Year 2006: Historical Tables (Washington: GPO, 2005), Table 6.1.

that, for the most part, were delivered directly by the federal government, shrank as well. Rising to replace these programs were grants to state and local governments and payments for individuals (notably Social Security, Medicare, and Medicaid). Payments to individuals doubled as a share of the federal budget in the second half of the twentieth century when government spending had returned to relatively stable patterns.

The dramatic shift from hard to soft programs, especially at the federal level, had equally dramatic implications for public administration. Soft policy, by its very nature, is harder to manage. There are beginnings but no ends; there can be progress, but rarely is there full success. Workers building a dam know when they start, when they finish, and whether it works. Roads have a start and a finish; they work or they do not. Engineers can test space satellites (even ones manufactured by contractors), they can watch them soar from launch pads, and they can assess whether their missions are successful. By contrast, good health care can improve and extend life, but it cannot delay death forever. Antipoverty programs can help individuals live a better life, but the gospels remind us, "The poor you will always have with you." The air can be cleaner, but it is impossible to remove all pollution, and new forms of pollution, like that from large hog and chicken farms, emerge.

In its first two hundred years, American governments accomplished a great deal. As the twentieth century ended, public officials committed the nation to even harder goals, where success was destined to be, at best, elusive. That demanded a change in the mindset of public administrators, who had to reach past the traditional approaches that worked well for hard policy to new strategies that could accommodate uncertain management technologies, vague and often conflicting goals, and the inevitability of less-than-full success that accompanied soft policies. For a field that for generations developed in pursuit of efficiency, this was a shocking change. In reviewing the legacy of the Great Depression and the twentieth century's two world wars, Waldo argued that efficiency had become one of the nation's defining values. "If democracy were to survive it had somehow to add efficiency to its ideals of liberty and equality. It had to bring efficiency out of factory, school, and home, where it was already a popular ideal, and make the nation as a whole an efficiency business."[24]

Efficiency, nonetheless, is very hard to attain in the context of soft programs. Yet the notion of borrowing lessons about efficiency from the private sector continued to drive public administration reform, to the horror of many public administrationists. Waldo sensed that efficiency was becoming an increasingly important virtue. The nation's expanding appetite for ambitious soft policy both underlined Waldo's argument and made it more difficult to achieve. The nation established more difficult goals and strove harder to achieve them. Public administration struggled to reform itself to produce the desired results. The rise of indirect tools and soft policy, however, led to recurring cycles of dissatisfaction with public administration, in theory and practice. These cycles in turn bred reform movements in government and new theoretical approaches in academia.

THE MOVEMENT TOWARD REFORM

Reform is rooted as deeply in administration as is the search for efficiency and leadership. The search for "good management" is eternal. But so too is the search for other, often competing values and objectives. While efficiency is an absolute, policymakers also constantly seek equality and liberty, flexibility and control, and these goals are rarely absolute. Every administrative strategy and tactic is the product of a delicate balance among such competing goals, and no balance ever remains stable for long. Because there is no stable equilibrium, and because policy goals themselves change, reform is a constant and inescapable force in the American administrative system. As Paul Light pointed out, reforms continually sweep the system like tides in the sea.[25] Waldo completed *The Administrative State* amid the establishment of the first Hoover Commission and its search for better government. Even if public administration found itself buffeted on all sides by doubt and skepticism, he argued that there was no doubt about one proposition: "that true democracy and efficiency are reconcilable."[26]

Even though there was no doubt in his mind that the two *could* be reconciled, there has been a huge, ongoing battle about how best to balance them. The twentieth century saw eleven major commissions dedicated to improving the efficiency and responsiveness of the executive branch. The commissions provide important indicators for two material facts: the reform issues that presidents have deemed most important and which strategies have seemed, at least to the commissioners, to offer the most promise. The batting average for the commissions as a whole are about the same as a good major league hitter: about one in three have had a significant impact. But beyond the question of impact are the deeper, enduring lessons that they teach as indicators of problems and favored solutions.

As the government's tools and strategies changed, so too did the focus of the reforms. Through the Nixon administration's Ash Council (1969–71), the reform commissions worked to propose top-down changes in government's organization and structure. These were traditional commissions, dedicated to classic principles, which viewed the organization and its framework as the basic building blocks of public administration. During the administration of President Jimmy Carter, with its focus on bottom-up, process-based efforts, that began to change. Some of the Carter reforms, such as the emphasis on zero-base budgeting, went nowhere. Others, such as civil service reform, created major alterations. Institutionally, the administration's major legacy was a traditional reorganization, which restructured existing agencies into new departments of energy and education. The Carter administrative reforms marked an important shift. They indicated the fact that shifting tools and more ambitious government strategies required more fundamental changes in how government worked—and that the more traditional focus on government agencies as the basic building blocks did not adequately address the major performance problems that were becoming increasingly apparent.

Those forces came into sharp focus with the Reagan administration's efforts to shrink the size of government and rely more on the private sector for the delivery of government services. The Grace Commission broke completely with the dominant Hoover Commission–style approach to reform. It did not ask how government could do its work better. Rather, it asked whether government should do some jobs at all. For those jobs that remained public functions, the commission pressed hard for contracting out the work and advanced other strategies for transferring operating responsibilities over to the private sector. The existing system of governmental administration,

TABLE 2.1
Major Efforts to Improve the Executive Branch, 1905–2000

Commission (date)	Improvement Efforts
Keep Commission (1905–9)	Personnel management, government contracting, information management
President's Commission on Economy and Efficiency (1910–1913)	The case for a national executive budget
Joint Committee on Reorganization (1921–24)	Methods of redistributing executive functions among the departments
President's Committee on Administrative Management (Brownlow Committee, 1936–37)	Recommended creation of the Executive Office of the President
First Hoover Commission (1947–49)	Comprehensive review of the organization and function of the executive branch; built on task force reports
Second Hoover Commission (1953–55)	Follow-up to first Hoover commission; focused more on policy problems than organizational structure
Study commissions on executive reorganization (1953–68)	Series of low-key reforms that produced quiet but important changes
Ash Council (1969–71)	Proposals for a fundamental restructuring of the executive branch, including merging existing departments into four new super-departments
Carter reorganization effort (1977–79)	Bottom-up, process-based effort to reorganize government; ended up mostly in failure; new cabinet departments created independently of effort Civil Service Reform Act (1978)
Grace Commission (1982–84)	Large-scale effort to determine how government could be operated for less money; heavy focus on privatization
National Performance Review (1993)	Effort to "reinvent" government to improve its performance
President's Management Agenda (2001)	Five-point agenda designed to create a results-oriented government

Source: Derived from Ronald C. Moe, *Reorganizing the Executive Branch in the Twentieth Century: Landmark Commissions,* report 92-293 GOV (Congressional Research Service, March 1992).

commission members concluded, produced such waste that the government could save $424 billion if the government adopted more efficient, market-oriented practices. Indeed, the commission found that citizens would be aghast if they knew that "one-third of all their taxes is consumed by waste and inefficiency in the Federal Government as we identified in our survey."[27]

Bill Clinton pushed aside the Grace Commission's work and launched the NPR, headed by Vice President Al Gore, to search for new ways of improving governmental efficiency. Like the Grace Commission, Gore's NPR believed that government was too inefficient. However, unlike the Grace Commission effort, which saw government as inherently less efficient than the private market, the NPR took a more positive approach to government. Relying heavily on Osborne and Gaebler's *Reinventing Government*, the NPR saw government's biggest problem as good people trapped in bad systems.[28] Their response to this problem was to flatten the bureaucracy, streamline its procedures, and give frontline workers more flexibility in doing what they knew had to be done.

Critics, especially within traditional public administration, roundly attacked the NPR because they believed it abandoned government's traditional commitment to the maintenance of democratic accountability over public bureaucracies in favor of private-sector management approaches. To be sure, both the NPR and *Reinventing Government* borrowed from some of the "liberation theology" movement sweeping private management: turn managers loose to do what they know how to do best. More centrally, however, the NPR grew from public-sector case studies in the Osborne and Gaebler book, as well as the experience of many frontline government workers. The roots of the NPR's arguments were far more public than private, and they grew from soil that said that bureaucrats, given the ability to do what most needed to be done, would pursue the public interest.

To be sure, the proposition was debatable. Indeed, in the early 1940s, Carl J. Friedrich and Herman Finer had a famous interchange on precisely this point. Like Osborne and Gaebler and the NPR, Friedrich argued that accountability had to grow from an administrator's innate integrity and that it therefore largely grew from professional training and practical experience.[29] Finer fiercely disagreed. He contended that accountability does—indeed, must—flow from control by outside forces with legal powers of oversight, such as Congress, the president, and the courts.[30] Neither academic experts nor practical politicians ever settled the Friedrich-Finer debate. Its conflicting principles have lived on and bookend recurring battles over how best to structure bureaucratic agents and their relationships to policymaking principals. The debate over the NPR simply reincarnated an old and unsettled—often unsettling—debate over how best to structure and reform government.

When George W. Bush took office, his administration predictably abolished the NPR and, just as predictably, launched its own reform effort. It moved away from the NPR's bottom-up approach toward a top-down, budget-driven strategy. Through a new "President's Management Agenda," the administration ordered agency managers to define the objectives of the programs they oversaw and to devise performance measures that would assess their success. The intent of the effort was similar to that underlying the Government Performance and Results Act (GPRA), passed just prior to the release of the NPR. Unlike GPRA, however, the Bush management initiative sought a direct link between policy decisions, budgetary allocations, and program results. And unlike the Grace Commission and the NPR, the Bush administration avoided recommendations by commission. Top officials in the president's Office of Management and Budget instead determined to create the input-outcome linkage through executive order and their leverage over the budget.

Neither the Grace Commission nor the NPR recommendations achieved much traction. Republicans continued to press for greater privatization of government programs through more aggressive contracting out, and the George W. Bush administration aggressively expanded that movement. The NPR produced significant procurement reforms and shrank the size of the federal work force. The broader objectives of each commission, however, proved far more difficult to pursue. The Bush administration did indeed claim at least modest success in connecting budget decisions with program results. But the reform proposals continued the same modest success that had marked previous reform efforts: a batting average of about .333—great for major league hitters but disappointing for government reformers.

Perhaps even more important was the lesson these efforts taught about the pursuit of government efficiency. All of these commissions, successful and unsuccessful alike, pursued efficiency as a central and inescapable goal of public programs. But as a century of reformers continued working on the problem, their strategies and tactics changed even as government's tools broadened and policy objectives became more ambitious. Beginning with the Grace Commission and continuing through the very different efforts of the NPR and the Bush management agenda, government reforms shifted their tack from restructuring public agencies to changing the processes through which they worked. The Grace Commission, the NPR, and the Bush management agenda pursued fundamentally different approaches. But they shared one important element: an avoidance of the traditional reform strategy of governmental reorganization. It was not that structure no longer mattered. Rather, it was that process—contracting out, empowering workers, measuring results—mattered more, at least to the reformers.

And process mattered more because policymakers and public managers alike worried far more about efficiency. They tried to accomplish far more difficult soft-policy goals using more indirect policy tools to do so. Moreover, taxpayers began insisting on more government efficiency. Beginning in the late 1970s with movements such as California's Proposition 13, taxpayers drew the line on higher taxes and bigger government. To be sure, the tax limitation movement was a bit disingenuous: taxpayers' taste for public services continued to increase even as their appetite for taxes diminished. But the rising pressures against taxes put policymakers and public administrators in a tight box of trying to do harder things, to do them through more indirect tools that challenged the administrative system, and to do them under severe resource constraints.

THE POSTMODERN ADMINISTRATIVE STATE
AND THE PUBLIC INTEREST

Although Waldo might have been surprised by the scale and scope of governmental change two generations after he first wrote his book, he surely recognized the core, fundamental challenges. Waldo was one of public administration's first and loudest voices making the case for a connection between democratic administration and the pursuit of efficiency. Because public administration in its infancy borrowed so heavily from Frederick Taylor and other private-sector thinkers, the field has always had a strong commitment to efficiency. Indeed, the creation of administrative principles in the 1930s, capped by the Brownlow Committee's recommendations in 1937 to consolidate federal agencies and strengthen the presidency, was a movement precisely devoted to making government more efficient.

For traditional public administration, there was never a strong tension between accountability and efficiency. More efficient bureaucracy was a matter of restructuring bureaucracy and improving its internal processes. Both structure and process relied on direct policy tools devoted to relatively hard policy goals. Administrators were thus directly accountable to their superiors and, ultimately, to policymakers, and their success in achieving hard policy objectives was relatively easy to measure. For latter-day public administration, by contrast, structure matters less. Indirect policy tools disrupt and complicate the chain of accountability from policymakers to service deliverers, and soft policy goals prove harder to measure. Reformers instinctively sensed this tension and began resorting to reforms based not on structure but on methods as varied as privatization, empowerment, and measurement of results.

Indeed, these changes mark the transformation from the modern to the postmodern administrative state, with government pursuing its policies through an ever-more-complex network of public, not-for-profit, and private providers. Crystal balls make dangerous toys, but even a casual look through a foggy ball suggests that, by the one hundredth anniversary of *The Administrative State* in 2048, these trends are likely to be even more firmly cemented. It is hard to imagine American government replacing its mixed system of publicly funded health care for the poor and elderly with a single government-provided health service or a retreat from government's reliance on private contractors for everything from space travel to social services.

If anything, the lines separating the public, not-for-profit, and private sectors are likely to become even more blurred. That in turn is likely to frame even tougher questions about how best to pursue efficient government in a democratic society. The structure and process of public institutions will probably still matter a great deal, but they are likely to provide decreasing opportunities for achieving democratic, efficient government. The postmodern administrative state is more likely to be shaped by information: its use as a strategic resource and its application as a tool for democratic accountability. Indeed, in a world where administrative systems are likely to be increasingly complex and where hierarchical controls provide weak leverage over programmatic outcomes, information—the process that can most easily leap bureaucratic walls and span a world of increasing globalization—is likely to be increasingly important in public administration. That, in turn, is likely to push administrators increasingly toward measurement of results as the most important tool for assessing accountability and efficiency.

A focus on results might provide accountability for outcomes, but it risks providing less leverage against the enduring and critical pursuit of accountability within governmental processes. Americans have long counted on government to provide services, but they have also counted on government to secure process goals such as equality of opportunity and fairness.[31] As information rises to become more important in ensuring accountability for results, *transparency* of information is likely to become far more important in ensuring accountability for process.

These trends pose stark challenges for public administration, whose leaders have never been comfortable venturing far from the field's roots in organizational structure. It is scarcely the case that structure will no longer matter, but it is not likely to matter as much, particularly as information rises to far greater importance. Mapping the course for public administration, in both theory and practice, will require energetic research and hard work. Along the way, Waldo offers an important guide. He warns in *The Administrative State* about the risks of "uncritical empiricism." Indeed, his warning suggests that too much focus on government's changes and challenges can risk dragging the field too far from enduring, critical questions. "Without faith or purpose," he warns, "individuals or societies stagnate."[32]

At the same time, Waldo's *Administrative State* teaches an even broader lesson. When pushed by practice into new territory, Waldo reached back to his roots in political theory. Indeed, the more he found himself and his field pressed by disconnects between events and theory, the more he sought first principles to guide his thinking. He acknowledged the challenge that, for example, the battle over the politics-administration dichotomy posed for the field in the late 1940s. In trying to resolve the dichotomy, he wrote at the end of his book, "if abandonment of the politics-administration formula is taken seriously, if the demands of present world civilization upon public administration are met, administrative thought must establish a working relationship with every major province in the realm of human learning."[33] Waldo sought solutions for new, difficult problems in old, lasting values. His book has its strongest, most important contribution not so much in telling today's readers the answers but, rather, by forcing them to think about the most important questions. *The Administrative State* thus provides an invaluable guide to a future postmodern administrative state, "so far like the present period," as Dickens put it. It provides as well a guide for understanding the challenges to which public administration must rise: ensuring the supremacy of the public interest in a world where government and its institutions will be but one among many players shaping public policy.

NOTES

1. Dwight Waldo, *The Administrative State: A Study of the Political Theory of American Public Administration*, 2nd ed. (New York: Holmes & Meier, 1984), lix, n. 6.

2. Ibid., xii, 7–14.

3. Norton Long, "Power and Administration," *Public Administration Review* 9 (Autumn 1949): 257–64.

4. Herbert Simon, *Administrative Behavior* (New York: Macmillan, 1947).

5. Robert Dahl, "The Science of Public Administration: Three Problems," *Public Administration Review* 7 (Winter 1947): 1–11.

6. Waldo, *Administrative State,* 178.

7. Ibid., 157.

8. David Osborne and Ted Gaebler, *Reinventing Government* (Reading, MA: Addison-Wesley, 1992).

9. Elaine Kamarck to Donald F. Kettl.

10. David H. Rosenbloom, "Editorial: Have an Administrative Rx? Don't Forget the Politics!" *Public Administration Review* 53 (November/December 1993): 503–7.

11. Ronald C. Moe, "Let's Rediscover Government, Not Reinvent It," *Government Executive* 25 (June 1993): 46–48; and Moe, "The 'Reinventing Government' Exercise: Misinterpreting the Problem, Misjudging the Consequences," *Public Administration Review* 54 (March/April 1994): 125–36.

12. H. George Frederickson, "Painting Bulls'-Eyes around Bullet Holes," *Governing* (October 1992): 13.

13. Jeffrey L. Pressman and Aaron Wildavsky, *Implementation* (Berkeley: University of California Press, 1973).

14. Waldo, *Administrative State,* 200.

15. Ibid., 28.

16. Ibid., xii.

17. Ibid., xiv.

18. Ibid., xv.

19. Ibid., xxi.

20. Frederick W. Taylor, *Principles of Scientific Management* (New York: Harper and Brothers, 1911). For an exploration of Taylor's management theories, see Robert Kanigel, *The One Best Way: Frederick Winslow Taylor and the Enigma of Efficiency* (New York: Viking, 1997).

21. Waldo, *Administrative State,* lii.

22. See Frederick C. Mosher, "The Changing Responsibilities and Tactics of the Federal Government," *Public Administration Review* 40 (November/December 1980): 541–48; Lester M. Salamon, "Rethinking Public Management: Third-Party Government and the Changing Forms of Government Action," *Public Policy* 29 (1981): 255–75; Lester M. Salamon, ed., *Beyond Privatization: The Tools of Governmental Action* (Washington, DC: Urban Institute, 1989); and Donald F. Kettl, *Government by Proxy: (Mis?)Managing Federal Programs* (Washington, DC: Congressional Quarterly Press, 1988). The best and most complete formulation of this approach is Lester M. Salamon, ed., *The Tools of Government: A Public Management Handbook for the Era of Third-Party Government* (New York: Oxford University Press, 2002).

23. This "hard" and "soft" distinction borrows from the notion of "hard" and "soft" foreign policy developed by Joseph S. Nye Jr., *The Paradox of*

American Power: Why the World's Only Superpower Can't Go It Alone (New York: Oxford University Press, 2003).

24. Waldo, *Administrative State*, 13.

25. Paul C. Light, *The Tides of Reform: Making Government Work, 1945–1995* (New Haven, CT: Yale University Press, 1997).

26. Waldo, *Administrative State*, 200.

27. President's Private Sector Survey on Cost Control, *Report to the President* (1984), www.uhuh.com/taxstuff/gracecom.htm (accessed October 15, 2003).

28. Osborne and Gaebler, *Reinventing Government*.

29. Carl J. Friedrich, "Public Policy and the Nature of Administrative Responsibility," in *Public Policy*, ed. Carl J. Friedrich and E. S. Mason (Cambridge, MA: Harvard University Press, 1940).

30. Herman Finer, "Administrative Responsibility in Democratic Government," *Public Administration Review* 1 (1941): 335–50.

31. For example, see Arthur Okun, *Equality and Efficiency: The Big Trade-off* (Washington, DC: Brookings Institution, 1975).

32. Waldo, *Administrative State*, 200.

33. Ibid., 203.

3

The Cultural and
Ideological Background

HOWARD E. McCURDY

A dministrative methods abound. Within countries around the world
and across time, the number of methods utilized to administer the
work of governments is astonishingly large. Bureaucracies, adhocracies,
merit systems, professional corps, prebends, patriarchies, government
corporations, government contracts, high reliability organizations,
nongovernmental organizations, privatized public services, administrative laws, and grants-in-aid expand a list of administrative methods
whose total possibly approaches the number of mammalian species in
the world.

What accounts for this bewildering array of methods, both contradictory and overlapping? During the first half of the twentieth
century, leading administrative scientists offered one suggestion. The
variation in administrative methods, they proposed, essentially rose
from ignorance. Lacking a deep understanding of administration, of-
ficeholders with little understanding of acceptable methods adopted
techniques based on their own personal experience and preferences.
Because experience and preferences differed, the number of methods
naturally proliferated.

The reformers who first made these observations believed that administrative methods could be freed from ignorance and personal experience and made scientific. As a consequence, they thought, well-trained
officials would be induced to adopt methods whose effectiveness had
been tested and verified, reducing the proliferation of methods in the
same manner that engineers who design airplanes are forced to obey the
laws of aerodynamics.

Yet there is a second explanation, one inspired by Dwight Waldo in his book *The Administrative State*. Waldo opened his classic work by reflecting upon the "material and ideological background" that underlay the rise of the administrative state. The implications of this starting point are profound. By beginning with the cultural setting of public administration, Waldo suggested its origins. The administrative state was not, in his view, the natural result of humans progressing up some predictable ladder of institutional development. Rather, it was a byproduct of a particular set of historical events and ideological preferences. While admitting that "the relationship of ideas to the existential world is a matter of profound scientific and philosophical dispute," he nonetheless pushed ahead with his assumption that the principles of public administration proclaimed by American reformers were profoundly affected by "the main currents of American thought."[1]

In the first chapter of his book, Waldo identified those currents. Commenting on "the ideological framework," Waldo suggested that American public administration was shaped by the commitment to democracy and the "mission of America" to spread it, the belief in a "higher law" or "fundamental moral order," acceptance of the "doctrine of progress," faith in science, and the gospel of efficiency.[2]

Taken from this perspective, administrative methods proliferate because ideologies proliferate and because the choice of methods can never be wholly separated from the ideological frameworks that people possess. Waldo demonstrated this proposition by revealing the normative preferences of twentieth-century reformers who claimed to be wholly objective in their selection of methods. Administrative methods were not objective, Waldo argued, but part of a much larger and longer debate over the nature of government. In this context, public administration could never be reduced to simple "facts," devoid of "values."

Waldo applied his analysis to the movement that produced scholarly works such as the *Papers on the Science of Administration* and advisory reports such as the *Report of the President's Committee on Administrative Management*.[3] The present chapter, and others in this volume, extend this analysis to movements before and beyond Waldo's writings. By extension, the analysis supports Waldo's view that administrative reforms reflect strong normative preferences.

As this chapter suggests, administrative methods differ because peoples' views of government differ. Their ideologies differ and the material backgrounds of their lives differ. Within a single society, moreover, the shaping factors shift with time. In a manner reminiscent of classical theories on the deterioration of governmental forms, both ideologies and administrative methods change because any single set contains weakness that other approaches mitigate.

A focus on purpose and constant readjustment is probably as close as scholars can come to a general theory of public administration. In that sense, administrative methods are relative, unfixed, ever changing. What is fixed, as Waldo noted, is not the methods that emerge, but their inevitable attachment to normative purposes. Administrative methods can only be understood through their association with purposes and preferences.

ETERNAL ISSUES, SHIFTING VALUES

Reformers in the first half of the twentieth century believed that they could avoid irresolvable issues of political philosophy by being pragmatic. They sought pragmatic solutions to practical problems by embracing the doctrine of efficiency. Luther Gulick called efficiency "axiom number one in the value scale of administration."[4] Efficiency provided a means for reformers to select administrative methods based solely on their capacity to achieve the objectives of the state. In the administrative sense, efficiency maximizes the achievement of objectives while minimizing the expenditure of money, people, and materiel.

Waldo characterized the reformer's use of efficiency as a "gospel," a system of beliefs that occupied a central place in the national culture. He ascribed its rise, in large part, to the public's preoccupation with industrialization in the first half of the twentieth century. Industrialization produced machines of ever-increasing power, such as railroad engines, airplanes, and cars. "Efficiency grew to be a national catchword in the Progressive Era as mechanization became the rule in American life," he wrote.[5] Strictly speaking, efficiency is a machine concept, referring to the work done or energy supplied relative to energy consumed. In the mechanical sense, friction accounts for the difference between energy-in and work-out. In the administrative realm, friction is viewed as waste.

Efficiency is a value bound in space and time, highly associated with the power-driven machine, economic rationality, and the business ethos that accompanied the Industrial Revolution. As Waldo noted, the word *efficiency* does not typically appear in the national discourse until the midpoint of the nineteenth century. Significantly, use of the term then declines within the rhetoric of recent administrative reform. David Osborne and Ted Gaebler do not place the term in the index to their seminal work, *Reinventing Government*. Instead, their purpose is creating what they call "entrepreneurial government," in which innovators acting on behalf of public purposes "use resources in new ways to maximize productivity and effectiveness." In establishing his support for the new public management, President William J. Clinton issued a statement committing his administration to changing "the culture of our national bureaucracy away from complacency and entitlement toward initiative and empowerment."[6] His statement began with a nod in the direction of cost cutting and efficiency, but ended with a commitment to the type of entrepreneurial leadership thought to guide business success in an era of rapidly changing technologies. Notions of entrepreneurship are largely incompatible with the mechanistic images of industrial organizations. Entrepreneurship is concerned with the creation of new business activities while the latter concentrates on improving the internal activities of existing workers. Given the emphasis upon entrepreneurship, discussions of management in the postindustrial era naturally moved away from efficiency toward innovation and initiative.

Dominant administrative values shift with place and time. "Every era," Waldo observed, "has a few words that epitomize its worldview." People in the Middle Ages were concerned with faith, grace, and salvation, and hence organized the construction of cathedrals. During the eighteenth century, philosophers emphasized natural rights and reason, and social movements, such as those that led to the American and French revolutions, occurred. During the nineteenth century, citizenship and suffrage expanded to include women, immigrants, and former slaves, and values such as representativeness and democracy dominated. The vocabulary of the Industrial Revolution stressed cause and effect, science, expertise, progress, and efficiency.[7] Innovation and entrepreneurship occupy a central place in the administrative language of the postindustrial era. Some people believe that an emphasis upon reliability will follow, as societies become more dependent on risky technologies.[8]

Administrative reformers writing in the first half of the twentieth century disparaged the proliferation of administrative values. They thought they were about to discover universal principles of good administration, an anticipation that arose from their belief that the quest for efficiency would provide a single standard against which administrative practices could be judged for all time. "In the science of administration, whether public or private, the basic 'good' is efficiency," Gulick wrote. Other values might impinge upon efficiency. For example, some people might value strong political parties. In the past, such preferences helped produce patronage and the spoils system. Gulick condemned the suggestion that alternative preferences might be allowed to influence public administration. "The continual intrusion of varying scales of value has served to hinder the development of all of the social sciences," he wrote. He suggested that all such values be treated as "environmental," meaning that they arise under special circumstances. The need for efficiency, on the other hand, was to be treated as universal. Students of administration might "explore relationships from the standpoint of efficiency within the framework provided." (He doubted that the spoils system was efficient for promoting strong political parties.) But more important, administrative scientists would consider "the effect of that framework upon efficiency itself."[9] (He knew that the spoils system destroyed efficiency in administration.)

Having settled upon a standardized value for the measurement of administration, early reformers announced that they were the first to deal with administrative practices in a systematic way. Writing in 1887, Woodrow Wilson suggested that people who had written about government before then had not much concerned themselves with administration. "The trouble in early times was almost altogether about the constitution of government . . . there was little or no trouble about administration . . . the functions of government were simple, because life itself was simple."[10]

Although Wilson's essay was not widely read at the time, it expressed a point of view repeated by people promoting the systematic study of public administration. People who had tinkered with administration in previous times had done so on the basis of their personal experimentation instead of what Wilson called "stable principle."[11] The systematic study of administration, the reformers promised, would change that. Gulick likened modern administrative studies to the process by which natural scientists had been able to achieve "remarkable control and great predictive accuracy" over natural phenomena. In the same way that chemistry had emerged from alchemy, Gulick expected a true science of administration to emerge from periods of mysticism and error. "At the present time, administration is more an art than a science; in fact there are those who assert dogmatically that it can never be anything else. They draw no hope from the fact that metallurgy, for example, was completely an art several centuries before it became primarily a science and commenced its great forward strides after generations of intermittent advance and decline."[12]

In a similar manner, Frederick Taylor characterized earlier efforts to understand administration as guided by ignorance and "rule of thumb." The result, he said, was "the great loss which the whole country is suffering through inefficiency in almost all of our daily acts." Like other reformers of that time, Taylor proposed to discover "clearly defined laws, rules, and principles" of management that could be used to improve productivity and motivate workers.[13]

By denigrating previous efforts to improve administration, people such as Wilson, Taylor, and Gulick sought to place management beyond the reach of preferences and philosophy. They sought to put it on firm scientific ground. "There are principles which can be arrived at inductively," wrote L. Urwick, an industrial engineer, "which should govern arrangements for human association of any kind." The principles could be examined "as a technical question, irrespective of the purpose of the enterprise . . . or any constitutional, political, or social theory underlying its creation." Urwick likened the work of people who ignored "sound principles" and fashioned organizations on the basis of individual preferences to the practice of "attempting to design an engine to accord with the whimsies of one's maiden aunt rather than with the laws of mechanical science."[14]

Administrative reformers such as Urwick, Taylor, Gulick, F. A. Cleveland, W. E. Mosher, J. M. Pfiffner, and J. M. Gaus embraced the scientific approach to administration. Yet the administrative principles they "discovered" were curiously unscientific. As Herbert Simon wrote in his critique of the administrative science movement, two "indispensable conditions" are necessary to complete a scientific study of administration. First, the desired effects of administration must be expressed in terms sufficiently concrete to allow their measurement. Second, the people studying the effects must utilize experimental controls that allow them to isolate the effects of administration from other factors impinging on the results.

"In the literature of administration," Simon wrote in 1946, "only a handful of research studies satisfy these fundamental conditions of methodology—and they are, for the most part, on the periphery of the problem of organization." As a consequence, reformers were obliged "to depend for their recommendations and conclusions upon *a priori* reasoning proceeding from 'principles of administration.'"[15] The principles were not scientifically derived; rather, they were the result of observing certain early twentieth-century organizations (armies and steel mills in particular), supplemented with deductive reasoning, in which certain principles produced others.

In spite of Urwick's promise to arrive at administrative principles inductively, most were discovered in a deductive fashion. The principle of unity of command, for example, was derived deductively from the scientifically established principle of specialization. Early studies of assembly-line methods established a substantial relationship between increased specialization and increased productivity—that much could be inductively observed. Managers who adopted specialized assembly-line methods incurred a penalty, however. Specialization overtly increased the need for higher levels of coordination. Since unity of command restricts the number of people to whom subordinates must report, it was thought to improve coordination. Through a process of deductive reasoning, administrative scientists hypothesized that unity of command would mitigate against the coordination problems accompanying the growth in specialization.

All of this seems logical in theory. The logic is deductive, however, and dangerous in practice. In deductive reasoning, conclusions are drawn from a set of premises that provide all of the information necessary to establish the conclusion. Scientific reasoning proceeds inductively in a much different way. An inductive conclusion is a proposition that contains more information than the experience upon which it is based. In a process of continual verification, the proposition is subjected to a series of tests that can disprove but never verify in an absolute sense. In the absence of scientific verification, deductive reasoning can be quite misleading.

Evidence that the principles might be deductively derived could be found in their vague and contradictory nature. Simon noted the tendency of administrative principles to appear in pairs, leading to the devastating observation that they resembled proverbs more than scientific laws. (Proverbs are formulated so as to confirm the predispositions of people seeking advice, no matter what those predispositions are. Hence, a person contemplating matrimony is warned to "look before you leap" while being told in a contrary fashion that "he who hesitates is lost.")

This does not imply that the principles of public administration early reformers proposed were wrong. Rather, it implies that they were not universal. The principles represented the preferences of people seeking to reform government in response to the demands of the Industrial Revolution and the desire to provide for the production of governmental services (from war making to social welfare) on a mass scale.

Even later reformers praised the workability of the bureaucratic model that emerged. Said Osborne and Gaebler, "During times of intense crisis—the Depression and two world wars—the bureaucratic model worked superbly." The model worked, they said, "not because it was efficient, but because it solved the basic problems people wanted solved." People wanted security, stability, fairness, and equity. They wanted highways, sewers, unemployment insurance, and public schools. They wanted to win wars whose outcome was determined as much through the movement of troops and material as through military tactics. The principles of administration produced "the basic, no-frills, one-size-fits-all services people needed and expected during the industrial era."[16]

THE PURPOSES OF GOVERNMENT

When one removes the foundation of efficiency upon which twentieth-century administrative reform was laid, the house of knowledge that rests upon that foundation becomes unstable. The choice of administrative methods begins to shift in response to changes in the outlook and values of people contemplating administrative reform. Such shifts are not wholly random. They tend to follow the purposes to which governmental reforms are put.

Governments pursue many purposes. Security of the citizenry, or public order, is a fundamental purpose of the state and one that defines the nature of governments worldwide. The use of government to promote liberty, or secure individual rights, is a Western tradition arising out of the Renaissance and the Age of Enlightenment. The desire to promote comfort or happiness motivates the functions of the modern welfare state. In more recent times, policy analysts have advanced the theory of public goods as a normative foundation for the effort to smooth the workings of markets.

Each of these purposes gives rise to a particular set of administrative practices. Contrary to the beliefs of twentieth-century reformers, the practices are not particularly new. Debates over their implementation can be traced back to the founding of the American republic.

Security

Preservation of security or public order is the most fundamental purpose governmental leaders can pursue. Max Weber defined government as a social institution that succeeds in acquiring a monopoly over the legitimate use of force within a given territory. The concept of legitimacy is probably unnecessary in this definition, because many heads of state throughout history have failed to seek the consent of ordinary people in order to rule. At the most fundamental level, a government consists of an organization capable of utilizing force and an apparatus for raising the revenue to support it.

The most basic administrative issue affecting the people who created the United States arose from the twin needs of security and finance. The founders were revolutionaries, a capital crime under British law. Five

TABLE 3.1

Relationship of Governmental Purpose to the Choice of Administrative Methods in the United States

Purpose of the State	Who Should Rule?	Separation of Powers	Role of Business	Centralization/ Decentralization	Big vs. Small Government
National security; economic development	Executive leadership	Energy in the executive	Government support for business and commerce	Favors centralization	Bigger than before
Protection of rights; extension of suffrage and citizenship	Representatives of society	Legislative supremacy	Business as a right of the people	Favors decentralization and local rule	Small, limited government
Industrial Revolution; social welfare state; national security	Politically neutral civil servants	Chief executive as general manager of government	Businesslike methods in public administration	Favors centralization	Big government
Supply and regulation of public goods	Entrepreneurs	Public/private partnerships	Business leaders as producers of public services	Decentralized and market-based	"Era of big government is over."

years after the signing of the Declaration of Independence, the American army was mired in New England under the command of George Washington. It consisted of some 4,500 soldiers, poorly outfitted and infrequently paid. Washington hoped to attack the British army stationed in New York City, well equipped and four times as large. The eventual colonial victory, which took place not in New York but in Virginia, was a consequence of superior management and contained lessons that strongly influenced the administrative views of the people who participated in the events.

The French government agreed to supply troops, of which six thousand had landed in Rhode Island the previous year, and a naval assault to assist the American cause. The French fleet under Admiral de Grass, however, was available for only two months, from mid-August until mid-October, and not in New York. Instead, de Grass proposed to enter Chesapeake Bay. In mid-August of 1781, the American commander began one of the most dramatic maneuvers in military history. Washington attempted to move six thousand American and French soldiers, undetected, to southeastern Virginia, where they would join the French fleet and five thousand revolutionaries from the American South under the marquis de Lafayette. Yet Washington did not have the funds or equipment needed to move the army, and American allies in the French government refused to advance any more.

The Continental Congress, meeting in the safe zone of Philadelphia, was controlled by farmers and merchants who distrusted the power of standing armies. In what historian Barbara Tuchman has characterized as "its abiding fear of centralized power," the Congress had refused for five years to appoint a single superintendent of finance to help fund the revolution. In 1781, the Congress relented and appointed Robert Morris of Maryland. Morris appealed to the states, cut government spending, and sought loans from Philadelphia bankers. In total, he raised sufficient funds, in Tuchman's words, to provide the dispirited Continental soldiers "with their first touch of hard cash since enlistment" and the funds necessary to move the army some five hundred miles from New England to southeastern Virginia, where with French help they defeated the British army under Lord Cornwallis at Yorktown.[17]

The administrative issues affecting the American republic during the Revolutionary War grew out of a clash between two great purposes of government. The clash occurred not because the delegates to the Continental Congress were less concerned with administrative efficiency than Washington and the leaders of the Continental army but because they were more concerned with the greater purpose of liberty. The British political scientist Samuel Finer once described governmental administration through what he characterized as an extraction-coercion cycle.[18] Most governments do not begin with a group of well-meaning citizens drafting a compact that explains the rights of individuals and the powers of government. Rather, they begin when a small group of individuals accumulate sufficient resources to subdue their rivals and then use the institutions that emerge, such as a revolutionary army or political party, to raise more funds. In that manner, the government grows, along with its control over the country and its ability to extract additional resources.

The people who created the American republic inherently feared such cycles of revenue taking and coercion. Republicans, as they were known, feared the accumulation of power that arose from what they viewed as the unchecked power of monarchies and the creation of standing armies. Federalists associated with George Washington and the continental army possessed a different set of concerns. They feared the accumulation of power in the hands of radical state legislatures and factions within the states. Shay's Rebellion in the winter of 1787 provided an illustration of the latter so vivid that it solidified support for the convening of the constitutional convention later that year. With a mob of debt-ridden farmers, Daniel Shay, a former captain in the colonial army, attempted to prevent the meeting of the county courts in western Massachusetts until a newly elected state legislature could be convened and pass a law relieving the farmers' debts.

The drafting of the American Declaration of Independence, with the prominence given to certain "unalienable rights," was a high achievement on behalf of a government devoted to promoting liberty. The U.S. Constitution, with its emphasis on "domestic Tranquility [and] common defence," served a different purpose. The clash between the two involved substantial administrative issues, a controversy well explored through Lynton Caldwell's famous interpretation of the administrative theories of Thomas Jefferson and Alexander Hamilton and the administrative histories of Leonard White.[19]

Arguing on behalf of the proposed U.S. Constitution, Hamilton criticized the "inefficiency" of the Articles of Confederation under which the Revolutionary War had been waged. "Dangerous ambition more often lurks behind the specious mask of zeal for the rights of the people," Hamilton observed in the first of the Federalist Papers, "than under the forbidden appearance of zeal for the firmness and efficiency of government."[20] Article 1, Section 8 of the constitution upon which Hamilton editorialized in the Federalist Papers lists the powers of the national government and by association the purposes of the view to which he subscribed. The list emphasizes the government's role in promoting economic development (issue debt, regulate trade, coin money, promote science) and securing the common defense (define piracy, declare war, raise armies, maintain a navy). Although that section describes the powers of Congress, it was to the nature of the executive that Hamilton most fervently wrote.

"Energy in the Executive is a leading character in the definition of good government," he wrote in Federalist Paper number 70. That energy was to be attained through the "decision, activity, secrecy, and dispatch [that] generally characterize the proceedings of one man."[21] On the question of who should rule, Hamilton favored "duration in office." Jefferson, by contrast, preferred a government in which officials held office for short periods of time out of a sense of civic duty (with little remuneration) so as to provide "a wise and necessary precaution against the degeneracy of the public servants." Whereas Hamilton was an advocate of a strong executive, Jefferson in principle favored the supremacy of the legislative branch. Hamilton favored centralization; Jefferson wrote in his autobiography that "it is not by the consolidation or concentration of powers, but by their distribution, that good government is effected."[22]

Anyone who like the young Woodrow Wilson believes that the founders of the American republic were preoccupied with constitutional issues to the detriment of administrative ones is not familiar with the details of the American founding. Conflict over the twin purposes of national security and liberty, with the former prevailing, characterized the waging of the American Revolution and the writing of the U.S. Constitution that followed.

Economic Development and Individual Liberty

With the replacement of the Federalist movement with the party of Jefferson and Jackson, the purpose of government shifted. The Federalist concern for security and promotion of commerce was replaced by issues arising from the expansion of territories, the abolition of slavery, the extension of citizenship, and the broadening of suffrage to include immigrants, freed slaves, and eventually women. With the change in purpose came a new set of administrative methods.

No administrative method had more impact than the creation of the spoils system. The Federalists—and many early Republicans—favored a civil service composed of talented, well-educated individuals. Herbert Kaufman has characterized this as an era of executive leadership.[23] The spoils system arose out of Jefferson's preference for simplicity in form and Jackson's desire for rotation in office. "I am for a government rigorously frugal and simple," Jefferson proclaimed and announced that the accounts of the national government "ought to be . . . as simple as those of a common farmer."[24] The principle of rotation, Jackson said in his first inaugural address, was necessary to correct those abuses "that have brought the patronage of the Federal Government into conflict with the freedom of elections . . . and have placed or continued power in unfaithful or incompetent hands."[25] Jackson's statement was a continuation of Jefferson's earlier complaint that vacancies in federal offices "by death are few; by resignation, none."[26] Conflicting political ideologies provided the motivation for inspecting the methods used to fill administrative offices.

Conflicting preferences for administrative arrangements also characterized the battle over the Bank of the United States, one of the most divisive political issues during the early nineteenth century. The original bank was chartered in 1791, part of Alexander Hamilton's plan to spur economic development in the United States. The bank provided many valuable administrative services. It offered a safe depository for public revenues, reduced the cost of transferring government monies, paid creditors and pensioners owed public funds, advanced monies to federal officials in anticipation of appropriations, and made loans to the government of the United States. It also performed important regulatory functions affecting banking practices in the states. When left to their own discretion, state bank officers issued what amounted to local currency—notes of indeterminate value and uncertain circulation that could be traded between financial institutions. The U.S. bank supplanted this practice by issuing notes backed by the federal government that possessed a common national value.

Farmers and merchants, especially those in the newly admitted and more western states, preferred to obtain credit on terms set by local banking institutions rather than accept conditions set by a central eastern bank. To the western farmers and merchants, the national bank represented centralized power, monopoly control, and the potential influence of eastern oligarchs and European investors. When Congress attempted to renew the bank charter in 1832, Andrew Jackson vetoed the bill. This was an unprecedented act. Most learned observers at that time believed that the president should exercise the veto only to protect the nation against unconstitutional acts, not as a way of expressing his disagreement with legislative policy.

Although Jackson admitted that "a bank of the United States is, in many respects, convenient for the Government," he believed banking to be a right of the people, like "farming, manufacturing, or any other occupation." The existing bank, he said in his veto message, was "subversive to the rights of the States, and dangerous to the liberties of the people." Its administrative practices tended to draw state banks into the sphere of national regulation instead of allowing them to serve local needs, a practice that Jackson characterized as "odious because it does not measure out equal justice to the high and the low, the rich and the poor." In Jackson's eyes, the national bank promoted centralized financial control, an approach that conflicted with his preference for decentralization, local preferences, and limited government.[27] As in earlier disputes, administrative methods and political preferences proved inseparable.

The Administrative State and the Ideology of Privatization

By the middle of the twentieth century, American reformers had run through three major approaches to public administration, corresponding closely to the three great purposes of government. The early Federalist emphasis upon security and economic development had produced a governmental apparatus larger and more centralized than its predecessor, with more "energy" in the executive branch and a devotion to the idea that government ought to be run by a corps of talented individuals. Both the Articles of Confederation under which the nation began and the republican reaction to Federalist rule favored the harmony implicit in a smaller and less centralized administration, legislative supremacy, and the patronage system. This corresponded to developments within the society as a whole that emphasized freedom from central control, the gradual expansion of suffrage, and the expansion of citizenship.

With the advent of the Industrial Revolution and the social welfare state, governmental administration shifted back toward a more executive-centered model. The shift occurred within industrializing nations worldwide. The resulting administrative reforms favored a large permanent bureaucracy, a general preference for centralization, and a politically neutral civil service. These were the conditions that created what came to be called the administrative state.

Reformers associated with the movement that produced the doctrines of the administrative state did not view the resulting arrangements as just another round in the preference cycle of pubic officials, but rather as an end point in the search for effective methods. Their devotion to efficiency as the ultimate purpose of administration, joined with what Waldo termed the "idea of progress," led many to view the principles as the perfection of administrative experimentation. As Waldo noted, students of administration "simply 'accepted' progress—its reality and desirability."[28] Progress is a biological concept, drawn from a frequent misinterpretation of the theory of evolution. In earth-bound biology, evolution has led from simpler to more complex life-forms. In the social realm, industrial economies and the bureaucracies that accompany them emerged from agricultural ones. The notion that industrialization and bureaucratization sit higher on the evolutionary scale is a normative judgment, however, that cannot be empirically sustained. It is the equivalent of suggesting that evolution exists for the purpose of creating human beings.[29]

The notion that the administrative arrangements to emerge from the Industrial Revolution represented the highest point on the scale of social organization was quickly demolished by an alternative point of view. The leading publications promoting the administrative science movement (Gulick and Urwick's *Papers on the Science of Administration* and the 1937 report of the Brownlow Committee) hardly had time to migrate to the used book shelf before dissenting views appeared. In 1940, the sociologist Robert Merton issued his classic essay on the shortcomings of bureaucracy (six years before the translation of Weber's famous essay on bureaucracy into English), and in 1937 the Brookings Institution issued its famous rebuttal to the Brownlow Committee report.[30]

The preferences that ultimately emerged from such dissents moved the administrative pendulum once more. Counteracting the trend toward administrative construction and expansion of the state, a number of political leaders announced that "the era of big government is over."[31] Newer calls for public servants to act as entrepreneurs contrasted sharply with the older commitment to restrain the politically neutral civil servant. The use of business firms to provide public services replaced the effort to make government more businesslike. The general predisposition in favor of executive control was balanced by the desire of legislators to oversee administrative process.

Not surprisingly, the shift in administrative methods was accompanied (and possibly encouraged) by a new perspective on the purpose of government. In a seminal 1954 article, the economist Paul Samuelson posed the question "Why should governments exist at all?" Avoiding conventional explanations, Samuelson observed that no decentralized pricing mechanisms (such as the market) could be used to determine the optimal level of goods characterized by collective consumption, repeating an earlier observation by Arthur Pigou that "certain specific acts of interference with normal economic processes" would be necessary to "make the national dividend a maximum."[32]

Significantly, Samuelson did not offer his insights as an empirical statement but rather as a normative observation about the ability of governments and markets to establish what another economist termed "mutually beneficial exchanges."[33] But the ideology of privatization, like the public administration movement that preceded it, was presented by its advocates as an empirical necessity. The tendency to convert preference statements into empirical necessities appears to be irresistible, even though changing preferences ultimately render such an insistence futile.

IMPLICATIONS: THE FELON AND THE BEAR

In his essay advocating the study of public administration, Woodrow Wilson wrote a famous statement in which he suggested how the search for effective administrative methods could be separated from the political preferences of public leaders. To make his point, he offered a parable. A sharpener of knives, he said, could improve his or her craft by observing the methods utilized by a person preparing a similar weapon for an awful crime. "If I see a murderous fellow sharpening a knife cleverly, I can borrow his way of sharpening the knife without borrowing his probable intention to commit murder with it."[34] By this statement, Wilson meant to suggest that administrative principles of universal benefit might be established, regardless of the type of regime for which they were invented. The belief in the existence of universal, objective principles of administration was an important component of the early public administration movement.

Not content to let the opportunity for drawing lessons from common experience slip away, Dwight Waldo offered another parable in *The Administrative State*. Waldo sought to make the point that administrative methods inevitably vary with the purposes of their creators. To demonstrate his point, he offered the parable of the bear. A rifle, he noted, was efficient for hunting a bear, but not for keeping it alive. "For the purpose of killing a bear . . . a large-bore rifle is more efficient than a bag of meal, but for the purpose of keeping a bear alive, the reverse is true." His observation produced a phrase that came to characterize his work: "efficiency *for what?*" In this sense, efficiency was not an end in itself but rather a concept "necessarily measured" in terms of the different values preferred by people operating in the public sphere.[35]

The choice of administrative methods, as this chapter has suggested, has varied not with the general intelligence of reformers but with shifting preferences concerning the purpose of government. Those shifts have followed cultural and ideological trends within the society at large. Yet the shifts have not been wholly random. In American public administration, for example, interest has shifted between centralization and decentralization, large government and small, and neutral civil servants and representative ones.

The tendency for one reform to follow another suggests an added dimension to this process. In his famous study of polities, the Greek historian Polybius proposed that each simple form of government contains a degenerate form. Thus monarchies through a process of gradual decline tend to degenerate into tyrannies. Aristocracies become oligarchies, and democracies descend into mob rule. This proposition was influential in molding the thoughts of the drafters of the U.S. Constitution, who sought to combine elements from each virtuous form as a means of checking the inherent weaknesses in all.

In a similar manner, simple administrative forms possess their own degenerative tendencies. Any single method carries the source of its own destruction. When Andrew Jackson, in his first inaugural address, proposed the practice of civil service rotation, he did so for a noble purpose. Yet within a half-century that principle of rotation had degenerated into a system of excessive political interference and spoils. The same could be said for the system of bureaucratic administration that replaced it. Bureaucrats were appointed for a noble cause, to restore impersonality to a government that had become too dependent upon favoritism and political rewards. Over time, however, the idea of experts in the bureaucracy acting impersonally came to be viewed as too elitist for the American polity.

From this perspective, the choice of administrative methods is not fated to change randomly but moves in response to political preferences and the excesses inherent in each administrative form. In a similar manner, the political preferences of public leaders may shift through cycles of attachment and excess. In discussing the vision of "the Good Life" that motivated the early public administration movement, Waldo noted the reformer's preference for features such as central planning and urbanization.[36] Those preferences suffered from their own excesses, however, ensuring that none would dominate the exercise of political power for all time. The result is likely to be a never-ending process of administrative reform, obdurately tied to a cycle of normative alternatives patterned on the purposes of the state.

NOTES

1. Dwight Waldo, *The Administrative State: A Study of the Political Theory of American Public Administration*, 2nd ed. (New York: Holmes & Meier, 1984), 14.

2. Ibid., 15–21.

3. Luther Gulick and L. Urwick, eds., *Papers on the Science of Administration*, repr. ed. (New York: Augustus M. Kelley, 1969); President's Committee

on Administrative Management, *Administrative Management in the Government of the United States* (Washington, DC: U.S. Government Printing Office, 1937).

4. Luther Gulick, "Science, Values and Public Administration," in *Papers on the Science of Administration*, ed. Gulick and Urwick, 192.

5. Waldo, *Administrative State*, 19.

6. Remarks by President Clinton Announcing the Initiative to Streamline Government, March 3, 1993, http://govinfo.library.unt.edu/npr/library/speeches/030393.html (accessed December 19, 2005); see also David Osborne and Ted Gaebler, *Reinventing Government: How the Entrepreneurial Spirit Is Transforming the Public Sector* (Reading, MA: Addison-Wesley, 1992), xix.

7. Waldo, *Administrative State*, 19.

8. Charles Perrow, *Normal Accidents: Living with High-Risk Technologies* (New York: Basic Books, 1984); Todd R. LaPorte and Paula M. Consolini, "Working in Practice but Not in Theory: Theoretical Challenges of 'High Reliability Organizations,'" *Journal of Public Administration Research and Theory* 1, no. 1 (1991): 19–47; Martin Landau and Donald Chisholm, "The Arrogance of Optimism: Notes on Failure-Avoidance Management," *Journal of Contingencies and Crises Management* 3 (June 1995): 67–80.

9. Gulick, "Science, Values and Public Administration," 192, 193.

10. Woodrow Wilson, "The Study of Administration," in *Classics of Public Administration*, 3rd ed., ed. Jay M. Shafritz and Albert C. Hyde (Pacific Grove, CA: Brooks/Cole, 1992), 12.

11. Wilson, "Study of Administration," 18.

12. Gulick, "Science, Values and Public Administration," 191.

13. Frederick Winslow Taylor, *The Principles of Scientific Management* (New York: W. W. Norton, 1911), 7, 16.

14. L. Urwick, "Organization as a Technical Problem," in Gulick and Urwick, *Papers on the Science of Administration*, 49, 85.

15. Herbert A. Simon, *Administrative Behavior: A Study of Decision-Making Processes in Administrative Organization*, 2nd ed. (New York: Free Press, 1957), 42–44.

16. Osborne and Gaebler, *Reinventing Government*, 14.

17. Barbara W. Tuchman, *The First Salute* (New York: Alfred A. Knopf, 1988), 241–42.

18. Samuel E. Finer, "State and Nation Building in Europe: The Role of the Military," in *The Formation of National States in Western Europe*, ed. Charles Tilly (Princeton, NJ: Princeton University Press, 1975).

19. Lynton K. Caldwell, *The Administrative Theories of Hamilton and Jefferson: Their Contribution to Thought on Public Administration* (Chicago: University of Chicago Press, 1944); Leonard D. White, *The Federalists: A Study in Administrative History, 1789–1801* (New York: Free Press, 1948).

20. *The Federalist Papers*, Federalist No. 1, author Alexander Hamilton, in Alexander Hamilton, James Madison, and John Jay, *The Federalist* (Cutchogue, NY: Buccaneer Books, 1992).

21. *Federalist Papers,* Federalist No. 70, author Alexander Hamilton.

22. Quoted in Caldwell, *Administrative Theories of Hamilton and Jefferson,* 26, 133, 136.

23. Herbert Kaufman, "Administrative Decentralization and Political Power," *Public Administration Review* 29 (January/February 1969): 3–15.

24. Quoted in Caldwell, *Administrative Theories of Hamilton and Jefferson,* 133.

25. Andrew Jackson, First Inaugural Address, March 4, 1829, The Avalon Project at Yale Law School, 2005, www.yale.edu/lawweb/avalon/presiden/inaug/jackson1.htm (accessed December 15, 2005).

26. Quoted in Paul P. Van Riper, *History of the United States Civil Service* (Evanston, IL: Row, Peterson and Company, 1958), 22.

27. Andrew Jackson, President Jackson's Veto Message Regarding the Bank of the United States, July 10, 1832, The Avalon Project at Yale Law School, 2005, www.yale.edu/lawweb/avalon/presiden/veto/ajveto01.htm (accessed December 15, 2005).

28. Waldo, *Administrative State,* 17.

29. See Stephen Jay Gould, *Wonderful Life: The Burgess Shale and the Nature of History* (New York: W. W. Norton, 1989).

30. President's Committee on Administrative Management, *Administrative Management in the Government of the United States; Investigation of Executive Agencies of the Government,* 75th Cong., 1st sess., 1937, S. Rep. 1275; Robert K. Merton, "Bureaucratic Structure and Personality," *Social Forces* 17 (1940): 560–68.

31. William J. Clinton, Address before a Joint Session of the Congress on the State of the Union, January 23, 1996, www.gpoaccess.gov/sou/, updated October 8, 2004 (accessed December 19, 2005).

32. Paul A. Samuelson, "The Pure Theory of Public Expenditure," *Review of Economics and Statistics* 36 (November 1954): 388; Arthur C. Pigou, *The Economics of Welfare,* 4th ed. (London: Macmillan, 1932), 173.

33. C. J. Dahlman, "The Problem of Externality," *Journal of Law and Economics* 22 (April 1979): 143.

34. Wilson, "Study of Administration," 25.

35. Waldo, *Administrative State,* 193.

36. Ibid., 68–69, 73.

4

The Criteria of Action

NORMA M. RICCUCCI

It is necessary to deny . . . that empiricism is the essence of science.

Dwight Waldo, *The Administrative State*

Writing more than fifty-five years ago, Dwight Waldo sought to understand why the scientific perspective had played such a large role in early efforts to understand the administrative state. From Luther Gulick's efforts to classify administrative studies as a social science to Frederick Taylor's promotion of "scientific management," people in the newly emerging field embraced the philosophy of scientific inquiry. Waldo noted that empiricism and experimentalism had played a prominent role in the development of the physical sciences. "But there is much in scientific method which is nonempirical and nonexperimental," he observed. Why then had administrative scholars so enthusiastically adopted the language of science? Typical of his work as a whole, Waldo saw the phenomenon in cultural terms. Administrative studies, he observed, were distinctly pragmatic, often drawing knowledge from common experience. Yet administrative scholars wanted people to respect that experience. What better way, Waldo suggested, than to cloak pragmatism in "the prestige of the 'philosophy of science.'"[1]

Caught between the pragmatic desire to derive knowledge from common experience and the impulse to appear scientific, people in the field of public administration have, throughout its history, struggled with the question of appropriate methods. The question that reflects the essence of the debate is "How do we know what we know?" Given

55

the field's propensity for administrative reform, how confident can people be that reforms produce the effects ascribed to them?[2]

Waldo struggled with these questions while examining three tendencies affecting the search for truth and reality in public administration. People in the field, he noted, had moved away from considerations of "higher law" and other traditional moral standards as a basis for administrative decisions. They had moved in the direction of utilitarianism (utility as the sole criterion for public action), pragmatism (an emphasis upon "workability"), and positivism (scientific observation). In the first edition of *The Administrative State,* Waldo noted the affinitive nature of these three movements relative to traditional political philosophy. With the advent of the behavioral revolution, he pointed out their radical differences. Pragmatism, he observed in the second edition, "held that values can be authenticated or proved by experience and experiment." The positivists, he continued, "held this to be a grave error." "Allying itself closely with science (as it perceived science), logical positivism asserted that values are outside the realm of the empirical world as addressed by science, and are beyond scientific authentication."[3] Logical positivists employed the scientific method in an effort to discredit the notion that common sense or general experience could be used to advance knowledge, especially where values were involved. This created a substantial difficulty, given Waldo's insight that administrative problems invariably contained philosophic issues. From the purely positivist point of view, this suggested that many administrative problems could not be addressed scientifically and should not be studied at all.

This issue of "appropriate" methods is an ageless one in public administration. It underlies every advancement achieved through practical reform or scholarly study. The examination that follows reviews the evolution of the debate regarding what Waldo called "the Criteria of Action"—the selection of techniques and methods employed in the study of administrative phenomena. The chapter then examines a number of fallacies associated with attempts to make public administration more "scientific." This discourse then serves as a template for an examination of the manner in which people in the field determine the effects of efforts at practical reform.

PUBLIC ADMINISTRATION: FACT OR VALUE?

When Woodrow Wilson advanced the widely known politics-administration dichotomy in his seminal 1887 article "The Study of Administration," he did so clearly in the context of practice. The determination of administrative methods in a governmental setting, Wilson argued, ought to be fully divorced from the values people brought to the debate. Wilson stated that "administration operates outside the proper sphere of politics. Administrative questions are not political questions."[4] Although untenable even then, Wilson's view represented a rational, intellectual attempt to escape from the corruption and inefficiency that permeated government service at the time.

Herbert Simon offered a similar dichotomy almost sixty years later in his pathbreaking *Administrative Behavior*. Many interpreted Simon's attempt to frame a fact-value dichotomy as a direct analogue to the politics-administration dichotomy. In addition, others, including Waldo, viewed Simon's classification as a call for the adoption of scientific "principles" that could be used for the *study* of public administration.

The search for principles permeates the history of scientific inquiry. Physical scientists discovered "laws of nature" and "principles of natural science," and in a similar manner early observers of administration sought to locate underlying principles. Taylor found "principles of scientific management," and Gulick located "principles of administration."[5] Yet these administrative efforts were fundamentally misplaced, Simon maintained, because they were rooted in knowledge derived from common experience rather than scientific inquiry.

Simon was heavily influenced by the behavioral revolution beginning to sweep the social sciences. The revolution found its historical roots in the philosophical movement known first as positivism, as advanced by Auguste Comte, and later logical positivism, as advanced by the Vienna Circle. For the movement's principal advocates, it came as no surprise that someone like Simon debunked the principles of administration and argued that a science of public administration could never be built upon a foundation of *practice*, as Taylor, Gulick, and others had called for. But, Simon argued, public administration could and *should* be studied from the viewpoint of scientific principles as rigorously applied in the social sciences.

The acquisition of knowledge about public administration, according to Simon, should be based in *fact:* empirically derived, measured, and verified. Values, he claimed, had no place in the study of public administration. Simon urged scholars to take as their primary unit of analysis the decisions that administrators made. Decisions could be studied scientifically, as to the effects they produced and the process for making them. Such inquiry in Simon's view could be value free and morally neutral, uncorrupted by the normative preferences of the people involved.

Parenthetically, Simon recognized that the administrators who made such decisions would not behave this way. The activities of actual administrators, he and James March recognized, were circumscribed by "boundaries of rationality."[6] Due to human limitations, decision makers in government did not maximize their preferences or find optimal solutions,[7] but rather they "satisficed." In practice, they made decisions that met minimum standards of satisfaction, sufficient for the task at hand. Simon expected persons engaged in the *study* of public administration to behave rationally and scientifically, but not the people toward whom those studies were directed.

Whereas leaders of the early public administration movement sought to discover principles of administration founded in practice, Simon and his followers championed research about administration based on scientific principles. Waldo responded in a satiric, mordant way:

> Facts, research, and measurement are deemed . . . to lie at the heart of science. Anything which is true—or at least significant—is a "fact." It is the duty of scientists to discover facts. The way one discovers facts is by engaging in "research." . . . The chief instrument or indispensable tool of research is "measurement." Measurement is in fact the criterion of genuinely scientific research. When measurement is possible, science at last has arrived. . . . In the spirit of the scientific maxim, "When we can measure, then we know," the assumption is made that measurement "solves problems."

Waldo maintained that Simon and his followers unjustifiably sought "to place large segments of social life—or even the whole of it—upon a scientific basis."[8]

Waldo elaborated that while some administrative matters may lend themselves to "treatment in the mode of natural science . . . administration is generally suffused with questions of value." He states, "A physical science problem is a problem of 'What is the case?' An administrative problem is characteristically a problem of 'What should be done?' Administrative study, as any 'social science,' is concerned primarily with *human beings,* a type of being characterized by *thinking* and *valuing.*"[9] For Waldo, many of the most important issues affecting the development of the administrative state were simply not amenable to the restrictive methods advanced or supported by logical positivism.

In "The Administrative State Revisited," a retrospective examination of his treatise that appeared in a 1965 issue of *Public Administration Review,* Waldo softened his criticism somewhat. He had been "bludgeoned," he said, by Herbert Simon in the early 1950s, causing him to examine more closely the central tenets underlying the philosophy of logical positivism. Upon close examination, Waldo recognized that there was a tendency for many, including himself, to view public administration as "*normative* theory, i.e., theory about how organizations *should* be constructed." A more contemporaneous treatment, he confessed, would recognize the possibility of an administrative theory that was "nonnormative."[10]

Waldo concluded that although he found the philosophy of logical positivism to be "acute and useful" in some ways, it was "limited and misleading in others." He went on to say that "Logical Positivism is content to take one area of human experience and treat it as the whole."[11] At the end, Waldo recognized that public administration might benefit from a combination of different methodologies.

PUBLIC ADMINISTRATION: ART OR SCIENCE?

In the same manner that people in the field of public administration have wrestled with the relationship between facts and values, they have since the inception of the field debated whether the practice of administration is an art or a science. As with the fact-value dichotomy, the issue lurking behind the art versus science debate arises from concern over appropriate methodologies. The issue has both a practical and a scholarly component:

1. Is public administration as practiced primarily an art, requiring intuition and experience, or can it be based on scientifically derived knowledge?
2. Does the search for public administration theory require artful insight, or can it be made wholly scientific?

The debate over the first issue begets another question: Are administrators "born" or can they be "made," that is, trained? The development of educational programs for public service in the first half of the twentieth century proceeded from the belief that a body of knowledge could be derived that, when taught to novices, could help them become better executives. Yet a contrary belief maintains that innate or "inborn" talents predispose certain persons to become leaders or exemplary managers, thus making them "natural born leaders."

The futile struggle that characterized the early study of public administration demonstrated that governmental management could not be reduced to easily derived and trainable principles that described the "one best way." On the one hand, the practice of public administration continues to require the artlike qualities associated with wisdom and experience. On the other hand, the practice of public administration

TABLE 4.1
What Is Public Administration?

Administration	vs.	Politics
↓		↓
Fact	vs.	Value
↓		↓
Science	vs.	Art
↓		↓
Logical Positivism	vs.	Metaphysics

requires scientific training insofar as persons need technical preparation to become public administrators. Few people would argue that untrained public servants as a whole perform as well as people trained in administrative skills. Indeed, the very existence of master of public administration (MPA) degrees represents a scientific and analytic endeavor (never, of course, sans politics). As Leonard White tells us, a society that becomes complex and mutable must continually rely on technical and scientific training of government administrators.[12] The common conception treats the practice of public administration as both art and science.

The second question asks whether public administration, in the scholarly search for "theory" or understanding, is an art or a science. Due to the inevitable presence of human beings, public administration can never be reduced to certainties such as those found in the natural or physical sciences. Yet public administration remains indeed a branch of the social sciences.

Beyond this simple taxonomy, the resolution of the art-science issue in the study of public administration intersects the perdurable debate over appropriate methodology. Here one can find three identifiable camps. One group claims that public administration theory can and must be scientific; another asserts that it has been, historically, an art; while a third sees elements of both art and science.

The first camp, comprised of early behaviorists and more lately people applying economic theories to the analysis of public policies, advocates a logical positivist approach. According to this group, there is no room for the metaphysical speculation, reason, or innate ideas that early rationalists allowed. Rather, the creation of administrative theory must be inductive and based on value-free, rationally derived, testable hypotheses. The goal of knowledge, they insist, is simply to describe the phenomena experienced. Empirically based, quantitative research is the only way, the "one best way," to seek and discover truth and reality. For some in this camp, quantitative data and research method drive ideas, concepts, and theory, rather than vice versa.

The second camp views the study of public administration as an art. For them, metaphysical concerns have a place in administrative research and theory building. They leave room for reasoning, dialectic, and deduction, and research that can be descriptive, prescriptive, and normative. The chief source of knowledge, argues this camp, is reason. The "new public administration," reacting in the late 1960s against the behavioral movement in public administration, is representative of this coterie.[13]

A third group in public administration sees the field as both art and science. Given the variegated and applied nature of the field, they maintain, public administrative research should be pluralistic. In their view, room exists not only for logical positivism and metaphysical speculation, but also for realism, relativism, rationalism, postmodernism, and even reductionism.[14] For this camp, there is no one best way to do research, and given the lack of a unified theory, public administration should not strive for an "appropriate" methodology. As Frederickson recently suggested, the field can greatly benefit from "a rapprochement between the . . . administrative sciences and the humanities." He goes on to say, "The analytical tools of social sciences help us *know* how organizations operate and how public managers function. But to know public organizations and their management is not to understand them. Understanding requires perspective, experience, judgment, and the capacity to imagine. These qualities have less to do with analytical skills and more to do with philosophy, language, art, and reason."[15] To this group, diversity of methods is the key to the acquisition of perspective.

Waldo was sometimes accused by his critics of ambivalence regarding his conception of appropriate methods for public administration. His scholarship, however, spanned substantial periods in the intellectual development of the field and much experimentation with methodologies. One would expect an insightful scholar to respond to those developments, especially one committed more to the accumulation of knowledge than to the defense of a particular approach.

ADMINISTRATIVE REFORM AND
THE SCIENCE OF KNOWING

Public administration in the realm of inquiry as well as practice has historically and typically been problem oriented: reformers, researchers, and analysts continually seek to identify and solve problems associated with the administrative state. Reformers offer initiatives, often conflicting, designed to promote efficiency in government, bolster democratic processes, and foster the value of law within the administrative state. Throughout the history of public administration, reformers have sought to increase executive power, often at the expense of other critical values within a democratic state such as accountability.[16] From Theodore Roosevelt's Keep Commission in 1905 to William Clinton's 1993 National Performance Review, presidents have traditionally sought to improve government efficiency and effectiveness by strengthening the powers of the executive branch. But did these reforms actually result in greater efficiency? Did they lead to stronger executive controls? Did, for instance, the reforms imposed by President Franklin Roosevelt's Committee on Administrative Management, better known as the Brownlow Committee, improve the efficiency of the executive branch? Did the creation of the Executive Office of the President, the passage of the 1939 Reorganization Act, and the implementation of Brownlow's recommendations within the Federal Security Agency and Federal Works Administration enhance the effectiveness of the federal government? How do we know one way or the other?

An examination of the politics underlying attempts to reorganize or reform the federal bureaucracy ultimately makes the determination of effectiveness difficult. FDR's experience with the Brownlow Committee proves instructive here.[17] Around the same time that the Brownlow Committee was established, the U.S. Senate and House of Representatives formed select committees on reorganization and commissioned a congressional study of executive branch organization to be carried out at the Brookings Institution. Legislators did so to ensure that the interests of the law-making branch, particularly as they arose from their constitutional responsibilities for the establishment and oversight of administrative agencies, would be represented. This move resulted in chronic tensions between the Brownlow Committee and the Brookings Institution over not simply the priority of various problems associated with reorganization but also the *methods* for defining them: the Brookings Institution relied on a survey method of functional analysis and classification of federal agencies, whereas the Brownlow Committee relied on the recommendations of the president and his advisors.[18]

Political conflicts and value judgments permeated the investigations into the desirability and feasibility of restructuring the executive branch of government. In the end, the two groups came to very different conclusions about the best means for improving efficiency in the federal bureaucracy, differences that ultimately undermined the acceptance of both reports. Balogh, Grisinger, and Zelikow describe the problem in this fashion:

> The Brownlow Commission examined the problem of administration from the perspective of the presidency, and thus understood the solution to be increased presidential power to manage administration. The Brookings Institution report began from the perspective of Congress and focused on cutting the costs of government. Thus, Congress and the administration had different data they could use to debate the functions of fiscal management and where the control should be. To make matters worse, conflicting expert reports diluted the public authority of supposedly neutral experts, as well as the political influence they normally wielded. Public administration advocates could no longer present themselves as purely technical or apolitical arbiters. Rather, questions of policy preferences and the role that the administration played in vetting those preferences were crucial to the debate.

The three writers conclude that the conflict between Brookings and the Brownlow Committee "revealed the fallacy of a single, scientific answer to the challenge of public administration."[19]

Several important observations can be drawn from this experience as well as other reform efforts. First, practical reform efforts are infused with political concerns and personal values. As Rosenbloom has said, administrative reforms that do not account for political processes, such as legislative self-interest, are doomed to the realm of fantasy, no matter how sweet their methodologies. "Even if federal administration is reinvented . . . Congress may manage to reinvent its leverage over the agencies," he concluded. In the end, he points to "an old lesson: if we want better government, we better talk politics."[20]

Given the very nature of political life, the "research lab" of government is, in effect, inescapably contaminated. Analysts and researchers add their own set of values by, for example, choosing a particular method for studying governmental issues. In the context of the aforementioned experience, the choice of whether to rely on the Brownlow Committee report versus the Brookings Institution study adds another dimension of value-laden choice or subjectivity. Ultimately, it becomes impossible to separate, as Simon and others called for, fact from value. While the advocates of a particular reform effort may purport it to be effective, observers may never know the actual effectiveness of the effort in a "purely" scientific sense.

The arguments presented here are not to diminish the importance of research in public administration. Rather, the purpose is to highlight the preeminence of politics and hence the inevitable presence of values in the study of public administration. The laboratory within which public administration operates is immersed in politics, inevitably affecting the outcome of any study.

Second, most administrative reformers, regardless of where they stand politically, claim to "know," through their own set of value-laden conceptual lenses and experiences, what will and will not work. Administrative reform is a highly developed form of American pragmatism, derived from a common cultural belief that, through tinkering and trial and error, experienced people can discover how things work and make them run better. Pragmatism allows people's values to be "authenticated" and proven by experience. "Pragmatism ... continues importantly as a part of public administration. ... As an integral part of the American experience ... our public administration, both self-aware and not self-aware, has a notable pragmatic temper. What has experience demonstrated? What will work best—or at least work? What does the situation permit or demand? Who wants what and why?"[21] In this sense, the scientific investigations of reformers, as a corollary, augment their own version of the "truth." The downside to this, of course, is the tendency of administrative reformers to then state their knowledge in the form of relatively useless "principles" for the general practice of administration.

In a related manner, the choice of methodologies supporting reform may have great symbolic value, but, because of politics, may be ultimately inconsequential. Advocates of logical positivism may claim that reality can be discovered more definitively through explanatory means, but, again, politics precludes an absolute finding of effectiveness in administrative reforms. The history of the National Performance Review (NPR), whose advocates sought to "reinvent" government, provides another useful example.

In 1993, the NPR was established under the guidance of Vice President Al Gore. Its proponents argued that their reforms would "make government *work better* and *cost less.*"[22] While there were many supporters of this movement, a number of public administration scholars virulently attacked the NPR. They did not center their attacks on the tenuous causal relationship between reinvention techniques and administrative effectiveness. (Given that reinvention principles were based on anecdotal evidence and personal testimony, this could have been a fruitful attack.) Rather, most of the critics charged that the philosophic underpinnings of the NPR failed to account for the fundamental principles of democratic and constitutional rule.[23]

A central part of their argument criticized the reformers' call for a shift from administrative bureaucracy to entrepreneurial organizations. Such a shift, the critics maintained, ignored the very nature of democratic government and its evolution in the United States.[24] Under the U.S. constitutional system, bureaucrats were not empowered to be independent entrepreneurs. Rather, they did their work within a system of checks and balances designed to limit the ability of any officeholder to act in a solely entrepreneurial fashion.

At the very outset, many scholars of public administration argued that the reforms proposed by the NPR, a priori, could *never* be effective in a democratic state, because the advocates of the NPR ignored politics and the practice of democracy.[25] Whatever research might support or dispute, the efficiency claims of NPR reformers would ultimately contain a bias because of the movement's failure to address democratic values. As Beryl Radin points out, most federal management reforms such as those emerging from the NPR prove ineffectual not because of weak methodological roots but because they do not "fit easily into the institutional structures, functions and political realities of the American system."[26] Perhaps Rosenbloom said it best in the title of his 1993 *Public Administration Review* article: "Have an Administrative Rx? Don't Forget the Politics!"[27]

When President George W. Bush succeeded William Clinton, he dismantled much of the apparatus of the NPR. Less than one month into his term, Bush issued Executive Order 13203, revoking Clinton's eight-year-old executive order establishing the National Partnership Council (NPC). The NPC required federal agencies to form labor-management partnerships as a means of fostering improved labor relations in the federal government. Bush's order owed more to a difference in political perspectives than concern about the effectiveness of the NPR or its weak methodological support. Again, politics came into play, thereby diluting the importance of methodological choices in supporting pragmatic reform.

In an effort to understand the dynamics of reorganization, the NPR was subjected to scientific inquiry. Yet the principles themselves, given the difficulty of separating managerial effects from philosophic preferences, proved difficult to study in a purely scientific manner. Even if such a separation were possible, the NPR principles might not prove worthy of study. As Peter Drucker, one of the nation's premier observers of private-sector management, caustically observed, the NPR recommendations contained the sort of advice that "even a poorly run manufacturer expects supervisors to do on their own—without getting much praise, let alone any extra rewards." In a typical business organization, Drucker said, the reforms would not be "trumpeted as reinvention" but would likely be relegated to "the bulletin board in the hallway."[28] Significantly, Drucker's insights were based on years of observed experience.

CONCLUSION

Administrative reforms aimed at improving governmental effectiveness will be pursued throughout time. That is a given. Scholars and practitioners concerned with the location of "appropriate" methodologies for truly knowing or determining the efficacy of those reforms, however, may be frustrated. In a field plagued with politics, and hence "values," methodological disputes aimed at removing values may prove largely irrelevant. Moreover, because the impact of governmental change is so strong—and the uncertainties are so high—conventional science may not be suitable for resolving differences in perspective.[29] The most sophisticated quantitative tools sought by logical positivists can never produce definitive scientific truths acceptable to all when political and policy preferences differ greatly. As Dwight Waldo argued throughout his career, promoters of scientifically neutral truth quickly find themselves allied with beliefs and values promoted by one or another normative political theory.

As a consequence, people studying public administration will never be forced into a single, binding methodological box. The history of recent efforts to redirect management studies illustrates this point particularly well. The public management movement as a research enterprise began, in part, as a neobehavioral response to the earlier call for a new public administration. (Dwight Waldo, then Albert Schweitzer Professor in the Humanities at Syracuse University, initiated and funded the conference that produced the new public administration, with its attempt to ensure the relevancy of values, both social and political.) As noted earlier, the new public administration arose, in part, as a reaction to the advent of administrative behavioralism, with its apolitical, value-free, generic focus. Lynn states that the public management movement began as "a jurisdictional claim by 'new' graduate programs in public policy to a domain 'owned' until the early 1970s . . . by another field: so-called traditional public administration."[30]

Efforts within the public management movement to shift the methodological focus of the field were largely unsustainable, because the dominant force within the scientific community of public administration, whether acting consciously or unconsciously, averted the actualization of such a paradigm. In an almost natural occurrence, scientists within the field, recognizing the disparate nature of the field, saturated and engulfed the efforts, thus ensuring that the scientific approaches to inquiry would remain diverse and pluralistic.

The advent of the "new public management" revived the debate around scientific investigation and methodology in public administration.[31] The new public management refers to efforts derived from reform efforts such as the NPR to improve the performance of government bureaucracies, especially through market-driven business practices. Aside from its overall thrust, the research approach adopted by people associated with the new public management has been questioned from epistemological and axiological standpoints by scholars who claim that its descriptive, case-study methods lack analytical rigor, thereby rendering it intellectually bankrupt.[32] Such propositions, as argued in this chapter, miss the point about the fundamental nature and essence of public administration and the body of research supporting it.

In the tradition of *The Administrative State,* the time has come for reasonable-minded scholars in public administration to accept diversity in research methods and to value different approaches equally. This will ensure that scientific imperialism is not tolerated in the field. Many topics and issues in public administration do not appropriately lend themselves to, for example, positivist approaches; others do. In an *applied* field such as public administration, which continues to be maligned from the standpoint of practice, even research on "best practices" serves a useful role. It helps in a modest way to improve the talents of people recruited for public service.

The study of public administration, an applied field that remains captive to politics, will be more consonant with its subject matter once its participants agree that knowledge can be derived from impressions both on the intellect and on the senses. The field will continue to absorb new methodologies, which can only strengthen rather than diminish it as a profession and area of inquiry.[33] In a field founded on pragmatism, as Waldo pointed out, public administration capably absorbs whatever works. Scientific research can produce insights that may justifiably be called verifiable. That still leaves room for a second area of concern, in which the fruits of that process—the insights gained—are examined with respect to their ultimate use and purpose.

NOTES

1. Dwight Waldo, *The Administrative State: A Study of the Political Theory of American Public Administration,* 2nd ed. (New York: Holmes & Meier, 1984), 168–69.

2. Frank J. Thompson, "Public Administration and Post-Reagan Reform: Boon or Barrier to Theory?" *Administration and Politics* 3 (Winter 1993): 12–16.

3. Waldo, *Administrative State,* xxxviii–xxxix, 78–79.

4. Woodrow Wilson, "The Study of Administration," *Political Science Quarterly* 2 (June 1887): 210.

5. Frederick Winslow Taylor, *The Principles of Scientific Management* (New York: W. W. Norton, 1911); Luther Gulick and L. Urwick, eds., *Papers on the Science of Administration* (New York: Augustus M. Kelley, 1969).

6. James M. March and Herbert A. Simon, *Organizations* (New York: John Wiley, 1958), 171.

7. It should be noted, however, that in his later teachings regarding artificial intelligence (AI), Simon suggested that it may be possible to find rational decision makers. Simon is considered to be one of the cofounders of the field of artificial intelligence, whereby computers and computer programs can be relied on to perform functions normally associated with human intelligence. But AI goes further to suggest that the computer programs can perform with greater intelligence than human action, particularly around reasoning and optimization. Herbert A. Simon, *Administrative Behavior* (New York: Macmillan, 1945); Herbert A. Simon and Joseph B. Kadane, "Optimal Problem-Solving Search: All-Or-None Solutions," *Artificial Intelligence* 6 (1975): 235–47.

8. Waldo, *Administrative State,* 56–57.

9. Ibid., 171. Waldo went on to say that "it is submitted that the established techniques of science are inapplicable to thinking and valuing human beings." However, when he revisited these arguments in 1965, he stated that this was a "half-truth," confessing that "it is simply not the way I would now put and argue my opinions." Dwight Waldo, "The Administrative State Revisited," *Public Administration Review* 25 (1965): 13.

10. Waldo, "Administrative State Revisited," 13.

11. Ibid., note 14.

12. Leonard D. White, *Introduction to the Study of Public Administration,* 4th ed. (New York: Macmillan, 1955).

13. Frank Marini, ed., *Toward a New Public Administration: The Minnowbrook Perspective* (Scranton, PA: Chandler, 1971).

14. Felipe Fernández-Armesto, *Truth: A History and a Guide for the Perplexed* (New York: St. Martin's Press, 1997); Philip Kitcher, *Science, Truth, and Democracy* (New York: Oxford University Press, 2001).

15. H. George Frederickson, "Can Bureaucracy Be Beautiful?" *Public Administration Review* 60 (January/February 2000): 51–52.

16. See, for example, David H. Rosenbloom, "Public Administrative Theory and the Separation of Powers," *Public Administration Review* 43 (May/June 1983): 219–27; Herbert Kaufman, "Emerging Conflicts in the Doctrines of Public Administration," *American Political Science Review* 50 (December 1956): 1057–73.

17. Examples abound here. Consider, for instance, the effort to introduce scientific management reforms to the federal government, which met its demise because of politics. In 1906, disciplines of Frederick Taylor, after having some success in the private sector, attempted to apply scientific management principles to a military arsenal in Massachusetts. This led to a major strike, albeit illegal, by the workers, which in turn led to congressional hearings and a five-year investigation into the feasibility of scientific management for the federal government. In the end, Congress prohibited its use in and application to the federal government.

18. See Fritz Morstein Marx, ed., *Elements of Public Administration* (New York: Prentice Hall, 1946).

19. Brian Balogh, Joanna Grisinger, and Philip Zelikow, *Making Democracy Work: A Brief History of Twentieth Century Federal Executive Reorganization* (Charlottesville, VA: Miller Center of Public Affairs, 2002), 28, 31.

20. David H. Rosenbloom, "Have an Administrative Rx? Don't Forget the Politics!" *Public Administration Review* 53 (November/December 1993): 506; Rosenbloom, *Building a Legislative-Centered Public Administration* (Tuscaloosa: University of Alabama Press, 2000).

21. Waldo, *Administrative State,* xxxviii.

22. Al Gore, *From Red Tape to Results: Creating a Government That Works Better and Costs Less: The Report of the National Performance Review* (Washington, DC: U.S. Government Printing Office, 1993), xxiii.

23. See, for example, Rosenbloom, "Have an Administrative Rx?"; Ronald C. Moe, "The 'Reinventing Government' Exercise: Misinterpreting the Problem, Misjudging the Consequences," *Public Administration Review* 54 (March/April 1994): 111–22; H. George Frederickson, "Comparing the Reinventing Government Movement with the New Public Administration," *Public Administration Review* 56 (1996): 263–70.

24. Charles Goodsell, "Reinventing Government or Rediscovering It?" *Public Administration Review* 53 (January/February 1993): 85–86.

25. See, for example, Rosenbloom, "Have an Administrative Rx?"; Robert F. Durant, "Wither the Neoadministrative State? Toward a Polity-Centered Theory of Administrative Reform," *Journal of Public Administration Research and Theory* 10 (January 2000): 79–109.

26. Beryl A. Radin, "Government Performance and Results Act (GPRA) and the Tradition of Federal Management Reform: Square Pegs in Round Holes?" *Journal of Public Administration Research and Theory* 10 (January 2000): 111.

27. It should be noted that many scholars who may not have subscribed to the underlying premises of the NPR and its consumer-driven managerialism

pointed to the importance of reform and innovation in the federal government. See James R. Thompson and Patricia W. Ingraham, "The Reinvention Game," *Public Administration Review* 56 (May/June 1996): 291–98.

28. Peter Drucker, "*Really* Reinventing Government," *Atlantic Monthly* (February 1995): 50.

29. Silvio O. Funtowicz and Jerome R. Ravetz, "Three Types of Risk Assessment and the Emergence of Post Normal Science," in *Social Theories of Risk*, ed. Sheldon Krimsky and Dominic Golding (Westport, CT: Praeger, 1992), 251–73; Funtowicz and Ravetz, "Science for the Post-Normal Age," *Futures* 25 (1993): 739–55.

30. Laurence E. Lynn Jr., *Public Management as Art, Science, and Profession* (Chatham, NJ: Chatham House, 1996), 1–2.

31. Norma M. Riccucci, "The 'Old' Public Management v. the 'New' Public Management: Where Does Public Administration Fit In?" *Public Administration Review* 61 (March/April 2001): 172–75.

32. See Laurence E. Lynn Jr., "The Myth of the Bureaucratic Paradigm: What Traditional Public Administration Really Stood For," *Public Administration Review* 61 (March/April 2001): 144–60.

33. See, for example, David Rosenbloom, "Public Administration Theory and the Separation of Powers," *Public Administration Review* 43 (May/June 1983): 219–27; Richard J. Stillman, *Preface to Public Administration: A Search for Themes and Direction* (New York: St. Martin's Press, 1991); Donald F. Kettl and H. Brinton Milward, eds., *The State of Public Management* (Baltimore: Johns Hopkins University Press, 1996).

5

Who Should Rule?

PATRICIA W. INGRAHAM

Dwight Waldo worried about intellectual foundations—of academic thought, of citizenship, of government, and of public administration as a discipline. He worried about the potential for intellectual rootlessness and its impact on the discipline and on the government to which he had committed his life's work. Waldo worried about the manifestations of intellectual rootlessness in the politics-administration dichotomy and in the split between political science and public administration. He worried, perhaps most of all, about the continued failure to define the "proper" role of administration in American government. How, he wondered, could we possibly understand the American state if we failed to understand the fundamental roles played by public administrators in their governing responsibilities? How indeed could we understand administration if we failed to recognize its multifaceted roots—in many disciplines, theories, and perspectives—none central, but all-important? Underlying all of these concerns was Waldo's fundamental belief that good administration was central to good government. He was fervent in his admonishments that administrators could be "good" not only if they were fully aware of the political world in which they worked but also only if they developed carefully formed ideas about how that world should look. "Government work," therefore, was as much about defining government as in carrying out its tasks. It was, in Waldo's view, a noble calling worthy of respect and prestige.

In his chapter titled "Who Should Rule?" Waldo addressed the issues posed by the rise of an administrative class with a claim to governmental power. He traced the genesis of this development to the advent of expertise and professionalism and the notion that public administration "in itself is a subject-matter field or technique in which one can specialize, a science and art one can learn."[1] Having established the basis for this claim, he then proceeded to examine the qualifications recommended for people holding such positions: their education, qualifications, virtues, and skills. "What we are dealing with is a theory of a governing class," he insisted, pressing hard to resolve questions regarding the nature of public administration in the modern democratic state.[2] He acknowledged that the advice proffered by people contemplating the nature of this new administrative class was full of "conflicts and inconsistencies," a point he reemphasized in the second edition of *The Administrative State.* "These are not irrelevant or captious questions," he emphasized. "These are things we have a right to know about our new Ruling Class."[3]

In his lecture on the occasion of his receipt of the American Political Science Association's Gaus Award in 1987, Waldo forcefully restated these arguments and also expressed his frustration with the inability of others to see their importance. Decrying the "lower status" he perceived administration to be assigned, Waldo argued,

> The lower things with which Public Administration is now deeply engaged are such matters as the common defense, education, safety and health, economic development and the elimination of poverty, problems of freedom and equality, law enforcement and the administration of justice, the preservation and development of resources, social and physical mobility, population planning, recreation and the amenities, the development of science and the use of technology; and with the interactions of all such matters with governmental theories, institutions, and processes, at all levels of government at home and abroad.[4]

Waldo was especially perplexed by the tendency of Americans to believe that public affairs in the modern democratic state "need not be 'managed' but will run themselves."[5] Ever the restless scholar, he searched for explanations of this incongruity. Early on, he perceived the ill fit of administration with democratic theory to be at least partially due to the commingling in the United States of Greek and Roman traditions or philosophies of the state. This is not surprising, given that he approached the issue from the perspective of his doctoral research—political philosophy, not public administration, was his course of study. In the Gaus lecture, he noted that the Grecian civic culture and the Roman imperial tradition influenced most Western constitutional development. But in the American case, he said, we kept them more distinct: "Our politics are Greek, but our administration is Roman."[6]

The ramifications of these differences are many and too complex to be analyzed in a single chapter. The most important conclusion for our purposes is that an easy fit between politics (or governing) and administration would not be likely under this umbrella of dual philosophies. But it can also be argued that the status of administration in this setting is not necessarily that of a lower order. Indeed, the invocation of a noble Roman order calls to mind Woodrow Wilson's earlier comment that it was the task of administration to "straighten the path" of government.[7]

THE IDEAL ADMINISTRATOR

Waldo's discussion of "Who Should Rule" in chapter 6 of *The Administrative State* reflects the duality of these philosophies and his theories. The discussion was intended to refute what he considered scientific management's underlying principle—the idea that neutral expertise could serve as a validator of administration's rights to position and influence in a democratic government.[8] At the same time, he was quick to acknowledge the contributions that scientific management theory had made in the two generations of its ascendance.[9] Scientific management and the "dichotomy" it suggested, he argued, did permit creative approaches to some important issues in government. It also permitted the application of highly specific expertise to increasingly complex governmental issues.

Waldo moved very quickly from this endorsement, however, to a discussion of why those contributions were inadequate to establish scientific management as a theory of administrative legitimacy in government. The bounded expertise and limited role that scientific management advocated simply did not match government's needs when the problems it confronted were unpredictable and complex in increasingly unknowable ways. Waldo's administrator was a different kind of expert. Waldo concluded *The Administrative State* with this admonition: "If abandonment of the politics-administration formula is taken seriously, if the demands of present world civilization upon public administration are met, administrative thought must establish a working relationship with every major province in the realm of human learning."[10]

He returned to the point in his conclusion to *Public Administration in a Time of Turbulence*, arguing that, "we know too little of the effects of our actions—or inactions" for neutral, limited expertise to be effective.[11] He consistently held that while the quality of expertise might be elusive, its broad pursuit was critical to effective administration. This was not an argument for the primacy of public administrative knowledge and values in government, as some associated with the new public administration suggested. Rather, Waldo argued that the spanning capability of broad knowledge, if housed in problem-solving institutions such as he believed public bureaucracies could be, was a critical part of democracy.

MODERN REFORM

What would Dwight Waldo make of current descriptions of government as "hollow," of reform rhetoric urging the privatization of government tasks to ensure their proper undertaking, of a consistent reform pressure to make government "more like business"? If his response to the arguments advanced at the Minnowbrook Conference—which he sponsored as the Schweitzer Chair at the Maxwell School—are a guide, he would be, at best, bemused.[12] He was not certain of the theoretical foundations of new public administration, and he continued to believe throughout his life that fervent advocacy did not solve the rootlessness problem for American administration.

Waldo's response to contemporary reform undoubtedly would have also included his skepticism about scientific management. Current reform nostrums, like those before them, do not address the core responsibilities of and given to government.[13] On the contrary, many modern reforms retreat to perspectives similar to those of scientific management theorists—for example, administrative action should be carefully circumscribed, administrative actions are primarily implementing actions, and administrative legitimacy is defined and bounded by politics.

One element of "hollow government" did, however, ring true to Dwight Waldo's view of emerging governmental reality. As Waldo observed administrative developments and emergent values throughout the 1960s and 1970s, he came closer and closer to the conclusion that the responsibility of administrators in government was to serve as the connectors among critical groups or centers of necessary expertise. The question he addressed morphed from "Who should rule?" to "What is government?" to "How do we govern?" This last question is of central relevance as we consider contemporary administrative and management reforms, which inexorably move the administrative state toward more diffuse settings and structures of expertise and authority.

To some extent, the rootlessness that Waldo perceived in administration has been transferred to the broader issue of government itself. This has created new demands for knowledge and expertise for which Waldo's concerns not only remain relevant but take on new dimensions. It is important, therefore, to analyze the fit between Waldo's *Administrative State* and the views of governance and public service now apparently on the minds of reformers.

"WHO SHOULD RULE" AND THE NATURE OF PUBLIC SERVICE

As already demonstrated, Dwight Waldo did not concur with the image and role of public service created by scientific management theorists. Further, he did not believe that administrators were of a "lower" or subservient class in government. *The Administrative State* and later work affirmed Waldo's belief that contributing to effective government was a value-laden and proactive undertaking, based increasingly on *understanding* and *linking* critical areas of expertise. In *Public Administration in a Time of Turbulence*, he noted the continuing gap between this conviction and the practical reality of the state of public administration theory as he interpreted it:

> We lack beliefs, which can perform the function of getting agreement, motivating action, informing the solution of problems, defining institutional functions, and specifying operational relationships. The most widely touted formulation of the past generation, the fact-value dichotomy, for all of its *logical* strengths, does not even come close to serving the *political* function of the politics-administration formulation. *The popularity of the former may in fact have hindered the devising and justifying of "solutions.*[14]

The patterns of beliefs that Waldo envisioned are somewhat clearer than the actual nature of the administrators who would embody them. Indeed, it requires some leaps of faith to assume that the "Roman" influence on administration to which Waldo referred so frequently was not just the code of laws he describes, but also a fundamental structure for action allowing administrators to possess and pursue democratic values.

In addition, the distinctions that Waldo draws between the civic and democratic values necessary for the melding of administration and politics are somewhat unclear, as is the nature of the expertise necessary to link to multiple required knowledge centers. On the issue of education necessary for a government administrator, Waldo observed in 1978 that the field of public administration education was becoming increasingly diverse, both in terms of its location within departments, schools, and universities and in terms of content.[15] He attributed this to public administration programs per se paying inadequate attention to policy and implementation, schools of business management becoming more interested in government management, and political science departments adopting a somewhat "warmer" attitude toward public administration than in the early 1970s.[16] Again, he emphasized that "contributions from a wide range of sources, not from one or a few disciplines, will be necessary if the education is to meet its challenges successfully."[17] In other words, he saw such diversity as critical to success.

Nonetheless, Waldo's Greco-Roman, Renaissance, international expert presents a daunting prototype for the contemporary public servant working in a service increasingly populated by narrowly defined technical or scientific expertise. Members of this service are more likely to be accountants and engineers than the more broadly trained and educated administrators Waldo envisioned. Further, it is unlikely that Waldo would be pleased by the current tendency of schools of policy and public affairs to move toward increasingly sophisticated econometric analysis rather than a broader understanding of politics, policy, and the world. He would undoubtedly be horrified to know that his signature course at the Maxwell School of Citizenship and Public Affairs, "Public Administration and Democracy," is sometimes referred to as the "dinosaur" of public administration by outside observers.

But this very challenge—how to prepare and educate administrators for their future—was a prescient concern for Dwight Waldo. His adamant belief in broad talent and skills fits very well with the networked organizations and work now endemic in all sectors of society. Waldo's discussion of the politics/administration dichotomy is also, in many ways, as fresh as when he wrote *The Administrative State*. The continuing reality is that *both* the politics-administration split and the fact-value split have continued to inform contemporary government and administration. They have also fundamentally shaped reform content. Whatever might be said about the new public management's roots in economic theory, it can as easily be argued that the reform's ancestry includes the scientific management theorists and others who argued for the separation of politics and administration and the "partitioning" of administrative expertise from the policy decisions directing its use.[18] The presence of such roots in reform provides modern testimony to Dwight Waldo's conviction that administration's legitimacy should be grounded in democratic governance.

ADMINISTRATIVE REFORM AND WALDO'S VALUED ADMINISTRATOR

Toward the end of his life, Dwight Waldo became mystified by the speed at which governments around the world were reshaping and reforming their governments.[19] New public management reforms, led by the dramatic changes in New Zealand, provided a model for change notable for coherent principles and the consistency of their application in widely diverse governmental settings.[20] The reinventing government approach, more shapeless conceptually and theoretically, represented a more participative view of reform and also wreaked changes on governments worldwide. These reforms, discussed in more detail later, occurred concurrently with what Kettl termed the "blurring of boundaries" between government, the private sector, and nonprofit organizations.[21] As noted, the blurring was consistent with Waldo's identification of the need for administrators to reach out to multiple centers of expertise and to cross organizational and governmental boundaries in the course of problem solving. The difficulty, of course, is that most of the reformers clearly viewed administration in much more limited ways.

The internationalization and globalization that Waldo predicted has also occurred in extraordinary dimensions. Indeed, one of the notable characteristics of modern governments has been their inability to isolate themselves from world events and from global changes. In this setting, administrators did not fare too well. The quality and cost of administration, the inability of government to effectively solve emergent problems, and the difficulties of ensuring administrative responsiveness to political direction were commonly cited reasons for reform.[22] The public service emerged in a more positive light in the post-September 11, 2001, world, but reform in the name of effectively combating terrorism followed quickly. Each of these developments will be discussed in turn, with an eye toward dissembling the multiple influences from a perspective similar to that of Dwight Waldo.

In describing the new public management and reinventing government movements, Kettl notes, "Governments were reforming their administrative systems, simultaneously and on a massive scale, unlike anything seen since the turn of the twentieth century . . . public officials were charting their own course into the twenty-first century, largely without intellectual or moral support from academia."[23] The latter part of Kettl's comments refers to the limited academic foundation for the reinventing government movement. In fact, although reinventing government seemed to have sprung full-blown from a single book by David Osborne and Ted Gaebler, it did have conceptual roots in earlier thinking about empowerment of citizens and employees and earlier efforts to clarify accountability. Some ideas, such as those related to total quality management, were transformed into bottom-up, participative reform ideas such as reinvention laboratories.[24]

In contrast, advocates of the new public management could not have been more explicit in acknowledging their academic and theoretical roots. The language of the legislation creating the New Zealand reform cited an academic literature including William Niskanen and others and drew very clearly on principal-agent theory in creating the contract system for management of many public services.[25] This contract system also specified the boundary between politics and administration and between policy choice and policy implementation. The designers of these reforms did not cite scientific management theorists, but they would have found their case well supported in that literature as well.

Despite these differences, fundamental ideas in the two reform movements were remarkably similar and pointed in common directions for government and its administrators in every nation where the reforms took hold. These ideas included smaller but more effective government ("doing more with less" in reinvention terms), clearer and more direct accountability mechanisms, privatization of many previously governmental functions, and a clear separation of policy and operations. Officials in the United States, while lagging behind other nations in adopting the reforms and not changing government either as decisively or as clearly as many other nations, adopted enough of the ideas to make a difference in perspectives and views about the role of public administration.[26]

In the United States, two elements of change were most notable. The first was that reinvention—particularly at the national level—became identified with downsizing government. A primary target of cuts were the midlevel managers of government organizations—the "overhead controllers" of government. This changed the role of top-level career administrators because it gave them new liaison and communication responsibilities throughout their organizations. At the same time, many internal organizational processes were changed or eliminated, and most administrators struggled to understand new systems. This internal, multilevel change and uncertainty provided one new dimension of the "blurring" of administration. The second dimension of uncertainty arose from the executive desire to change in the absence of clear (or any) congressional and statutory direction to do so. Finally, particular components of reinvention, such as the reinvention laboratories, created conflicting signals about the legitimacy of the change and the role public administrators should have in shaping it.[27]

These dimensions of uncertainty were exacerbated by realities within the politics of change. The reform ethos did not take place within an environment that fundamentally supported administrative legitimacy. Quite the contrary. New public management and reinventing government posed direct challenges to the legitimacy of administrative action as political leaders perceived it. In the United States, the lack of clarity proved particularly difficult: administrators were expected to simultaneously create a "smaller, better, faster" government, to "do more with less," and to find "new solutions to old problems."

Although the political climate and antibureaucracy attitudes were similarly harsh in nations such as New Zealand, Australia, and Great Britain, new expectations were put forward with greater clarity in these settings. Further, structural and legal changes were put in place to support the new expectations. In the United States, new expectations for administrators were presented with no concomitant structural or legal change, save diminution in the middle levels of their organizations.[28] While clear elements of the politics-administration dichotomy appeared in these actions, those elements did not serve to clarify the relative responsibilities of politicians and administrators—as original advocates of the dichotomy had advocated—but only further complicated the relationship. Laurence Lynn Jr. argues that the reforms muddied the situation not only because they reverted to simplistic models of administration but also because they fundamentally ignored the constitutional environment in which administration exists. "Traditional habits of thought exhibited far more respect for law, politics, citizens and values than customer oriented managerialism or civic philosophies that, in promoting community and citizen empowerment, barely acknowledge the constitutional role of legislatures, courts, and executive departments."[29]

This followed a situation for federal administrators that had already been characterized as "ubiquitous anomie." Aaron Wildavsky, who used the term in 1988, wrote, "Civil servants by themselves cannot do much to improve the situation because their situation is the effect and not the cause. The cause lies in ideological dissensus within the political strum, profound disagreements over equality, democracy, and hence the role of government, disagreements that create conflicting expectations that no conceivable cadre of civil servants can meet."[30] Quite clearly, conflicting perspectives and proposals for action did not come together in the reinventing years. Subsequent reforms, such as those undertaken in the George W. Bush administration, were more sweeping. Legislative actions approving the Department of Homeland Security and reforming the Department of Defense, as well as proposed civil service changes government-wide, contained the source of what some thought might become significant changes in the structure and procedures of public administration—and perhaps in public perceptions of administration as well.

But is there a difference in the perception of the administrator's role? Put another way, could Waldo's enlightened administrator find a happier home within these reforms? Probably not. First, both of the U.S. departmental reforms were somewhat like the first congressional acts to create a civil service 125 years ago: they were stimulated by a major external event or crisis and were not the product of "normal" policy processes. In 1883, a national tragedy—the assassination of a president—helped to crystallize clearly needed civil service reforms that had been percolating for some time and to clarify the place that a professional public service could occupy in a democratic system. In 2001, the events of September 11 forced a reexamination of the ways in which politics—presidential politics, congressional politics, oversight, and, to some extent, overmanagement—had perversely shaped important national organizations. The conglomerate Department of Homeland Security was intended to solve that problem. The organizations pulled into the new Department of Homeland Security encountered serious problems reconciling fit and redefining mission as department leaders pressed for an integrated organization, however.[31] Possibly it can be argued that gathering together multiple agencies with some fundamental mission commonalities is a clarifying act that contrasts with previous narrowness and insularity in policy choice and serves a legitimizing purpose. It can also be argued that renewed confidence in the work of public servants in the post-September 11 months had the legitimizing effect of blunting years of dissatisfaction with, and cynicism about, public service. Post–2001 events, such as Hurricane Katrina and the actions of federal agencies in response, undoubtedly countered that effect.

The impact of reform has also been shaped by the move to privatization, or the transfer of previously governmental services to the private or not-for-profit sectors. This activity was a major component of new public management. In the United States, it continued to be manifest in the reforms pursued by the Bush administration through the President's Management Agenda and the priorities of the president's Office of Management and Budget. The impact on administration was at least threefold. First, the content of many administrative jobs changed as government moved away from direct service provision. The responsibility of the job thus became hollower, as the administrator moved beyond probable expertise and education to a different kind of job: that of a contract administrator. Second, the accountability of the administrator, while now more indirect, remained intact. Finally, this more complex web of responsibility and authority devalued longer term institutional expertise, for which administration has been valued, and transferred much—if not all—of that expertise into the private or not-for-profit sector.

This environment of networked management—or administration in the "hollow state"—has been extensively discussed in organization theory and public administration literature.[32] Kettl describes one of the implications of the development as the "fuzzy boundary" issue: "The policy-administration, public-private-nonprofit, bureaucratic level, and labor-management fuzzy boundaries create substantial coordination problems. But the biggest coordination problem—the one for which organizational alchemists have for millennia sought the philosopher's stone—is coordination *between* bureaucracies."[33] In reaching conclusions about the impact of the fuzziness, Kettl argues that complex networks have been layered on top of hierarchical organizations and thus must be managed differently. As a result, "public managers need to rely on interpersonal and inter-organizational processes as complements to—as sometimes as substitutes for—authority."[34] In startling ways, this fits with Waldo's vision of the administrator as a "gatherer" of expertise and knowledge from many sources and as a problem solver par excellence.

In other ways, however, the demands outlined by Kettl point to the very real tensions induced by the continued presence of rigid hierarchies and hierarchical processes (e.g., the classification and compensation systems in the federal civil service) and the stark limits on action that they present. Again, Waldo's theme of ensuring a legitimate foundation for administration and then providing discretion for necessary action seems both common sense and appropriate. It is not reflected, however, in current reform reality.

NOT WHO SHOULD RULE, BUT WHO CAN GOVERN?

It is easy to suspect that even Dwight Waldo's head would be spinning as he considered the implications of these reforms and continuing cross-pressures on administrative action. The legitimacy of administrators and their activities in public policy processes remains a lively topic for debate. The nature of administrative jobs continues to change at a very rapid pace. At the same time, reforms in the United States have consistently produced new expectations for administrators but have rarely created the tools or conditions to satisfactorily meet them. Despite the reality of the intersection of politics with the administrative functions of government; the role of administrative actors in policy design, implementation, and evaluation on a constant basis; and the deepening needs for broad expertise, reforms such as reinventing government and new public management placed their faith in oversimplified and discredited nostrums. Scientific management remains alive and well. Contemporary demands on administrators have only heightened the primacy of scientific management's core value: efficiency, now in the guise of performance.

In the second edition of *The Administrative State,* Waldo recalled that he had intended in writing his dissertation to explore ideas related to "Theories of Expertise in the Democratic Tradition."[35] One of the ideas he originally intended to explore, for example, was "that the businessmen who have allegedly built this civilization know best how to govern it" and "that those who have taken law as a vocation are entitled to roles of privilege and power in a government dedicated to the rule of law."[36] Electoral politics and reform movements in the intervening years seem to offer not a thorough questioning of the ideas Waldo posed but a simple acceptance of them. Waldo's search for legitimacy in the administration of democratic government would continue today, were he here to pursue it.

If anything, reforms have heightened the complexity of the conundrums Waldo explored. Expertise, though valued, is thought to be as appropriately housed in contract operations as in more permanent government agencies. Professionalism, and the questions of whether professionals of any stripe have the ability to stake a special claim on legitimacy, remains a problem but rarely emerges even in academic debate. The final issue for our purposes here is the extent to which both expertise and professionalism fit with the idea of Waldo's valued administrator. How do they contribute—or not—to the demands of the contemporary administrative state?

Waldo's conviction that the administrator should be a proactive actor in the democratic arena is an important part of his enduring legacy. Waldo's valued administrator was interactive in ways that were shaped by democratic values, but also shaped the values. He placed enormous faith in education and the acquisition of expertise in that pursuit. He strongly believed that expertise would be broad based. His continued fascination with the burgeoning of schools of public administration, public affairs, and public policy barely masked a constant hope that the education and expertise provided by these schools would somehow manage to provide a magic bullet as well.

In most respects, however, the movement that Waldo envisioned toward the education of broadly informed and multidimensional administrators has not developed. Rather, the reform trend of looking back to the separation of policy and operations has been accompanied by the development in many schools of policy and management of a model of an antiseptic administrator: a skilled expert, to be sure, but one with grounding in models and methods of economics. The value base is one dimensional; the inclusiveness toward history, political theory, and even political science is not there.

It is also fair to say that the emergent new neutrality in administration has limited the ability of administrators to proactively shape ideas about government, except to reemphasize the value of efficiency. Certainly it was neither the public administration community nor public policy scholars that shaped the fundamental ideas of reforms such as reinvention. As Don Kettl reports, the influence of academic thought on the course of the Clinton administration's reinvention ideas was "really—none."[37]

At the same time, perhaps the nature of administration and the nature of public service have changed so dramatically that the prescience of Waldo's prescriptions is only now becoming clear. The increasing role of both the private and not-for-profit sectors in providing government services, the increased transparency and porosity of organizational boundaries, and the dramatically changed ways of communicating and connecting expertise and capability are profoundly changing government. Constraining structures are changing as well. Boundaries, though they still exist, are becoming increasingly insignificant. Reforms now under way in the U.S. Department of Homeland Security, the U.S. Department of Defense, and other federal agencies emphasize intra-agency and interagency—as well as international—coordination and communication.[38] As network theorists have clearly demonstrated, these more flexible structural arrangements are necessarily founded on values broader than efficiency—effectiveness, collaboration, and coordination must be more emphatically present. Hopefully, they will be reinforced by strong core democratic values. Should that be true, it will not have been a windmill Dwight Waldo saw in the distance. His impossible dream may become a component of contemporary reality.

NOTES

1. Dwight Waldo, *The Administrative State: A Study of the Political Theory of American Public Administration,* 2nd ed. (New York: Holmes & Meier, 1984), 93.

2. Ibid., 97.

3. Ibid., 99.

4. Dwight Waldo, "Public Administration for Their Time Is a Public Administration for Our Time Also," John Gaus Lecture. Excerpts printed in *PS* (March/April 1987): 905.

5. Waldo, *Administrative State,* 99.

6. Waldo, "Public Administration for Their Time," 906.

7. Woodrow Wilson, "The Study of Administration," *Political Science Quarterly* 2 (June 1887): 186–202.

8. Brack Brown and Richard Stillman, *A Search for Public Administration: The Ideas and Career of Dwight Waldo* (College Station: Texas A&M University Press, 1979), 31.

9. It is important to note that Waldo described his quest as one for theory and argued that he found scientific management ripe for theoretical dissection. Other analysts, such as Lynn, argue that Waldo's analysis of scientific management excludes consideration of the treatment that the democratic environment and the U.S. Constitution actually received in some of the work. L. E. Lynn Jr., "The Myth of the Bureaucratic Paradigm: What Traditional Public Administration Really Stood For," *Public Administration Review* 10 (March/April 2001): 359–79.

10. Waldo, *Administrative State,* 203.

11. Dwight Waldo, *Public Administration in a Time of Turbulence* (New York: Chandler, 1971), 275.

12. Frank Marini, ed., *Toward a New Public Administration: The Minnowbrook Perspective* (Scranton, PA: Chandler, 1971).

13. D. H. Rosenbloom, "Have an Administrative Rx? Don't Forget the Politics!" *Public Administration Review* 53 (November/December 1993): 503–7.

14. Waldo, *Public Administration in a Time of Turbulence,* 265 (emphasis mine).

15. Note that Waldo made a distinction between "government" administration, which draws its values from the public and from politics, and "public" administration, which he deemed to be more encompassing.

16. Brown and Stillman, *Search for Public Administration,* 173–74.

17. Ibid., 175.

18. J. Boston, J. Martin, J. Paillot, and P. Walsh, *Public Management: The New Zealand Model* (Wellington, NZ: Oxford University Press, 1996); Donald F. Kettl and John DiIulio, *Inside the Reinvention Machine: Appraising Governmental Reform* (Washington, DC: Brookings Institution, 1995).

19. Personal note to author from Dwight Waldo.

20. C. Pollitt and G. Bouckaert, "Evaluating Public Management Reforms: An International Perspective," *International Journal of Political Studies/ Revista Internacional de Estudos Politicos,* special issue (2002): 141–66.

21. Donald F. Kettl, *The Transformation of Governance: Public Administration for Twenty-First Century America* (Baltimore: Johns Hopkins University Press, 2002).

22. Patricia W. Ingraham, "A Laggard's Tale: Civil Service Reform in the United States," in *Comparative Civil Service Reform,* ed. Hans Bekke, James Perry, and Theo Toonon (Bloomington: Indiana University Press, 1999), 147–66; Pollitt and Bouckaert, "Evaluating Public Management Reforms."

23. Kettl, *Transformation of Governance,* 21.

24. Hal G. Rainey and Edward Kellough, "Civil Service Reform and Incentives in the Public Service," in *The Future of Merit: Twenty Years after the Civil Service Reform Act,* ed. James P. Pfiffner and Douglas A. Brooks (Washington, DC: Woodrow Wilson Institute, 2000), 127–45.

25. Boston, Martin, Paillot, and Walsh, *Public Management.*

26. Patricia W. Ingraham and Daniel P. Moynihan, "Reinvention and Reform in the United States," in *Public Sector Reform around the World,* ed. J. Halligan (London: Edward Elgar, 2004), 84–110.

27. J. R. Thompson, "The Reinvention Laboratories: Strategic Change by Indirection," *The American Review of Public Administration* 30 (March 2000): 46–49.

28. Ingraham and Moynihan, "Reinvention and Reform in the United States."

29. L. E. Lynn Jr., "The Myth of the Bureaucratic Paradigm: What Traditional Public Administration Really Stood For," *Public Administration Review* 61 (March/April 2001): 154–55.

30. Aaron Wildavsky, "Ubiquitous Anomie: Public Service in an Era of Ideological Dissensus," *Public Administration Review* 48 (July/August 1988): 753.

31. D. P. Moynihan, "Homeland Security and U.S. Public Management Policy Agenda," *Governance* (forthcoming).

32. K. Provan and H. B. Milward, "Governing the Hollow State," *Journal of Public Administration Research and Theory* 10 (April 2000): 359–80.

33. Kettl, *Transformation of Governance,* 67.

34. Ibid., 168.

35. In the introduction to the second edition of *The Administrative State,* Waldo strongly emphasized that, at the time the book was written, he was *not* a scholar of public administration. In fact, he noted, he had taken no courses on the subject during his doctoral study. Waldo, *Administrative State,* ix.

36. Ibid., ix–x.

37. See chapter 2 of this volume.

38. P. W. Ingraham, "The Federal Public Service: The People and the Challenge," in *Institutions of Democracy: The Executive Branch,* ed. Joel Aberbach and Mark Peterson (New York: Oxford University Press, 2005).

6

The Separation of Powers

DAVID H. ROSENBLOOM

In chapter 7 of *The Administrative State*, Dwight Waldo reviewed the contorted theories that scholars in the early public administration movement developed to explain the alignment of the two functions of governing, politics and administration, with the constitutional three-branch separation of powers. Waldo found their writings to be "hostile to the tripartite separation of powers," unable to pass "the test of consistency," and based on a "constitutional history [that] has been misread, distorted." Their problem, to put it in more contemporary terms, is that two won't go evenly into three. Waldo explains, "Almost without exception the [orthodox] writers accept it as plain fact that there are but two parts or functions in the governmental process: decision and execution, politics and administration; that administration is a realm of expertise from which politics can be and should be largely excluded."[1]

The orthodox solutions to the two function–three branch conundrum generally required constitutional change or circumvention in the name of better administration. Strikingly, the more things change, the more they remain the same. When it comes to the separation of powers, contemporary administrative prescriptions for reform and reorganization have much in common with orthodox thinking.

This chapter reviews Waldo's treatment of the separation of powers issue and demonstrates the manner in which the U.S. Congress and federal courts, beginning in the 1940s and 1950s, framed institutional responses to the administrative state that increased their roles in the administrative process. It then considers the challenges these developments posed to public administrative theory, with its traditional emphasis on the subordination of federal agencies through executive hierarchy. In their search for efficiency and effectiveness, major contemporary reform proposals echo this orthodox insistence that Americans aggrandize the role of the presidency in controlling public administration. This chapter presents an alternative to the persistent reform bias in favor of treating administration exclusively as an executive function. Drawing on ideas from Waldo's *Administrative State*, it considers the virtues of a "democratic-constitutional scorecard" for evaluating the potential impact of reform and reorganization proposals on the separation of powers doctrine and the broader values embedded in it.

UNTENABLE THEORIES: TWO INTO THREE WON'T GO

"The problem of separation of powers has been of prominent and continuing interest to administrative writers," Waldo noted in *The Administrative State*.[2] He then proceeded to skewer several orthodox authors for their unbending and unproductive belief that good government requires a constitutional order to embrace a dichotomy between politics and administration. His main attention was devoted to the following writers.

Frank Goodnow. As every student of American public administration knows, Goodnow maintained that all governments possess two primary functions, "the expression of the will of the state and the execution of that will." "These functions," Goodnow announced, "are, respectively, Politics and Administration."[3] Waldo observed the manner in which Goodnow began from a simple and appealing proposition and ended with "complications" ("convolutions" would be a better term) that made his theory of two into three untenable, if not unintelligible. Waldo pointed out that the clarity of the original proposition disintegrated, as Goodnow conceded that "it is impossible to assign each of these functions to a separate authority, not merely because the exercise of governmental power cannot be clearly apportioned, but also because, as political systems develop, these two primary functions of government tend to be differentiated into minor and secondary functions." In practice, those "minor and secondary functions" involve the executive, legislature, and judiciary in both politics and administration. Because, as Goodnow observes, "politics must have a certain control over administration," a mixing of branches and functions is inevitable.[4] In Waldo's view, Goodnow never satisfactorily resolved this mixing.

Only by radically changing the American separation of powers doctrine could the branches be made to fit Goodnow's dichotomy of functions. Waldo suggested that Goodnow was a latent parliamentarian, sympathetic to a radical change in American constitutional philosophy in order to achieve his administrative theory.

W. F. Willoughby. "Examination will show," Willoughby argued, that the separation of powers doctrine "cannot stand the test of scientific analysis." According to Willoughby, democratic government consisted of five powers or functions: executive, legislative, judicial, administrative, and electoral. He believed that the constitutional framers committed a major error in failing to "make any direct provision for the exercise of administrative powers." The administrative function consisted of "actually administering the law," whereas the executive or presidential function involved the "political duties of the titular head of the nation." From Willoughby's constitutional perspective, administration should be subordinate to the legislative function. Unlike Goodnow, however, Willoughby did not favor a parliamentary system. He advocated Congress acting as a board of directors while the president fulfilled his constitutional duties as "administrator-in-chief," responsible for taking "care that the laws be faithfully executed."[5] Waldo found Willoughby's concepts to be flawed, as they require the president to separate his executive functions, which are political, from his administrative ones, which are presumably not. Similarly, members of Congress, participants in an intensely political institution, would have to distinguish their policymaking responsibilities from their role as the board of directors over administration.

Harvey Walker. Walker followed Goodnow in arguing for a strong division between policy and administration: "There are only two phases to any business, public or private. One is to make the decision as to what is to be done. That is legislation. The other is to see that the decision is carried out. That is administration."[6] Unlike other thinkers, Walker did not wish to entrust the oversight of administration to an elected executive, at least not at the state level. Instead, as Waldo explained, Walker advocated "a small, unicameral legislature, responsible for the selection of a state-manager and a legislative auditor." Similar to the theory of city management, "the state-manager would be a professional administrator, responsible for state administration."[7] Waldo was wholly unconvinced of Walker's logic, finding the notion of administrative insulation from the executive and legislative branches to be thoroughly incompatible with American constitutional philosophy.

The President's Committee on Administrative Management (the Brownlow Committee). The presidential advisory committee led by Louis Brownlow took yet another tack. Its members circumvented the separation of powers problem by substantially enhancing presidential authority over administration while diminishing the constitutional role of Congress. In the committee's words, the separation of powers should be understood to place "in the President, and in the President alone, the whole executive power of the Government of the United States."[8] This advice came to dominate much administrative thought over the following decades. Unless one follows Willoughby's distinction between executive and administrative functions, however, this was clearly wishful thinking on the committee's part. The executive power may reside with the president, but administrative oversight is shared with the legislature. Willoughby more correctly viewed Congress as the "final authority in respect to the organization and work of the administrative branch."[9] Although Waldo does not press the point, the president has only two specific constitutional powers over domestic administration that are not shared with Congress: requesting written opinions from the principal officers of the executive departments and making recess appointments when the Senate is not in session (U.S. Constitution, Article II, section 2). In their advice, the members of the Brownlow Committee distorted rather than confirmed the separation of powers.

Luther Gulick. A member of the Brownlow Committee, Gulick could have claimed the title of "Mr. Orthodoxy." He wrote much, with much inconsistency, over his career. In representing Gulick's views on the separation of powers, Waldo concentrated on Gulick's 1933 essay titled "Politics, Administration, and the New Deal." According to Gulick, "The reason for separating politics from administration is not that their combination is a violation of a principle of government. The reason for insisting that the elected legislative and executive officials shall not interfere with the details of administration . . . is that this division of work makes use of specialization and appears to give better results than a system where such a differentiation does not exist."[10] The problem with this reasoning, as Waldo and other critics came to realize, grew out of the discretion afforded public administrators. Gulick stated that the acts of public employees constituted "a seamless web of discretion and action."[11] Philosophically, Congress and the president might not have a right to intervene in administration, but they have a constitutional duty to participate in policy making. To the extent that policy and administration represent a "seamless web" in the work of public employees, legislative and presidential intervention is inevitable.

At the time Waldo wrote *The Administrative State,* several of his contemporaries had already criticized the politics-administration dichotomy and offered more realistic interpretations of the relationship between politics and administration. Waldo wondered how the dichotomy could deal with the obvious administrative role in policy making, which he found to be "a lacuna in the literature." He concluded that the politics-administration dichotomy was "inadequate" and expressed confidence that the field was "on the way to a more adequate philosophy of the powers and functions of government, their nature and interrelation."[12]

CONGRESSIONAL RESPONSE TO
THE ADMINISTRATIVE STATE

The Administrative State is a condensed version of the Ph.D. dissertation Waldo submitted to Yale University's Department of Political Science in 1942. Published in 1948, it failed to consider the 1946 congressional response to the full-fledged post–New Deal, post–World War II administrative state and could not have anticipated the reaction of the federal judiciary to the growth of administrative power that began a few years later.[13]

In 1952, Justice Robert Jackson observed that American administrative agencies had become "a veritable fourth branch of the Government, which has deranged our three-branch legal theories."[14] Jackson, a keen observer of the American system, could hardly have failed to recognize this constitutional development. Through the New Deal and the world war that followed, American administrative agencies grew into power centers that were large, unwieldy, diffuse, and difficult to control. The president had acquired some leverage over this administrative apparatus through the creation of the Executive Office of the President (EOP) and by gaining a stronger role in federal budget making in the late 1930s. Presidential influence surpassed that possessed by Congress or the federal judiciary, although by most accounts it was still inadequate for presidential control.[15] If they wished to maintain rough coequality with the presidency, members of the legislative and judicial branches had to establish new or better means of influencing administrative decision making. As James Madison perceptively explained in Federalist Paper number 51, "The great security against a gradual concentration of the several powers in the same department, consists of

giving to those who administer each department, the necessary constitutional means, and personal motives, to resist encroachments of the
others. . . . Ambition must be made to counteract ambition. The interests of the man, must be connected with the constitutional rights of the
place."[16]

Congress asserted its interest in greater influence over federal administration in a self-conscious, concerted fashion. The courts promoted
theirs more incrementally through a variety of decisions beginning in
the early 1950s and crystallizing in 1975. The nature of judicial decision
making suggests that the judges' response to the administrative state
was more evolutionary than strategic. However, judges issued more
than enough judicial statements concerning the challenges of controlling bureaucracy to suggest they were concerned with the "derange-
ment" of America's separation of powers.[17]

The year 1946 was a watershed in the development of U.S. public
administration because Congress essentially "repealed" the politics-
administration dichotomy. During debate on the Administrative Procedure Act of 1946 (APA), members of Congress noted that civil
servants had "assumed the function of making laws" and exercised
"legislative and judicial powers." Lawmakers complained that "what
they do is binding upon the citizen exactly as statutes or judgments are
binding." Administrative rule making is policy making. If administrators made policy, then politics and administration were combined, not
separated. The APA was premised in part on an idea expressed by Representative Francis Walter (D-PA). "Day by day Congress takes account of the interests and desires of the people in framing legislation,"
he said. Commenting upon the policymaking tasks of federal bureaucrats, Walter argued that there was "no reason" why civil servants
should not do the same "when they exercise legislative functions
which the Congress has delegated to them."[18]

If administrative agencies engage in legislative functions, it is axiom-
atic that Congress should supervise the performance of those functions. By stripping away the fiction of the politics-administration
dichotomy, Congress removed the foundation for the administrative
independence advocated by Goodnow, Walker, and other orthodox
writers. In addition, the Brownlow Committee's prescription of a se-
verely limited role for Congress in the administrative state cannot be
sustained when agencies clearly exercise legislative lawmaking authority, albeit under the guise of "rule making."

Congress did not confine itself to regulation of administrative procedures as a means of exercising greater control over administration. The
1946 Legislative Reorganization Act provided a legal foundation, for

the first time in U.S. history, for the principle that Congress, through its standing committees, exercise "continuous watchfulness" of the agencies under their jurisdictions.[19] The term "continuous watchfulness" was deliberately ambiguous, though certainly broad enough to accommodate direct legislative efforts to correct maladministration of the laws. The act also provided for expanded and better qualified committee staff, partly to assist with oversight of administration. During the floor debate on the Legislative Reorganization Act, legislators frequently discussed the need for nonclerical personal staff to help constituents deal with federal agencies (i.e., "casework"). Provisions for this purpose were voted down in the House of Representatives out of concern that additional staff would be expensive and unnecessary. In the upper chamber, however, the volume of casework justified the appointment of such staff, and the Senate began doing so in 1947. Members of the House gradually followed suit.

In 1946, Congress also enacted the Employment Act. Within Congress, this was widely viewed as a means of gaining greater legislative control over the administrative allocation of public works projects. As with the APA and the Legislative Reorganization Act, this aspect of the Employment Act was premised on the inseparability of administrative and political decision making.

Overall, the congressional response to the administrative state enabled Congress to treat administrative agencies as its extensions for the performance of legislative functions. Congress regulated agency procedures through a substantial body of administrative law,[20] supervised agencies on a day-to-day basis, and gained the wherewithal to intercede in administrative decision making to promote the interests of constituents, districts, and states. The congressional role in administrative processes expanded in the decades that followed. In 1993, Congress legislated a role for itself in the strategic planning activities of administrative agencies.[21] Congress established its power to review and negate agency final rules in 1996, a role considered in the 1940s.[22] In contrast to the 1930s, when congressional oversight of administration was weak, one is more apt to hear complaints about legislative micromanagement or interference in administration today than laments that Congress is relatively powerless to combat administrators who "usurp power."[23]

Congress undertook these reforms, moreover, for reasons that departed substantially from the values inherent in the development of the traditional administrative state. As Luther Gulick and others noted, the primary aim of traditional administrative reform rested with the pursuit of efficiency. Such a pursuit was premised on the belief that the purpose of the administrative machine could be separated from considerations of how well it ran. For the most part, Congress proved less interested in promoting administrative efficiency than in overseeing and regulating administration to make it more transparent, open to public and stakeholder participation, less burdensome and invasive of individual rights, and more responsive to the members' constituency and district-oriented interests. Understandably, lawmakers were less enamored of the doctrine that administrative procedures could be separated from political concerns such as these.

JUDICIAL RESPONSE

The judicial response to the creation of the administrative state was more diffuse, but ultimately coherent. It rested on four pillars. First, beginning in the 1950s, the federal courts empowered private individuals to employ a wide array of constitutional rights to protect themselves in their encounters with public administrators. Clients or customers, public mental health patients, prisoners, property owners, contractors, and even public servants can all assert substantial constitutional rights as part of the administrative process. These rights simply did not exist prior to the 1950s. To a lesser extent, the courts extended similar rights to individuals confronted by police and other "street-level bureaucrats." Much of the so-called rights revolution of the third quarter of the twentieth century constrained administrative action. Judges accomplished this by strengthening the "unconstitutional conditions" doctrine, which limits the conditions that administrative agencies can attach to the receipt of benefits, jobs, contracts, permits, and licenses; by applying a new and invigorated equal protection doctrine to administrative actions; and by developing a "new property" doctrine, which redefines many governmental benefits, such as civil service jobs, as individuals' property subject to the protection afforded by the Constitution's due process clauses.

Second, the courts relaxed the requirements necessary to establish standing, a prerequisite for citizens wishing to seek judicial remedies for improper administrative decisions. Once a formidable barrier to bringing suits, by 1975 Kenneth Culp Davis would conclude that "the present law of standing differs no more than slightly, if it differs at all, from the simple proposition that one who is hurt by governmental action has standing to challenge it."[24] Easier standing meant that more cases alleging administrative abuse could be brought to the federal courts, which gave judges additional opportunities to expand individual rights.

The availability of new rights provides the judiciary with greater potential to intervene in public administration. Enforcement powers help realize that potential. The third pillar arose around the willingness of the courts to develop "remedial law." This concept enables judges to enforce their decisions by supervising the management of administrative facilities and activities such as prisons and public schools, mental health hospitals, and personnel systems. The experience of public servants in the city of Boston is an exemplar of this particular judicial response to the growth of the administrative state. In 1981, federal and state judges "presided over" administrative activities amounting to 48 percent of the city's operating budget, essentially for the purpose of remedying past breaches of individual rights and preventing future violations of them.[25]

The fourth pillar made public employees and executive officials at all levels of government potentially personally liable for their constitutional torts—that is, for their violations of individuals' constitutional rights. By 1975, the Supreme Court had fully abandoned the historic presumption that public administrators generally possessed absolute immunity from civil suits for money damages in response to actions taken within the framework of their jobs.[26] Instead, public servants typically now possess only qualified immunity and may be held personally liable if they violate "clearly established statutory or constitutional rights of which a reasonable person would have known."[27] Rights can be "clearly established" even in the absence of a precedent with materially similar facts. Rather, the question is "whether the state of the law" gives the administrator "fair warning" that an action will be unconstitutional.[28] In a self-interested way, qualified immunity creates a direct incentive for public administrators to understand the constitutional law regulating their official actions. Because "constitutional law is what the courts say it is,"[29] qualifying the scope of administrators' immunity this way enables judges to use the Constitution as a basis for prescribing appropriate administrative practices. Emblematic here is the burgeoning field of "constitutional audits" in prison administration, in which the activities of public administrators are reviewed for their constitutional propriety.[30]

While it was crystallizing, constitutional scholars viewed the judicial response to the administrative state as an extraordinary development. During the 1970s, books with titles such as *Government by Judiciary* and *The Jurocracy* appeared.[31] By the twenty-first century, however, deep judicial involvement in public administration was considered a normal feature of the U.S. governmental scene. It is doubtful that many were surprised in 1995 when the *Washington Post* published an editorial explaining "Why the Courts Are Running D.C." and supporting the judges for doing so.[32]

Neither the congressional nor judicial responses sought to reduce presidential power over administration. This is an important point. The U.S. president, ostensibly the chief executive, was not viewed as part of the problem by lawmakers and judges. Rather, the legislative and judicial responses to the growth of administrative power sought to enhance the capacity of Congress and the federal courts to play major roles in directing the administrative state. In some instances, congressional and judicial decisions even strengthened presidential control.[33]

CAN THREE GO INTO ONE?

In 1939, Lewis Meriam noted that "under our system of divided powers, the executive branch of the national government is not exclusively controlled by the President, by the Congress, or by the courts. All three have a hand in controlling it, each from a different angle and each in a different way."[34] At the time, Meriam's statement was prospective, in the sense that none of the branches had developed the sufficient means to control the emerging administrative state. By the last quarter of the twentieth century, however, actual practices had confirmed Meriam's observation. Federal public administration was subordinate to all three branches of government, and each brought distinct institutional values and perspectives to the supervision of agency decision making and other actions. Reflecting on a 1983 article on the separation of powers, Waldo succinctly observed,

> For each of the three constitutional branches . . . there is a body of doctrine, set of values, collection of instruments, and repertoire of procedures. For the executive branch this "cluster" is administrative, managerial, bureaucratic, and the emphasis is on effectiveness and efficiency. For the legislative branch the cluster is political and policy making, and the emphasis is upon the values of representativeness and responsiveness. For the judicial branch the cluster is legal, and the emphasis is on constitutional integrity on one side and substantive and procedural protections for individuals on the other.
>
> Realistically our public administration does consist of varying mixtures of these three approaches or clusters.

Waldo had stern advice for those who would confine administrative studies to matters of management, efficiency, and effectiveness. "It is not just undesirable, it is impossible," he said, "to narrow the concerns of public administration" to the perspective imposed by any one cluster. "Our task," he concluded, "is to find the proper way to put the three together."[35]

CONTEMPORARY REFORM AND
THE SEPARATION OF POWERS

Contemporary reformers disagree with this point of view. They argue that legislative and judicial involvement under the separation of powers doctrine has yielded a convoluted, process-obsessed, and input-oriented public administration. Such administration, in their view, cannot respond to customers or produce the cost-effective results citizens presumably want. To them, the post-orthodox administration that became conventional in the United States after 1946 has produced a proliferation of red tape, legislative interference, and litigiousness making governmental administration wasteful and ineffective compared to the private sector.

The National Performance Review (NPR), introduced by the Clinton-Gore administration in September 1993, sought to reestablish the primacy of cost-effectiveness. Its proponents called for a "reinvention" of federal administration to make it "work better and cost less." In spite of their forward-looking rhetoric, however, the fundamental assumptions and prescriptions regarding the separation of powers advanced by NPR advocates had much in common with orthodox thinking. In the first NPR report, Vice President Al Gore attempted to resuscitate the politics-administration dichotomy, observing that administrative improvement "is not about politics" and did not depend on "which party is in power." More generally, the dichotomy reappeared in one of reinvention's major themes, the notion that government should "steer more, row less."[36] The report echoed the advice of the 1937 Brownlow Committee in its call for Congress to reduce its involvement in federal administration. Among Gore's chief complaints were:

> Congressional appropriations often come with hundreds of strings attached. . . . As the federal budget tightens, lawmakers request increasingly specific report language to protect activities in their districts. . . . Even worse, Congress often gives a single agency multiple missions, some of which are contradictory. . . . One place to start liberating agencies from congressional micromanagement is the issue of reporting requirements. . . . In fiscal year 1993, Congress required executive branch

agencies to prepare 5,348 reports. Much of this work is duplicative. . . .
Meanwhile, trapped in this blizzard of paperwork, no one is looking at
results.[37]

Vice President Gore and the NPR staff issued a large number of prescriptions aimed at reducing the congressional role in federal administration. They advocated strengthening the executive budget process, making it more difficult for Congress to ignore or reject the president's budget proposals. They proposed biennial budgets, aimed at reducing the amount of time lawmakers spend on budgetary decisions and their ability to use budgets as a means of controlling agency activities. They recommended that Congress restrict its use of line items, earmarks, and full-time equivalent personnel floors. "Congress should permanently allow agencies to roll over 50 percent of unobligated year-end balances in all appropriations for operations," the reform group suggested as a means to encourage administrative cost savings and promote budgetary independence. They also sought enhancement of the president's recision power, making it easier for him (or her) to counteract congressional spending decisions. "Reduce the burden of congressionally mandated reports," the group implored.[38]

Some lawmakers supported these actions in the name of better administration. Many lawmakers called upon the president to mitigate their own collective inability to reduce wasteful pork-barrel and district-oriented spending, as they did with the Defense Base Closure and Realignment Act (1990) and with the ultimately unconstitutional Line Item Veto Act of 1996.[39] From a broader perspective, however, the 1946 congressional framework for administrative involvement rests on a fundamental element of American constitutional theory—the belief in legislative supremacy (or at least coequality) in a system of separated powers. The framework also contributes to incumbents' electoral advantages by allowing them to serve as the advocates of constituency interests when the latter are aggrieved.[40] Short of a major crisis, change in the name of cost-effective, results-oriented administrative reform is unlikely to trump political and constitutional philosophy and political advantage.

In fact, one could easily argue that some of the reforms designed to improve federal administration in the last decade of the twentieth century strengthened legislative oversight of administration. The Government Performance and Results Act (1993) and the Congressional Review Act (1996) enlarged the potential involvement of Congress by granting the legislative branch a role in agency strategic planning and creating a new institutional process for nullifying final administrative rules. The movement toward a performance budget for the federal government, contained in the Government Performance and Results Act, would also enhance congressional oversight.

By contrast, President George W. Bush is a strong proponent of executive power. His ideas about federal administration sound very much like those of Al Gore during the 2000 election campaign. Bush reported that "my policies and my vision of government reform are guided by three principles: government should be citizen-centered, results oriented, and wherever possible, market-based."[41] This repeated the rhetoric of the NPR. The enhancement of administrative capability, however, was not to come at the expense of executive control. "In 34 years" in Washington, Vice President Richard Cheney observed, "I have repeatedly seen an erosion of the powers and the ability of the president of the United States to do his job." The American presidency, Cheney added, had been weakened "because of the unwise compromises that have been made over the last 30 or 35 years."[42] He and Bush promised to strengthen the office, its autonomy, and its authority for dealing with administrative agencies. Like the Brownlow Committee and the NPR, Bush favored a reduction of the congressional role in federal administration. Following Brownlow, but departing from Gore, his administration also preferred centralizing executive power in the White House and in the EOP.

The Bush administration deliberately sought to reduce congressional participation in federal administration by withholding information from it. When asked why the administration had refused to release some information considered vital by Congress, former press secretary Ari Fleischer replied, "Is it because we have something to hide? No." Rather, Fleischer continued, the promotion of confidential discussions was "the best way to have a healthy discussion inside an administration and that serves the President." Speaking for the Republican administration, Fleischer, apparently straight-faced, elaborated, "The pendulum probably shifted too far toward the Congress, in terms of probing the administration, during the Clinton years. . . . I think there's been a healthy rebalancing so the executive can have the authority to get the job done."[43]

Sometimes relying on an expansive vision of "executive privilege" and other times just stonewalling, the Bush administration quickly developed a reputation for not being forthcoming. Vice President Cheney refused to release information regarding the composition of the National Energy Policy Development Group to the General Accounting Office (GAO).[44] Attorney General John Ashcroft's expressed repeated disdain for congressional requests seeking information related to the

Department of Justice's antiterrorism activity. The congressional reaction to Ashcroft provided a rare vestige of legislative bipartisanship. Republican Senator Charles Grassley (IA) likened the process of "getting information" from the Department of Justice to "pulling teeth."[45] His Democratic colleague, Patrick Leahy (VT), averred that in his three decades of service, "I have never known an administration that is more difficult to get information from that the oversight committees are entitled to."[46]

In another case, Secretary of Health and Human Services Tommy Thompson unsuccessfully attempted to consolidate (i.e., limit) information flowing from his department. Congress, preferring "choirs to soloists" when it comes to information sources, refused to appropriate $28 million for Thompson's vision of "one department, one voice."[47] The administration's massive effort to outsource several hundred thousand "commercial-like jobs" in the federal administrative establishment significantly reduces congressional oversight of appropriations and work performance and renders inapplicable a number of federal transparency statutes, such as the Freedom of Information Act.[48] As political scientist Thomas Mann summarized with regard to the Bush administration, "They are consumed with secrecy. They have cut Congress off."[49]

The Bush administration relied extensively on units and functionaries within the EOP in its efforts to centralize executive control over federal administration. On inaugural day, 2001, Bush's White House chief of staff, Andrew Card Jr., issued a controversial—and possibly illegal—memorandum asking federal agencies to postpone the effective date of final rules for sixty days.[50] More dramatically, Bush initially sought to "go it alone" in the war on terrorism by using an executive order to establish the original Office of Homeland Security (OHS) within the EOP.[51] Eventually this arrangement, which left the OHS budget scattered in more than two thousand accounts, could not be sustained.[52] The Constitution places the power to create federal departments and agencies in Congress. After much political wrangling, Congress and the administration agreed on a new Department of Homeland Security, though not before OHS Secretary Tom Ridge riled Congress by citing the separation of powers as grounds for his refusal to testify formally with respect to the OHS' request for a $38 billion appropriation for fiscal year 2003.[53] Congress granted the new department a number of flexibilities that enhanced the authority of its political appointees in dealing with career personnel. For example, the department was exempt from standard federal labor relations requirements, hiring rules, job classification systems, pay rates and systems, and adverse actions appeals procedures.[54]

Officials in the Bush administration relied heavily on the U.S. Office of Management and Budget (OMB), part of the EOP, to promote the President's Management Agenda.[55] OMB plays a centralizing role in four of the agenda's five government-wide initiatives: competitive sourcing (i.e., determining whether the government's "commercial jobs" should be outsourced), improved financial performance, expanded electronic government, and budget and performance integration.[56] In another centralizing move, OMB's Office of Information and Regulatory Affairs took a strong role in overseeing agency rule-making activities, including substantive evaluation of proposed rules.[57]

EVALUATING ADMINISTRATIVE REFORM: A MADISONIAN APPROACH

In Federalist Paper number 47, James Madison warned that "the accumulation of all powers, legislative, executive, and judiciary, in the same hands, whether of one, a few, or many, and whether hereditary, self-appointed, or elective, may justly be pronounced the very definition of tyranny."[58] The growth of the administrative state in the first half of the twentieth century deranged the separation of powers doctrine precisely because administrative processes combine legislative, executive, and judicial powers—often within the same agency. Congress and the federal courts responded to this accumulation by integrating the separation of powers doctrine into federal administration and by strengthening tripartite control over the administrative agencies. Federal administrators must now adhere to legislative values and processes when they perform legislative functions and judicial values when they adjudicate. Congress and the judiciary have substantially enhanced their ability to oversee and direct administration. Consequently, modern public administrative theory and practice are much more compatible with the political theory of U.S. democratic constitutionalism than when Waldo penned *The Administrative State.*

Administration is also much more cumbersome, as contemporary reformers often contend. In *Immigration and Naturalization Service v. Chadha* (1983), the Supreme Court fully agreed that the separation of powers, along with other constitutional provisions, "impose burdens on governmental processes that often seem clumsy, inefficient, even unworkable."[59] However, the justices also reaffirmed the fundamental need to adapt administrative principles to constitutional arrangements. In the contest between administrative and constitutional principles, the latter are supreme. The Constitution cannot be rearranged in the name of cost-effectiveness, except by amendment: "There is no support in the

Constitution or decisions of this Court for the proposition that the cumbersomeness and delays often encountered in complying with explicit constitutional standards may be avoided. . . . With all the obvious flaws of delay, untidiness, and potential for abuse, we have not yet found a better way to preserve freedom than by making the exercise of power subject to the carefully crafted restraints spelled out in the Constitution."[60]

Major public administrative reforms have both political and efficiency effects. If one agrees with the Supreme Court in *Chadha*, as Waldo did,[61] then proponents of reform incur an obligation to measure the effects of change on democratic constitutionalism as well as on more conventional administrative values such as efficiency and flexibility. Otherwise, important democratic-constitutional values, such as freedom of information, may be weakened through inattentiveness.[62] In short, reformers need a scorecard that assesses the compatibility of proposed reforms with democratic and constitutional values.

A "democratic-constitutional scorecard" would join a variety of scorecards for measuring and tracking organizational change.[63] The Bush administration attached an "executive branch management scorecard" to its proposed 2003 budget.[64] At a minimum, a democratic-constitutional scorecard would grade proposed administrative reforms and reorganizations with respect to their probable impacts on (1) the vibrancy of the separation of powers, (2) individual rights vis-à-vis public administration, (3) public participation and stakeholder representation, and (4) executive branch transparency as contemplated by administrative law statutes and the Constitution's "receipts and expenditures" clause.[65] Actual scoring could be done by any number of knowledgeable governmental, academic, or informed observers. Competing scorecards might be useful in promoting full evaluation of reforms and reorganizations. Almost any reasonable scorecard format would protect against the weakening of democratic-constitutional values by default or neglect, a concern that runs very strongly throughout *The Administrative State*.

In *The Administrative State*, Waldo asks, "Is not efficiency for efficiency's sake meaningless? *Is efficiency not necessarily measured in terms of other values?*" One might ask the same of public management generally, as Waldo often did.[66] He considered the difficulty of reconciling democratic and bureaucratic values to be a challenge "that pervades our society: our institutions, our organizations, our associations, private and mixed, as well as our governmental and business entities."[67] How can reformers say that their reform and reorganization proposals score high on "executive branch management" if they simultaneously weaken democratic constitutionalism by diminishing the separation of powers or curtailing individual rights, public participation, representation, and transparency?

NOTES

1. Dwight Waldo, *The Administrative State: A Study of the Political Theory of American Public Administration,* 2nd ed. (New York: Holmes & Meier, 1984), 104, 111, 121.

2. Ibid., 104.

3. Quoted in ibid., 106.

4. Ibid., 106, 107. Goodnow is unclear on how the judicial function fits into the expression and execution of the will of the state, although, as Waldo points out, he indicates that the courts make law and administer justice. Ibid., 106, note 10.

5. Quoted in ibid., 109–11.

6. Quoted in ibid., 112.

7. Ibid., 113.

8. Quoted in ibid., 114.

9. Quoted in ibid., 111.

10. Quoted in ibid., 118. Gulick was the chief target of Herbert Simon, "The Proverbs of Administration," *Public Administration Review* 6 (Winter 1946): 53–67.

11. Quoted in Waldo, *Administrative State,* 118.

12. Ibid., 121. In his preface to the second edition, Waldo notes that this expectation was not "borne out" and admits that the original chapter 7, republished in the second edition, has "an air of antiquity." Ibid., xlii.

13. David H. Rosenbloom, *Public Administration and Law* (New York: Marcel Dekker, 1983), and Rosenbloom and Rosemary O'Leary, *Public Administration and Law,* 2nd ed. (New York: Marcel Dekker, 1997); Rosenbloom, *Building a Legislative-Centered Public Administration* (Tuscaloosa: University of Alabama Press, 2000). See also Rosenbloom, "Retrofitting the Administrative State to the Constitution: Congress and the Judiciary's Twentieth-Century Progress," *Public Administration Review* 60 (January/February 2000): 39–46; and Rosenbloom, "Whose Bureaucracy Is This, Anyway? Congress' 1946 Answer," *PS: Political Science and Politics* 34 (December 2001): 773–77.

14. *Federal Trade Commission v. Ruberoid,* 343 U.S. 470, 487 (1952; dissenting opinion).

15. In 1952, President Harry Truman mused while contemplating president-elect Eisenhower's arrival in the White House: "He'll say, Do this! Do that! *And nothing will happen.* Poor Ike—it won't be a bit like the Army. He'll find it very frustrating." Richard Neustadt, *Presidential Power* (New York: John Wiley and Sons, 1969), 9.

16. George W. Carey and James McClellan, eds., *The Federalist*, Federalist No. 51, author James Madison (Indianapolis, IN: Liberty Fund, 2001), 268.

17. Justice William O. Douglas was a leader in advocating greater subordination of public administration to constitutional values. Among his statements were the following: "The bureaucracy of modern government is not only slow, lumbering, and oppressive; it is omnipresent" (*Wyman v. James,* 400 U.S. 309, 335 [1971]); "The sovereign of this Nation is the people, not the bureaucracy" (*U.S. v. Richardson,* 418 U.S. 166, 201 [1974]); and "Today's mounting bureaucracy, both at the state and federal levels, promises to be suffocating and repressive, unless it is put into the harness of procedural due process" (*Spady v. Mount Vernon,* 419 U.S. 983, 985 [1974]).

18. *Administrative Procedure Act,* Public Law 79-404, *U.S. Statutes at Large* 60 (1946): 237. Quoted in Rosenbloom, *Building a Legislative-Centered Public Administration,* 7, 38–39.

19. *Legislative Reorganization Act,* Public Law 79-601, *U.S. Statutes at Large* 60 (1946): 812, sect. 136.

20. The list includes the *Administrative Dispute Resolution Acts,* Public Law 101-552, *U.S. Statutes at Large* 104 (1990): 2736, and Public Law 104-320, *U.S. Statutes at Large* 110 (1996): 3870; *Federal Advisory Committee Act,* Public Law 92-463, *U.S. Statutes at Large* 86 (1972): 770; *Freedom of Information Act and Amendments,* Public Law 89-487, *U.S. Statutes at Large* 80 (1966): 250, and Public Law 93-502, *U.S. Statutes at Large* 88 (1974): 1561; *Government in the Sunshine Act,* Public Law 94-409, *U.S. Statutes at Large* 90 (1976): 1241; *Inspector General Act,* Public Law 95-452, *U.S. Statutes at Large* 92 (1978): 1101; *Negotiated Rulemaking Act,* Public Law 101-648; *U.S. Statutes at Large* 104 (1990): 4969; *Paperwork Reduction Acts,* Public Law 96-511, *U.S. Statutes at Large* 94 (1980): 2812, and Public Law 104-13, *U.S. Statutes at Large* 109 (1995): 163; *Privacy Act,* Public Law 93-579, *U.S. Statutes at Large* 88 (1974): 1896; *Regulatory Flexibility Act,* Public Law 96-354, *U.S. Statutes at Large* 94 (1980): 1164.

21. *Government Performance and Results Act,* Public Law 103-62, *U.S. Statutes at Large* 107 (1993): 285.

22. *Small Business Regulatory Enforcement Fairness Act,* Public Law 104-121, *U.S. Statutes at Large* 110 (1996): 857. The provision for congressional review of agency rules is often called the Congressional Review Act.

23. Statement by Representative Earl Michener (R-MI) in 1940. Quoted in and see Rosenbloom, *Building a Legislative-Centered Public Administration,* 7, for the full context.

24. Kenneth Culp Davis, *Administrative Law and Government* (St. Paul, MN: West Publishing, 1975), 72.

25. Robert Turner, "Governing from the Bench," *Boston Globe Magazine,* November 8, 1981, 12ff.

26. *Wood v. Strickland,* 420 U.S. 308 (1975).

27. *Harlow v. Fitzgerald,* 457 U.S. 800, 818 (1982). Public administrators retain absolute immunity when engaged in judicial functions and integral

legislative activity. See *Butz v. Economou,* 438 U.S. 478 (1978), and *Bogan v. Scott-Harris,* 523 U.S. 44 (1998).

28. *Hope v. Pelzer,* 536 U.S. 730, 741 (2002).

29. *Owen v. City of Independence,* 445 U.S. 622, 669 (1980).

30. Malcolm Feeley and Roger Hanson, "The Impact of Judicial Intervention on Prisons and Jails," in *Courts, Corrections, and the Constitution,* ed. John DiIulio Jr. (New York: Oxford University Press, 1990), 26.

31. Raoul Berger, *Government by Judiciary* (Cambridge, MA: Harvard University Press, 1977); Donald Horowitz, *The Jurocracy* (Lexington, MA: Lexington Books, 1977).

32. "Why the Courts Are Running D.C.," *Washington Post,* August 15, 1995, p. A16.

33. Paul Light, *The Tides of Reform* (New Haven, CT: Yale University Press, 1997), 206, observes that "Congress was still quite capable of loaning the keys to administrative reform to the presidency" for paperwork reduction, and it "still shows a surprising readiness to defer to the commander in chief with regard to the war on waste." The Supreme Court's decisions in *Vermont Yankee Nuclear Power Corp. v. Natural Resources Defense Council,* 435 U.S. 519 (1978); *Chevron v. Natural Resources Defense Council,* 467 U.S. 837 (1984); and *Heckler v. Chaney,* 476 U.S. 821 (1985), give agencies greater independence from judicial review with regard to rule making, statutory interpretation, and discretionary nonenforcement.

34. Lewis Meriam, *Reorganization of the National Government: Part I: An Analysis of the Problem* (Washington, DC: Brookings Institution, 1939), 131.

35. Brack Brown and Richard Stillman, "A Conversation with Dwight Waldo: An Agenda for Future Reflections," *Public Administration Review* 45 (July/August 1985): 463–64. Waldo's observations are based on David H. Rosenbloom, "Public Administrative Theory and the Separation of Powers," *Public Administration Review* 43 (May–June 1983): 219–27.

36. Al Gore, *From Red Tape to Results: Creating a Government That Works Better and Costs Less: The Report of the National Performance Review* (Washington, DC: U.S. Government Printing Office, 1993), iv, 7.

37. Ibid., 13, 34.

38. Ibid., 20, 34.

39. *Defense Base Closure and Realignment Act,* Public Law 101-510. *U.S. Statutes at Large* 104 (1990): 1808; *Line Item Veto Act,* Public Law 104-130, 110 (1996): 1200. The latter was declared an unconstitutional effort to give the president lawmaking power in *Clinton v. City of New York,* 524 U.S. 417 (1998).

40. Rosenbloom, *Building a Legislative-Centered Public Administration,* chap. 4.

41. George W. Bush, "Building a Responsive, Innovative Government," *Federal Times,* June 26, 2000, 15.

42. Quoted in Victor Kirk, "Congress in Eclipse as Power Shifts to Executive Branch," *Government Executive,* April 7, 2003, p. 1, www.govexec.com/dailyfed/0403/040703nj1.htm (accessed April 7, 2003).

43. Alexis Simendinger, "Results-Oriented President Uses Levers of Power," *Government Executive*, January 25, 2002, p. 7, www.govexec.com/dailyfed/0102/012502nj2.htm (accessed January 25, 2002).

44. *Walker v. Cheney*, U.S. District Court for the District of Columbia, Civil Action No. 02-0340 (December 9, 2002).

45. Kirk, "Congress in Eclipse," 6.

46. Adam Clymer, "Justice Dept. Balks at Effort to Study Antiterror Powers," *New York Times*, August 15, 2002, p. A14.

47. Rick Weiss, "HHS Sought 'One Voice' from Its Many Mouths: Hill Rejected Centralized Information Flow," *Washington Post*, March 12, 2003, sec. A, p.19.

48. U.S. Office of Management and Budget, *Competitive Sourcing: Conducting Public-Private Competition in a Reasoned and Responsible Manner* (Washington, DC: U.S. Office of Management and Budget, 2003), 3.

49. Quoted from Kirk, "Congress in Eclipse," 7.

50. Cindy Skrzycki, "Critics Assail Review of 'Final' Rules," *Washington Post*, May 29, 2001, sec. E, p. 6.

51. Simendinger, "Results-Oriented President," 1.

52. Bill Miller, "$37 Billion for Homeland Defense Is a Start, Bush Says," *Washington Post*, January 25, 2002, sec. A, p. 15.

53. Liza Porteus and Lisa Caruso, "Dems Continue to Rap Ridge for Failure to Testify on Hill," *Government Executive*, April 12, 2002, www.govexec.com/dailyfed/0402/041202cdam1.htm (accessed April 12, 2002).

54. Brody Mullins, "Bush, Senate GOP Win Big on Homeland Security Bill," *Government Executive*, November 19, 2002, www.govexec.com/dailyfed/1102/111902cd1.htm (accessed November 19, 2002).

55. Katherine Peters, "Agencies to Receive More Money Scrutiny, OMB Chief Says," *Government Executive*, January 24, 2002, www.govexec.com/dailyfed/0102/012402kp1.htm (accessed January 24, 2002); Tom Shoop, "Bush Budget Rips Agencies' Management in Key Areas," *Government Executive*, February 4, 2002, www.govexec.com/dailyfed/0202/020402ts1.htm (accessed February 4, 2002).

56. The fifth initiative is "strategic management of human capital" and contains a budget component linked to downsizing. See U. S. Office of Management and Budget, *The President's Management Agenda* (Washington, DC: U.S. Office of Management and Budget, 2001).

57. David H. Rosenbloom, *Administrative Law for Public Managers* (Boulder, CO: Westview, 2003), 77–78.

58. Federalist No. 47, author James Madison, 249.

59. *Immigration and Naturalization Service v. Chadha*, 421 U.S. 919, 959 (1983).

60. *Immigration and Naturalization Service v. Chadha*.

61. Dwight Waldo, *The Enterprise of Public Administration* (Novato, CA: Chandler & Sharp, 1980), 103–4, placed "Obligation to the Constitution" first on a list of public administrators' ethical obligations.

62. See Suzanne J. Piotrowski and David H. Rosenbloom, "Nonmission-Based Values in Results-Oriented Public Management: The Case of Freedom of Information," *Public Administration Review* 62 (November/December 2002): 643–57.

63. Perhaps the most popular approach is Robert Kaplan and David Norton, "The Balanced Scorecard—Measures That Drive Performance," *Harvard Business Review* 70, no. 1 (1992): 71–79; and Kaplan and Norton, *The Balanced Scorecard* (Boston, MA: Harvard Business School Press, 1996).

64. Shoop, "Bush Budget Rips Agencies' Management."

65. U.S. Constitution, article I, section 9, clause 8.

66. Waldo, *Administrative State,* 193.

67. Waldo, *Enterprise of Public Administration,* 89.

7

The Thinning of Administrative Institutions

LARRY D. TERRY

[S]tudents of administration remain generally of the opinion that the values and practices of American Business can be accepted for governmental administration with only slight reservations. There is an aura of explicit doubt and skepticism about all of these tenets.

Dwight Waldo, *The Administrative State*

In *The Test of Time: An Essay in Philosophical Aesthetics*, the British philosopher Anthony Savile examined the meaning of the concept "test of time" as it relates to works of art. Savile suggested that works of art pass the test of time because of "survival of attention," that is to say, they hold our attention because of their high quality, excellence, or merit. According to Savile, "Great art is bound to be influential," and such art "leaves its mark on what follows."[1]

Dwight Waldo's *The Administrative State*, by most accounts, is a work of art that has withstood the test of time. As the essays in this book attest, *The Administrative State* has been extremely influential; it has left a mark by raising a number of "big questions" ranging from the role of administration in our constitutional democracy to the difficulty of wholeheartedly adopting or displacing private-sector practices to governmental administration.[2] Many of these big questions remain at the center of scholarly discussions today. Chief among them are Waldo's remarks regarding the wholesale adoption of private-sector management practices by governmental agencies. Waldo's concerns are especially relevant when viewed from the perspective of what observers of government call an increasingly "hollow state."

Waldo spread his insights into the relationship between business and public administration throughout his book; he wrote no single chapter on the subject. A section on the "businessman as administrator" appears in the chapter titled "Who Should Rule?" In it, Waldo observed, "There is in the early writings a strong presumption that the businessman is the 'expert' who is entitled to rule. The businessman has built this civilization; so he is morally entitled and mentally equipped to run it."[3] In an earlier section on "business influence," he notes that the concept of "administration-is-business had become a creed, a shibboleth."[4] He was referring to movements and writings influencing public administration during the first part of the twentieth century, but he might as well have been commenting on the mood affecting American administrative reform in the first part of the twenty-first century.

THE CONCEPT OF THE HOLLOW STATE

H. Brinton Milward, Keith Provan, and Barbara Else introduced the term "hollow state" into the public affairs community. Drawing on the private-sector idea of the hollow corporation, Milward and his associates used the metaphor of the hollow state to "describe the nature of the devolution of power and decentralization of services from central governments to subnational governments, and by extension to third parties—nonprofit agencies and private firms—who increasingly manage in the name of the state." Stated simply, the hollow state refers to the extent to which governments do or do not directly provide services. Although scholars have used other phrases to describe this phenomenon, the metaphor of the hollow state is now widely recognized as the term of choice among those who talk and write about the changing nature of the public sector.[5]

When Milward and his coauthors directed attention to the hollow state, the phenomenon was in its adolescent stages of development— but rapidly maturing as administrative technologies such as contracting out, other forms of privatization, and deregulation gained widespread popular and political support. As the march toward an increasingly hollow state progressed with deliberate speed, writers across a spectrum of disciplines sought to understand its nature, characteristics, and administrative requirements, as well as its implications for democratic governance.[6] These efforts provided important insights into the hollow state phenomenon.

Much is now known about the hollow state. The phenomenon requires public managers to develop special competencies and skills to effectively function in the hollow state.[7] The emergence of nongovernmental partners as deliverers of public services has raised important questions about democratic accountability and, in turn, the legitimacy of the remaining state.[8] The primary administrative technologies used to create the hollow state are known to be integral components of a global revolution in public management broadly described as the new public management (NPM).[9] This revolutionary approach to public management and its impact on governmental administrative institutions forced to function in an increasingly hollow state is the focus of this chapter.

In the context of *The Administrative State*, these developments raise serious questions about the capacity of government officials to carry out their work. The NPM philosophy and practices associated with it have created an increasingly hollow state with *thinning* administrative institutions. Thin administrative institutions are "fragile" institutions.[10] Fragile institutions lack the integrity and the capacity to effectively serve the public good. To borrow a phrase from the progressive movement that launched the early concern with public administration, weak administrative institutions lack the capacity for "good government." This is a matter of great concern for persons in the public administration community, for, as Alexander Hamilton wisely wrote in Federalist Paper number 27, the confidence of the American public in its government is "proportioned to the goodness or badness of its administration."[11] The thinning of administrative institutions exacerbates the erosion of public confidence in government.[12] As a matter of political theory, the inevitable cycle of thinning and the eroding of public confidence in government deserves serious consideration. It raises troubling questions about the long-term stability of constitutional democracy.

The analysis that follows begins with a brief discussion of the NPM. This discussion is guided by the premise that the NPM movement is, in many respects, a response to the crisis of the Western state created by market libertarians.[13] Special attention is devoted to the two dominant approaches of the NPM movement, *liberation management* and *market-driven management*. An examination of the concept of thin institutions follows. This examination draws on the institutional theories of Philip Selznick and Richard Scott, which offer a theoretical framework for examining and assessing the capacity of administrative institutions.[14] Employing this framework and concrete examples, this discussion illustrates the manner in which NPM reforms contribute to the thinning of administrative institutions. The chapter concludes with an assessment of the implications for constitutional democracy, especially in the United States.

CRISIS, REFORM, AND THE NEW PUBLIC MANAGEMENT

The Dutch scholars Arjen Boin and Paul 't Hart offer a convincing insight into the relationship between crisis and reform. In a probing analysis of public leadership in troubled times, Boin and 't Hart argue that crises provide golden opportunities for the reform of institutional structures and long-standing policies. While Boin and 't Hart challenge aspects of the crisis-reform nexus, they acknowledge that political leaders use, and in some instances create, crises to generate momentum for governmental reform.

Boin and 't Hart assert that "reform leadership is an exercise in creative destruction," in the sense that "old structures must be destroyed before new ones can be implemented." They advise reform-minded public leaders to "exploit the crisis damage" and "build support for nonincremental reform" by portraying such crises as rising from "flaws in the existing institutional order."[15] The scholars advise leaders exploiting crises in attempts to generate reform to make frequent, strong public pronouncements about their commitment to drastic change.

Boin and 't Hart's crisis-reform thesis and related reform imperatives help to illuminate the nature of global governmental reform in recent times. As with Prime Minister Margaret Thatcher in Great Britain and Ronald Reagan in the United States, political leaders of the "market libertarian" persuasion sought to create a sense of crisis as a means of achieving wide-ranging public-sector restructuring.[16] To achieve this end they used multiple strategies, including "rhetoric and policy decisions to undermine the capabilities of the state, turning the macrocrisis of Western society into a crisis of the Western state."[17] They redirected general public discontent toward the administrative state and public servants, creating a movement that demanded radical changes in the fundamental nature of the state.[18] Daniel Cohn astutely observes that "neoconservative governments, led by committed market libertarians" sought to change the "purposes and operating values of the state."[19] According to Cohn, the reformers sought to turn the dominant political philosophy of the Keynesian welfare state on its head. Market libertarians were unified in their goal of protecting the market from political demands emerging from the society at large. This was a radical departure from the older goal of protecting society from the market's demands.

Market libertarians, with the support of various pragmatists, successfully turned the macrocrisis of Western society into a crisis of the Western state. In English-speaking democracies especially, political leaders exploited public discontent by blaming the state for slow economic growth, inflationary wage pressures, and a multitude of other economic and social sins. Consistent with the arguments advanced by Boin and 't Hart, market libertarians communicated a sharply honed message: the illnesses of Western societies could be cured only by drastically reforming the public sector and implementing management technologies compatible with the new "Schumpeterian workfare state."[20] This required dismantling and abandoning traditional administrative management practices associated with the Keynesian welfare state and replacing them with management technologies conveniently organized under the label of the NPM.[21]

THE NEW PUBLIC MANAGEMENT AND RESTRUCTURING OF GOVERNANCE

Government officials worldwide responded to the market libertarian message. In countries as diverse as New Zealand, Zambia, Japan, Italy, Portugal, Turkey, Chile, France, Singapore, and Australia, public officials aggressively pursued sweeping reforms and adopted NPM practices.[22] With an evangelical zeal, NPM believers sought to convert others by enthusiastically proclaiming that the "New Public Management was here to stay."[23] The meaning of this statement is not entirely clear. Exactly what is the "New Public Management"? The answer to this question has been the subject of intense debate.

At least as far back as 1991, when Christopher Hood published his seminal article "A Public Management for All Seasons?" scholars and practitioners have been debating the meaning of NPM in journals and at professional conferences.[24] They have debated the origins and theoretical foundation of NPM, questioned whether NPM represents a separate and distinct field of management studies, and pondered whether NPM is a passing fad.[25] Although this debate is far from over, consensus on the theoretical foundation of NPM has emerged. Scholars agree that managerialism, public-choice theory, transaction-cost economics, and principal-agent theory shaped the nature of the concept.[26] This complex mixture of theoretical perspectives produced what has been described elsewhere as "the neomanagerialist ideology," also known as "neomanagerialism."[27]

Neomanagerialism provides the philosophical foundation for two different concepts associated with the NPM. The first of these, *liberation management*, is based on the idea that public managers are competent and highly skilled individuals familiar with good management practices.[28] Consequently, managerial malfeasance does not offer a plausible explanation for the supposed poor performance of public agencies. If managerial incompetence does not explain the shortcomings of administrative institutions, what does? While critics of liberation management do not offer a single, unambiguous response to this question, proponents of liberation management do. The central problem, they say, rests with the bureaucratic system, with its burdensome rules, controls, and procedures. Stated a bit differently, the dysfunctional bureaucratic system incarcerates public managers, limiting their freedom to improve government performance.[29] To achieve better results, from this perspective, public managers must be freed (liberated, many say) from what reformers condemn as senseless red tape. As Peter Aucoin notes, advocates of liberation management argue that politicians and others "must let managers manage."[30] How are public managers to secure their freedom from an evil, oppressive bureaucratic system? Supporters of liberation management offer a variety of interrelated strategies ranging from deregulating the internal management of public agencies to decentralizing and streamlining various administrative processes such as procurement, human resource management, and budgeting.[31]

The second concept, *market-driven management*, provides a lightning rod for people engaged in the scholarly discussion of NPM.[32] Two basic premises guide market-driven management. One is the presumed advantages of competition, the other the perceived superiority of private-sector technologies and practices. With regard to competition, supporters of market-driven management rely on neoclassical economics and its admiration for the efficiency of markets.[33] From this perspective, competition provides an opportunity for the creation of marketlike mechanisms within government that attempt "to reform the public sector from the inside."[34] Proponents of market-driven management make the compelling argument that exposing public managers to market forces motivates them to improve their performance.[35] In the world of market-driven management, competition is a proven strategy to "make managers manage."

Respect for the perceived superiority of private-sector management practices motivates many people who observe public and business administration. Champions of market-driven management argue that any effort to distinguish between public and private management is misguided and urge public-sector managers to learn from their private-sector brethren. This certainly makes sense if one presumes that "management is management" and that the route to prosperity runs through business enterprise.[36]

Guided by the neomanagerialist ideology, supporters of both liberation and market-driven management sought to radically transform the role of the public manager in governmental affairs.[37] Public managers were strongly encouraged to reinvent themselves, relying primarily on private-sector management theory rather than theories of democratic governance.[38] They were instructed to become innovators and risk takers, radically altering institutional structures, practices, and norms.[39] In other words, public managers were told to assume the role of public-sector entrepreneurs.

In the United States, reformers embraced the public-entrepreneurship model as the most widely recognized model of administrative leadership. Just why Americans grew infatuated with public entrepreneurship is puzzling, given the country's history of political thought. As the critics of public entrepreneurship note, the concept directly conflicts with democratic theory.[40] The theory of democratic constitutionalism in the United States postulates a system of checks and balances in which administrative officials share powers with judges, legislators, and other executives, with none acting alone. Champions of public entrepreneurship have not let such criticism go unanswered: they contend that public entrepreneurship poses no threat to democracy if it is "civic regarding."[41] Moreover, proponents assert that little empirical evidence has been presented to substantiate the claim that public entrepreneurship poses a threat to democracy.[42]

The spirited debate concerning NPM and public entrepreneurship has focused attention on the extent to which the neomanagerialist philosophy undermines or strengthens values highly prized in the U.S. constitutional democracy. While effectiveness, efficiency, and economy are respected, the protection of values such as accountability, fairness, justice, and representation receives more attention. Missing from this debate, however, is a discussion of the long-term effects of NPM philosophy and practices on the integrity of administrative agencies. This is an important issue within the context of reinvention and reform. Public entrepreneurs, especially those who embrace the neomanagerialist ideology—and with it, the principles of liberation and market-driven management—express contempt for established institutional structures, practices, and norms. Armed with a multitude of reform strategies such as privatization, contracting out, user chargers, vouchers, decentralization, and downsizing (to name a few), these new public managers seek to radically transform the administrative institutions of modern government.

While the issue is not yet settled, accumulating evidence suggests that the NPM philosophy may have produced unintended consequences. By contributing to an increasingly hollow state, NPM practices have weakened the capacity of many public agencies and the ability of their managers to carry out their work. Rather than freeing managers to be entrepreneurs, the practices may be imprisoning them in weak institutions. If this proves true, then both liberation management and market-driven management will have contributed to a phenomenon described herein as the *thinning* of administrative institutions. This concept is explained in more detail in the following section, drawing on the institutional theories of Philip Selznick and Richard Scott.

THINNING ADMINISTRATIVE INSTITUTIONS: AN ANALYTICAL FRAMEWORK

Philip Selznick's *Leadership in Administration: A Sociological Interpretation* is widely regarded as a classic work in the area of institutional theory. Selznick's exposé on institutional leadership addresses a variety of topics ranging from the importance of defining an institution's mission to the defense of institutional integrity. The latter is of special interest here.

Selznick's discussion of institutional integrity originally appeared in a 1952 book analyzing communist party organization and tactics.[43] With the publication of *Leadership in Administration*, the concept began to attract serious attention. In discussing the processes associated with the "institutional embodiment of purpose," Selznick explained the meaning and importance of institutional integrity. Effective leaders, he suggested, acted to protect the "institution's distinctive values, competence and role." This is what he meant by the defense of institutional integrity. As a counterpoint, Selznick contended that an institution's integrity was vulnerable to the processes of corruption when values were "tenuous or insecure."[44]

More that thirty years later, in the *Moral Commonwealth: Social Theory and Promise of Community*, Selznick offered a more complex and developed notion of institutional integrity. Although the essence of the concept remained the same, Selznick examined integrity from the perspective of the "moral institution." After discussing the concept of identity and character as components of institutional integrity, Selznick explained the idea of integrity this way:

A test of moral character is the idea of *integrity*. This idea brings morality to bear in a way that respects autonomy and plurality of persons and institutions. The chief virtue of integrity is fidelity to self-defining principles. To strive for integrity is to ask: What is our direction? What are our unifying principles? And how do these square with the claims of morality? . . . Integrity involves wholeness and soundness. . . . Integrity has to do with principles, and therefore with principled conduct. . . . What counts as integrity, and what affects integrity, will be different for a university press or a commercial publisher; for a constitutional court and a lower court; for a regulatory agency and a highway department. Each type of institution has special functions and values; each has a distinctive set of unifying principles.[45]

Selznick's notion of institutional integrity is central to the idea of "thin institutions." The analogy of ice on a frozen lake provides a useful way of clarifying this point. When the ice on a frozen lake is several inches thick, it can support the weight of ice skaters and those who wish to engage in the sport of ice fishing. The thicker the ice, the more integrity or strength it possesses. In this case, one can speak of the ice on the lake as safe and sound. With *thin* ice, however, a totally different scenario unfolds. The thinner the ice, the less likely it will be able to safely support the weight of skaters and fishermen. Thin ice lacks integrity. Consequently, one can say that thin ice on a lake has a high probability of collapse if subjected to too much weight. Obviously, the exact point at which the thinly layered ice is likely to collapse depends upon the density of the ice and the amount of weight applied to it. This analogy can be applied to administrative institutions as well. Richard Scott's institutional framework, when combined with a modified version of Selznick's idea of institutional integrity, is helpful here.

In a comprehensive overview of the institutionalist approach to organization theory, Scott provides an analytical framework that identifies three essential elements or "pillars" of an institution. He describes these pillars as *regulative, normative,* and *cognitive* systems. An institution's regulative system is designed to constrain and standardize behavior. According to Scott, the regulative system is primarily concerned with "rule-setting, monitoring, and sanctioning activities." In the tradition of Chester Barnard, Scott states that "regulatory processes involve the capacity to establish rules, inspect others' conformity to them, and as necessary, manipulate sanctions—rewards or punishments—in an attempt to influence future behavior."[46]

The institution's normative system consists of norms and values that define desirable outcomes and the manner in which organizational members are expected to go about achieving preferred objectives. Scott

TABLE 7.1
Institutional Elements and Carriers

| | Elements | | |
Carriers	Regulative	Normative	Cognitive
Cultures	Rules	Values	Categories
	Laws	Expectations	Typifications
Structures	Governance	Regimes	Structural isomorphism
	systems	Authority	Identities
	Power systems	systems	
Routines	Compliance	Conformity	Performance programs
	Obedience	Performance	Scripts
		of duty	

Source: Adapted from W. Richard Scott and Soren Christensen, *The Institutional Construction of Organizations* (Thousand Oaks, CA: Sage Publications, 1995).

suggests that this system emphasizes "normative rules that introduce a prescriptive, evaluative, and obligatory dimension into social life." The normative system performs the important function of stabilizing the norms and values viewed as compulsory within the institution and internalizing those values in day-to-day behavior. "Shared norms and values," as Scott notes, are "regarded as the basis of a stable social order."[47]

The third pillar, cognitive systems, concentrates on what has been characterized as constitutive rules embedded in cultural systems. Constitutive rules assist organizational members as they attempt to interpret and make sense out of their world, especially as it relates to determining "what kinds of action can be taken by what kind of actors."[48] The cognitive system sensitizes organizational members to the "socially mediated construction of a common framework of meaning."[49]

Scott uses the concepts of regulative, normative, and cognitive systems as the foundation for building a definition of institutions. With the preceding discussion as a backdrop, he offers the following definition: "Institutions consist of cognitive, normative, and regulative structures and activities that provide stability and meaning to social behavior. Institutions are transported by various carriers—culture, structures, and routines—and they operate at different levels of jurisdiction."[50]

Table 7.1 depicts the three pillars and the processes that carry them through the organization. When combined with a somewhat modified version of Selznick's idea of institutional integrity, Scott's institutional framework provides a valuable analytical device for examining the capacity of administrative institutions. From this perspective, institutional integrity refers to the overall strength of an institution's regulative, normative, and cognitive systems insofar as they provide stability and meaning to social behavior. A *thin* institution lacks integrity due to the erosion and, in turn, weakening of its regulative, normative, and cognitive systems. This conceptualization of thin institution can be used to assess the effect of the NPM on the capacity of administrative agencies.

NEW PUBLIC MANAGEMENT REFORMS AND INSTITUTIONAL *THINNING*

As noted earlier, liberation management and market-driven management provide the motive behind the NPM. Advocates of liberation management argue that public managers must be liberated from a bureaucratic system plagued by cumbersome rules, regulations, and red tape. Proponents of market-driven management labor under the assumption that increased competition and strict adherence to private-sector management practices promote enhanced public management, thereby improving the performance of administrative agencies. While both liberation management and market-driven management have produced some positive results, each has also contributed to the thinning of administrative institutions. Many public agencies now lack the required integrity to fulfill their mandated responsibilities.

The Thinning of Regulative Systems

In their zeal to eliminate rules, regulations, and so-called red tape, advocates of liberation management fail to recognize the important role that rules and regulations play in strengthening the integrity of administrative institutions. As noted by Scott and other prominent organization theorists, rules are a stabilizing force; they structure conduct in organizations.[51] William Ocasio makes this clear when he states, "Rules are embodied in the policies, programs, procedures, routines, and conventions around which organizational activities are constructed. They comprise the knowledge, capabilities, beliefs, values, and memory of the organization and its members and are invoked in response to internal and external stimuli. Rules are . . . tools that both empower and control the social construction of organizational practices. They are . . . a guide for organizational adaptation and change."[52]

Indiscriminate attacks on rules and red tape are often misguided. Herbert Kaufman's oft-quoted maxim that "one person's red tape may be another's treasured procedural safeguard" suggests the importance of rules.[53] Yet people who march under the banner of liberation management treat rules and regulations like viruses, as germs to be eliminated. The manner in which this approach leads to thin regulative systems can be illustrated with a case involving the General Services Administration (GSA) and the Federal Aviation Administration (FAA).

The GSA administers the federal government's credit card program. GSA officials frequently enter into contractual agreements with commercial banks to secure credit cards that federal employees use for official business. According to the U.S. General Accounting Office, the use of commercial credit cards by public employees is "intended to streamline procurement and payment procedures and reduce administrative burdens by reducing the number of procurement requests, purchase orders, and vendor payments issues." According to General Accounting Office auditors, credit card purchases produce "lower costs and *less red tape* for both the government and the vendor community."[54]

In the spirit of liberation management, the Department of Transportation and the Appropriations Act of 1996 exempted the FAA from various governmental acquisition regulations. Congress gave the FAA the autonomy and authority to develop its own procurement procedures. Agency officials in turn adopted a decentralized acquisition system, giving regional offices the ability to establish their own purchase-card activities as well as methods for monitoring and controlling the use of such cards. Through the FAA's specialized purchase-card program, agency acquisition managers were liberated from the red tape of the procurement process.

In September 2001, the Department of Transportation's Office of the Inspector General released a report critical of the FAA purchase-card program.[55] This report prompted Congressman Don Young, head of a transportation oversight committee, to ask the General Accounting Office to review FAA purchasing controls and activities. What the General Accounting Office found was disturbing. Its report highlighted numerous weaknesses in the FAA's purchase-card controls and stated that such weakness "resulted in instances of improper, wasteful, and questionable purchases, as well as missing assets."[56] As a consequence of their investigation, government auditors identified $5.4 million dollars in improper purchases.

One can view the FAA's brief journey into the world of liberation management as an example of institutional empowerment. From another perspective, it is a textbook case of "bad administration" and misuse of taxpayer funds. Either way, it represents the consequences of thinning the regulative systems that support institutional integrity.

The Thinning of Normative Systems

As mentioned earlier, the institution's normative system performs the function of determining and reinforcing desired values. NPM practices, especially those associated with market-driven management, thin the normative systems of administrative institutions. This is readily apparent as an unintended effect of the increased use of downsizing, a strategy for lowering costs and increasing productivity.

Downsizing entails the divestiture of human assets.[57] At the federal level, many agencies adopted downsizing as a management response to the calls for "reinventing government" promoted by the Clinton administration. The General Accounting Office reports that the non-postal civilian work force grew smaller as a result. Downsizing reduced the federal work force from approximately 2.3 million employees in fiscal 1990 to fewer than 1.9 million in 1999.[58] In conjunction with their efforts to downsize through retirement and attrition, a number of federal agencies drastically reduced or froze their hiring efforts for extended periods of time. While serving to reduce the size of the work force, these measures also "reduced the influx of new people with new skills, new knowledge, new energy and ideas."[59] The manner in which downsizing was implemented resulted in consequences of an institutional nature. In an earlier report addressing the adverse consequences of poorly planned and executed downsizing, the General Accounting Office offered the following assessment: "A lack of adequate strategic and workforce planning during the initial rounds of downsizing by some agencies may have affected their ability to achieve organizational mission. Some agencies reported that downsizing in general led to such negative effects as *loss of institutional memory* and an increase in work backlogs."[60]

As these comments suggest, downsizing served to thin the normative systems of government agencies. The loss of "institutional memory" and the departure of "institutional elders" reduced the cognitive base to which institutional values and norms were secured. Institutional elders possess the knowledge, expertise, and valuable information about an organization's history that promotes institutional norms. With the massive exodus of institutional elders, agencies lost much of the resources necessary to transmit and protect values and norms. This weakened their integrity.

The Thinning of Cognitive Systems

Cognitive systems assist organizational members as they seek to interpret and make sense of their world. Both liberation management and market-driven management have altered constitutive rules—the view of what remains essential to government operations—thereby complicating the sense-making process used by managers in many agencies. Managers often proceed from the assumption that their agency has a particular history and mission. External pressures associated with the reinvention movement, however, required them to become isomorphic—that is, they take on the same form or appearance even though their agencies possess different ancestries.[61] Understandably, managers experienced difficulty adapting to the wider belief systems and cultural frameworks imposed on them. Along with the elimination of important rules and the loss of institutional memory, the thinning of cognitive systems weakened institutional integrity.

CONCLUSION

This chapter opened with a quote from *The Administrative State* in which Dwight Waldo warned practitioners of governmental administration about the dangers of blindly accepting the philosophy of American business. On its face, the philosophy of liberation management and market-driven management seem reasonable. When applied to business activities, they have produced spectacular results. Yet when applied to public administration, they tend to produce a hollow state in which the regulative, normative, and cognitive elements of institutional integrity grow thin.

The ideas embodied in liberation management and market-driven management, if swallowed whole, do not serve constitutional government well. Thin institutions are weak institutions; weak institutions lack the capacity for "good" administration. As noted frequently, good administration is a necessary requirement for maintaining public trust in democratic government.

NOTES

1. Anthony Savile, *The Test of Time: An Essay in Philosophical Aesthetics* (Oxford, UK: Clarendon Press, 1982), 210.

2. Robert Behn, "The Big Questions of Public Management," *Public Administration Review* 55 (July/August 1994): 313–24; John Kirlin, "The Big Questions of Public Administration in a Democracy," *Public Administration Review* 56 (September/October 1996): 416–23; Francis X. Neumann Jr., "What Makes Public Administration a Science? Or, Are Its 'Big Questions' Really

Big?" *Public Administration Review* 56 (September/October 1996): 409–15; Donald Schon, *Displacement of Concepts* (London: Tavistock, 1963).

3. Dwight Waldo, *The Administrative State: A Study of the Political Theory of American Public Administration*, 2nd ed. (New York: Holmes & Meier, 1984), 91.

4. Ibid., 38.

5. H. Briton Milward, Keith Provan, and Barbara Else, "What Does the Hollow State Look Like?" in *Public Management Theory: The State of the Art*, ed. Barry Bozeman (San Francisco: Jossey-Bass, 1993), 310. As Milward, Provan, and Else note, scholars have used terms such as the "shadow state," "government by proxy," "third-party government," and the "contracting regimes" to describe the hollow state phenomenon.

6. B. Guy Peters, "Managing the Hollow State," *International Journal of Public Administration* 17 (March 1994): 739–56; H. Brinton Milward, "Symposium on the Hollow State: Capacity, Control, and Performance in Interorganizational Settings," *Journal of Public Administration Research and Theory* 6 (April 1996): 193–95; Milward and Keith Provan, "Governing the Hollow State," *Journal of Public Administration Research and Theory* 10 (April 2000): 359–79.

7. E. S. Savas, *Privatization and Public-Public Partnerships* (New York: Chatham House, 2000); Donald F. Kettl, *Sharing Power: Public Governance and Private Markets* (Washington, DC: Brookings Institution, 1993); H. Brinton Milward, "Implications of Contracting Out: New Roles for the Hollow State," in *New Paradigms for Government: Issues for the Changing Public Service*, ed. Patricia Ingraham and Barbara S. Romzek (San Francisco: Jossey-Bass, 1994), 41–62; Jonas Prager and Swati Desai, "Privatizing Local Government Operations," *Public Productivity and Management Review* 20, no. 2 (1996): 185–203; Bruce A. Wallin, "The Need for a Privatization Process: Lessons from Development and Implementation," *Public Administration Review* 57 (January/February 1997): 11–20; Joycelyn M. Johnston and Barbara Romzek, "Contracting and Accountability in State Medicaid Reform: Rhetoric, Theories, and Reality," *Public Administration Review* 59 (September/October 1999): 383–99; David M. Van Slyke, "The Mythology of Privatization in Contracting for Social Services," *Public Administration Review* 63 (May/June 2003): 296–315.

8. Peters, "Managing the Hollow State"; Eugene Bardach and Cara Lesser, "Accountability in Human Services Collaborative—For What? And For Whom?" *Journal of Public Administration Research and Theory* 6 (April 1996): 197–224; Larry D. Terry, "Administrative Leadership, Neo-Managerialism and the Public Management Movement," *Public Administration Review* 58 (May/June 1998): 194–200; Richard Box, Gary Marshall, B. J. Reed, and Christine Reed, "New Public Management and Substantive Democracy," *Public Administration Review* 61 (September/October 2001): 608–19.

9. Peter Aucoin, *The New Public Management: Canada in Comparative Perspective* (Montreal: Institute Research on Public Policy, 1995); Jonathan Boston, J. Martin, J. Paillot, and P. Walsh, *Public Management: The New Zealand Model* (New York: Oxford University Press, 1996); Christopher

Hood, "A Public Management for All Seasons?" *Public Administration Review* 69, no. 1 (1991): 3–19; Hood, "Contemporary Public Management: A New Global Paradigm," *Public Policy and Administration* 10, no. 2 (1995): 104–17; Hood, "The New Public Management in the 1980s: Variations on a Theme," *Accounting, Organizations, and Society* 20, no. 2/3 (1995): 93–109; Donald Kettl, "The Global Revolution in Public Management: Driving Themes, Missing Links," *Journal of Public Policy Analysis and Management* 16, no. 3 (1997): 446–62.

10. Louise Comfort, "Governance under Fire: Organizational Fragility in Complex Systems," in *Governance and Public Security,* ed. Alasdair Roberts (New York: Syracuse University Press, 2002), 113–27.

11. *The Federalist Papers,* Federalist No. 27, author Alexander Hamilton, in Alexander Hamilton, James Madison, and John Jay, *The Federalist* (Cutchogue, NY: Buccaneer Books, 1992).

12. Joseph S. Nye, Phillip D. Zellikow, and David C. King, *Why People Don't Trust Government* (Cambridge, MA: Harvard University Press, 1997); Gary Orren, "Fall from Grace: The Public Loss of Faith in Government," in *Why People Don't Trust Government,* ed. Nye, Zellikow, and King.

13. Daniel Cohn, "Creating Crises and Avoiding Blame: The Politics of Public Service Reform and the New Public Management in Great Britain and the United States," *Administration and Society* 29, no. 5 (1997): 584–616.

14. Philip Selznick, *Leadership in Administration: A Sociological Interpretation* (Evanston, IL: Row and Peterson, 1957); Selznick, *The Moral Commonwealth: Social Theory and the Promise of Community* (Berkeley: University of California Press, 1992); W. Richard Scott, *Institutions and Organizations* (Thousand Oaks, CA: Sage Publications, 1995).

15. Arjen Boin and Paul 't Hart, "Public Leadership in Times of Crisis: Mission Impossible?" *Public Administration Review* 63 (September/October 2003): 549.

16. C. James, "The Rise and Decline of Market Liberals in the British Labour Party," in *The Labour Party after 75 Years,* ed. M. Clark (Wellington, NZ: Victoria University, 1992), 11–27.

17. Cohn, "Creating Crises and Avoiding Blame," 596.

18. Larry D. Terry, "Public Administration and the Theatre Metaphor: The Public Administrator as Villain, Hero, and Innocent Victim," *Public Administration Review* 57 (January/February 1997): 53–61.

19. Cohn, "Creating Crises and Avoiding Blame," 586.

20. Bob Jessop, "Towards a Schumperterian Workforce State? Preliminary Remarks on Post Fordist Political Economy," *Studies in Political Economy* 40, no. 1 (1993): 7–39; Jessop, "Towards a Schumpeterian Workfare Regime in Britain? Reflections on Regulation, Governance, and Welfare State," *Environment and Planning* 27, no. 9 (1995): 1613–26.

21. Michael Barzelay, *Breaking through Bureaucracy: A New Vision for Managing Government* (Berkeley: University of California Press, 1992); David Osborne and Peter Plastrik, *Banishing Bureaucracy: The Five Strategies for Reinventing Government* (New York: Addison-Wesley, 1997).

22. Shamsul Haque, "The Diminishing Publicness of Public Service under the Current Mode of Governance," *Public Administration Review* 61 (January/ February 2001): 65–82; Hood, "Contemporary Public Management"; Organisation for Economic Cooperation and Development (OECD), *Governance in Transition: Public Management Reforms in OECD Countries* (Paris: Organisation for Economic Cooperation and Development, 1995).

23. Sanford Borins, "The New Public Management Is Here to Stay," *Canadian Public Administration* 38, no. 1 (1995): 122.

24. Hood, "A Public Management for All Seasons?" L. R. Jones, Kuno Schedler, and Stephen Wade, *International Perspectives on the New Public Management* (Greenwich, CT: JAI Press, 1997); Larry D. Terry, "Symposium: Leadership, Democracy and the New Public Management," *Public Administration Review* 58, no. 3 (1998): 189–238; Fred Thompson, "The New Public Management," *Journal of Policy Analysis and Management* 16, no. 1 (1997): 165–76; Donald F. Kettl, "The Global Revolution in Public Management: Driving Themes, Missing Links," *Journal of Public Policy Analysis and Management* 16, no. 3 (1997): 446–62; L. R. Jones, "Symposium on Public Management Reform and E-Government," *International Public Management Journal* 2, no. 1 (2001): 97–124.

25. Gernod Gruening, "Origin and Theoretical Basis of New Public Management," *International Public Management Journal* 4, no. 1 (2001): 1–25; Michael Barzelay, "How to Argue about the New Public Management," *International Public Management Journal* 2, no. 2 (1999): 183–216; Laurence E. Lynn, "The New Public Management: How to Transform a Theme into a Legacy," *Public Administration Review* 58 (May/June 1998): 231–46; David Mathiasen, "The New Public Management and Its Critics," *International Public Management Journal* 1, no. 1 (1999): 90–111.

26. William F. Enteman, *Managerialism* (Madison: University of Wisconsin Press, 1993); Christopher Pollitt, *Managerialism and the Public Service: The Anglo-American Experience* (Cambridge, MA: Basil Blackwell, 1990); James Buchanan and Gordon Tullock, *The Calculus of Consent: Logical Foundations of Constitutional Democracy* (Ann Arbor: University of Michigan Press, 1962); Oliver Williamson, *The Economic Institutions of Capitalism* (New York: Free Press, 1995); Michael Jensen and William Meckling, "Theory of the Firm: Managerial Behavior, Agency Costs, and Ownership Structures," *Journal of Financial Economics* 3, no. 4 (1976): 305–60; Barry Mitnick, "The Theory of Agency: The Policing 'Paradox' and Regulatory Behavior," *Public Choice* 24 (1975): 227–42; Terry Moe, "The New Economics of Organizations," *American Journal of Political Science* 28, no. 4 (1984): 739–75; B. Dan Wood, "Principal-Agent Models of Political Control of Bureaucracy," *American Political Science Review* 83 (September 1989): 965–78.

27. This discussion of neomanagerialism and the NPM is drawn from Terry, "Administrative Leadership, Neo-Managerialism, and the Public Management Movement."

28. The term "liberation management" was popularized by Thomas Peter in his book *Liberation Management: Necessary Disorganization for the Nanosec-*

ond Nineties (New York: A. A. Knopf, 1992). The term, however, did not gain intellectual currency until Paul Light used it to describe one of his four "tides of reform." Light, *The Tides of Reform: Making Government Work, 1945–1995* (New Haven, CT: Yale University Press, 1997).

29. Al Gore, *From Red Tape to Results: Creating a Government That Works Better and Costs Less: The Report of the National Performance Review* (Washington, DC: U.S. Government Printing Office, 1993).

30. Aucoin, *New Public Management;* Boston, Martin, Paillot, and Walsh, *Public Management;* Kettl, "Global Revolution in Public Management."

31. Steven Kelman, "Public Choice and Public Spirit," *The Public Interest* 87 (Spring 1987): 80–94; David Osborne and Ted Gaebler, *Reinventing Government* (Reading, MA: Addison-Wesley, 1992).

32. Louis Gawthrop, "Public Entrepreneurship in the Land of Oz and Uz," *Public Integrity* 1, no. 2 (1999): 75–86; Linda deLeon and Janet Denhardt, "The Political Theory of Reinvention," *Public Administration Review* 60 (March/April 2000): 89–97; Robert Denhardt and Janet Denhardt, "The New Public Service: Serving Rather Than Steering," *Public Administration Review* 60 (November/December 2000): 549–59; Box et al., "New Public Management and Substantive Democracy;" Camilla Stivers, "Resisting the Ascendancy of Public Management: Normative Theory and Public Administration," *Administrative Theory and Praxis* 22, no. 1 (2000): 10–23.

33. Peters, "Managing the Hollow State," 739–56.

34. Elke Loffler, *The Modernization of the Public Sector in an International Comparative Perspective: Implementation in Germany, Great Britain, and the United States* (Speyer, Ger.: Gorshungsinstitut Fur Offentliche, 1997), 7; Mark Considine, *Enterprising States: The Public Management of Welfare-to-Work* (Oakleigh, Vic., Australia: Cambridge University Press, 2001), 28.

35. Boston, Martin, Paillot, and Walsh, *Public Management;* Kettl, "Global Revolution in Public Management."

36. B. Guy Peters, *The Future of Governing: Four Emerging Models* (Lawrence: University Press of Kansas, 1996), 28.

37. Barzelay, *Breaking through Bureaucracy;* Nancy Roberts and Paula King, *Transforming Public Policy: Dynamics of Policy Entrepreneurship* (San Francisco: Jossey-Bass, 1996); Mark Schneider, Paul Teske, and Michael Mintrom, *Public Entrepreneurs: Agents for Change in American Government* (Princeton, NJ: Princeton University Press, 1995).

38. deLeon and Denhardt, "Political Theory of Reinvention."

39. Sanford Borins, "Loose Cannons and Rule Breakers, or Enterprising Leaders? Some Evidence about Innovative Public Managers," *Public Administration Review* 60 (November/December 2000): 498–507.

40. deLeon and Denhardt, "Political Theory of Reinvention"; Gawthrop, "Public Entrepreneurship in the Land of Oz and Uz"; Larry D. Terry, "Why We Should Abandon the Misconceived Quest to Reconcile Public Entrepreneurship with Democracy," *Public Administration Review* 53 (July/August 1993): 393–95; Terry, "Administrative Leadership, Neo-Managerialism, and

the Public Management Movement"; Ronald Moe, "The Reinventing Government Exercise: Misinterpreting the Problem, Misjudging the Consequences," *Public Administration Review* 54 (March/April 1994): 111–22; Charles Goodsell, "Reinvent Government or Rediscover It," *Public Administration Review* 53 (January/February 1993): 85–87; James Stever, *The End of Public Administration: Problems of the Profession in the Post-Progressive Era* (Dobbs Ferry, NY: Transactional, 1988); Colin Diver, "Engineers and Entrepreneurs: The Dilemma of Public Management," *Journal of Policy Analysis and Management* 1 (Spring 1982): 402–6.

41. Carl Bellone and George Goerl, "In Defense of Civic Regarding Entrepreneurship or Helping Wolves to Promote Good Citizenship," *Public Administration Review* 53 (March/April 1993): 130–34.

42. Borins, "Loose Cannons and Rule Breakers."

43. Philip Selznick, *The Organizational Weapon: A Study of Bolshevik Strategy and Tactics* (New York: McGraw-Hill, 1952).

44. Selznick, *Leadership in Administration*, 90, 119, 120.

45. Selznick, *Moral Commonwealth*, 322–24.

46. Scott, *Institutions and Organizations*, 47, 52. Scott suggests that an institution's regulative system primary mechanism for control is coercion. Although he relies on DiMaggio and Powell's typology, the intellectual roots of using coercion as a control mechanism can be traced back to Chester Barnard's discussion of "methods of persuasion." Paul DiMaggio and Walter Powell, "The Iron Cage Revisited: Institutional Isomorphism and Collective Rationality in Organization Fields," *American Sociological Review* 48, no. 1 (1983): 147–60; Chester Barnard, *The Functions of the Executive* (Cambridge, MA: Harvard University Press, 1938), 142–48.

47. Scott, *Institutions and Organizations*, 54, 56.

48. W. Richard Scott and Soren Christensen, *The Institutional Construction of Organizations: International Longitudinal Studies* (Thousand Oaks, CA: Sage Publications, 1995), xviii.

49. Scott, *Institutions and Organizations*, 58.

50. Scott and Christensen, *The Institutional Construction of Organizations*, xiii.

51. Barry Bozeman, *Bureaucracy and Red Tape* (Upper Saddle River, NJ: Prentice Hall, 2000); James March and Johan P. Olsen, *Rediscovering Institutions* (New York: Free Press, 1989); DiMaggio and Powell, "Iron Cage Revisited"; John W. Meyer and Brian Rowan, "Institutionalized Organizations: Formal Structure as Myth and Ceremony," *American Journal of Sociology* 83, no. 1 (1977): 40–63; R. Cyert and James G. March, *A Behavioral Theory of the Firm* (Englewood Cliffs, NJ: Prentice Hall, 1963); Paul Appleby, *Big Democracy* (New York: A. A. Knopf, 1945); Fritz Morstein Marx, ed., *Elements of Public Administration* (Englewood Cliffs, NJ: Prentice Hall, 1946).

52. William Ocasio, "Institutionalized Action and Corporate Governance: The Reliance on Rules of CEO Succession," *Administrative Science Quarterly* 44 (June 1999): 386.

53. Herbert Kaufman, *Red Tape: Its Origins, Uses, and Abuses* (Washington, DC: Brookings Institution, 1977), 4.

54. U.S. General Accounting Office, "FAA Purchase Cards: Weak Controls Resulted in Instances of Improper and Wasteful Purchases and Missing Assets," GAO-03-405, March 21, 2003, 1, 5 (emphasis mine).

55. U.S. Department of Transportation Office of Inspector General, *Department of Transportation Use of Government Credit Cards*, FI-2001-095, September 24, 2001.

56. U.S. General Accounting Office, "FAA Purchase Cards," 2.

57. Susan R. Fisher and Margaret A. White, "Downsizing in a Learning Organization: Are There Hidden Costs?" *Academy of Management Review* 25 (January 2000): 244–51.

58. U.S. General Accounting Office, "Major Management Challenges and Program Risks: A Governmentwide Perspective," GAO-01-241, January 2001, 21.

59. Ibid., 22.

60. U.S. General Accounting Office, Testimony before the Subcommittee on Oversight of Government Management, Restructuring, and the District of Columbia, Committee on Governmental Affairs, U.S. Senate, "Management Reform-Continuing Attention Is Needed to Improve Government Performance." Statement of J. Christopher Mihn, GAO/T-GGD-00-128, 7.

61. DiMaggio and Powell, "Iron Cage Revisited."

8

Competition for Human Capital

JOHN CADIGAN

American public administration has evolved political theories unmistakably related to unique economic, social, governmental, and ideological facts.

Dwight Waldo, *The Administrative State*

Government is no longer a second- or third-rate industry. . . . Its successful conduct calls for the best brains and leadership available in the country. If we cannot increase the prestige of public employment and give assurance of satisfactory careers in it . . . the permanency of democratic institutions is far from assured.

W. E. Mosher, "The Making of a Public Servant,"
quoted in Waldo, *The Administrative State*

Throughout his career, Dwight Waldo worked to relate administrative theories to the social movements in which they arose. "Political theories must be construed in relation to their material environment and ideological framework," he wrote in the opening sentence to *The Administrative State*. American public administration was "unmistakably related to unique economic, social, governmental, and ideological facts."[1]

At the same time, Waldo believed that administrative practices derived from particular histories could be applied to broader circumstances. He did not expect, for example, that "the concepts of economy and efficiency may now be abolished because they are rooted in a

129

particular history we may not like." This outlook encouraged paradoxical statements in which contrary beliefs appeared in a single administrative theory. His views on the ideal public servant reflect such dichotomies. He did not like the early twentieth-century history that conferred administrative power on the politically neutral expert, much preferring a public service inhabited by administrators broadly knowledgeable of governmental affairs. Yet he recognized the advantages of expertise, even after the particular history that produced the notion of the politically neutral expert had passed. "We might discover ways in which they should be qualified and adapted in a changing world," he wrote of aged administrative concepts.[2]

Administrative concepts are rooted in social conditions, but certain administrative practices have value beyond the particular circumstances in which they arise. This conclusion often led Waldo to speak of administrative theory in terms of dichotomies: centralization and/or decentralization, stability and/or change, efficiency and/or "inefficiency"?[3]

Waldo did not like the narrow and deprecating attitude that modern economic analysis brought to the study of administrative theory. Toward the close of his career, he found in it the same lack of insight that had characterized scientific management decades earlier. Nonetheless, he appreciated the particular historical circumstances that elevated economic approaches to administrative affairs.

This chapter examines recent developments in public administration from the point of view of economics. (It was prepared by a bona fide economist, who like the young Waldo developed an interest in administrative theory without ever taking a public administration course.) The chapter examines the impact of recent historical events—in particular the war on terrorism—on the economic, political, and social climate in the United States and the resulting effects on the structure of the administrative state. Particular emphasis is given to the contemporary pressures affecting recruiting and retention in government organizations. The chapter takes a coldly realistic view of prevailing conditions, as befits analysis from an economist's platform. That history has served to accentuate budget deficits at all levels of government, reinforcing the movement to "reinvent government," with its emphasis on market competition, privatization, and outsourcing.

From an economic perspective, the use of privatization techniques pushes government into the marketplace. This raises significant questions about "who should rule." Historically, the ability of governmental leaders to attract qualified civil servants to serve in the modern administrative state has been based on the combined attractiveness of public service and job security. Particularly with the rise of the modern welfare state, governmental work has been viewed as a calling or an obligation of citizenship, rewarded in modern bureaucracies with the granting of tenure or job security.

Privatization and economic perspectives undermine the notion of public service as a noble calling. From an economic point of view, government work is nothing more than another set of occupations for which employers must compete in the open marketplace. Here recent history intervenes. The heavy burden of deficits produces circumstances in which public officials cannot match the pay and entrepreneurial opportunities available in the private sector. Nor do traditional incentives such as job security give assurance of satisfactory careers in public service. Privatization and the extensive use of contracts have undermined career opportunities and the job security that once made government work so attractive relative to the private sector.

Using military personnel policies as a case study, this chapter examines the difficulties government officials face as they compete with private-sector executives for labor—in this case, recruitment to the all volunteer military. This example highlights the particular difficulties associated with recruitment to what Waldo termed "the administrative class," given the particular historical circumstances shaping twenty-first-century American public administration. Importantly, the incentives to which public leaders turn as they recruit personnel affect not only the composition of the new work force, but its ability to "'efficiently'" provide services. History and economy interact to produce current theories of administration, though not in ways that Waldo might have preferred.

EFFECTS OF SEPTEMBER 11, 2001

In contrast to the record levels of economic growth and prosperity prevailing in the 1990s, the U.S. economy following the events of September 11, 2001, was characterized by doubt, uncertainty, and economic slowdown. While catastrophic, the losses directly inflicted by the attacks on New York City and Washington, D.C., represented only one aspect of this historical event. Decreases in consumer confidence and the heightened sense of uncertainty prevailing after the attacks restrained consumer spending. The slowdown in travel and tourism, accompanied by shrinking demand for transportation services, nearly bankrupted the airline industry. Pressures associated with the provision of increased security, including the need to more rigorously screen passengers and their luggage, increased overall transportation costs. In part, this led government officials to approve a $15 billion "bailout" of the airline industry.[4]

Across the economy, restraint in consumer spending reduced the demand for goods. In response, firms reduced demand for labor, contributing to increases in the unemployment rate and accelerating the slowdown in economic growth. In the fourth quarter of 2001, businesses cut industrial production by about 7 percent, reduced payroll by about 1.2 million, and cut worker hours worked by 3.8 percent. The unemployment rate rose from 4.9 percent in August 2001 to 5.8 percent in December 2001.[5] Uncertainty also influenced the performance of the stock market. Both the NASDAQ Composite Index and the Standard & Poor's 500 decreased 20 percent in value in the year following the attack.[6] Alan Greenspan confirmed that "the U.S. economy went through a significant cyclical adjustment in 2001 that was exacerbated by the effects of the terrorist attacks on September 11. That adjustment was characterized by sharp reductions in business investment and pronounced liquidations in business inventories and was compounded by the simultaneous economic difficulties of some of our major trading partners."[7] Economic recovery from the recession that followed September 11 was sluggish. Faced with uncertain demand for their products, business leaders deferred new hiring, relying instead on increased hours worked and part-time employees. The slowdown in growth led to an increase in demand for public services, including, for example, the extension of unemployment benefits by an additional thirteen weeks to more than 2 million workers unemployed in January 2003.

The events of September 11, 2001, also influenced the way in which U.S. leaders interacted with foreign nations. Foremost among these changes was the implementation of a new security strategy based on preemptive strikes and an increase in the U.S. role in constructing a world police force. The change in policy appeared in several speeches delivered by President George W. Bush in the aftermath of the attacks. In an address to a joint session of Congress on September 20, 2001, Bush stated, "Every nation, in every region, now has a decision to make. Either you are with us, or you are with the terrorists. From this day forward, any nation that continues to harbor or support terrorism will be regarded by the United States as a hostile regime."[8] This was followed in the January 2002 State of the Union Address by the following statement: "All nations should know: America will do what is necessary to ensure our nation's security. We'll be deliberate, yet time is not on our side. I will not wait on events while dangers gather. I will not stand by as peril draws closer and closer. The United States of America will not permit the world's most dangerous regimes to threaten us with the world's most destructive weapons."[9] The shift in policy led to a revision of the national security strategy: "The United States has long maintained the option of preemptive actions to counter a sufficient threat to our national security. The greater the threat, the greater is the risk of inaction—and the more compelling the case for taking anticipatory action to defend ourselves, even if uncertainty remains as to the time and place of the enemy's attack. To forestall or prevent such hostile acts by our adversaries, the United States will, if necessary, act preemptively."[10]

The immediate consequences of these policies—the wars in Afghanistan and Iraq—proved costly. Between September 11, 2001, and May 14, 2004, Congress provided $165 billion to fund the wars in Afghanistan and Iraq and to support antiterrorism efforts.[11] Concurrent reforms in intelligence services, military restructuring, and homeland security also proved time-consuming and costly. The time and resources required for "nation building" and the potential for conflict with other countries, including Iran and North Korea, exacerbated pressures to spend, further accentuating the demand for government services and persistence of budgetary shortfalls.

The terrorist attacks also affected social priorities. In a search for a sense of increased security, citizens became more willing to tolerate restrictions on personal freedom. The passage of the U.S.A. Patriot Act illustrates this point.[12] Among other provisions, the Patriot Act allows for detention of non-U.S. nationals if the attorney general believes such individuals may be terrorists or support terrorist activities. It permits broader law enforcement access to electronic communications and Internet sites, expands the ability of government officials to conduct "sneak and peek" searches, and extends the secrecy of grand jury proceedings in cases where intelligence or counterintelligence information is involved. The requirement for increased domestic surveillance further strained state and local budgets, as well as the legal system in general. Although similar responses followed the attack on Pearl Harbor, they were relatively short-lived. Current changes in domestic priorities may be sustained if future conflict in Iran and North Korea materializes, or if the threats associated with al Qaeda and the current military action in Iraq persist. Political support for increased centralization of intelligence services led to the passage of the Homeland Security Act. In one of the most significant efforts to restructure the federal administrative establishment, Congress passed legislation creating the Office for Homeland Security with an estimated annual budget in excess of $25 billion for fiscal year 2003, followed by the creation of the Department of Homeland Security.

Economic, political, and social forces associated with these events increased the demand for a variety of public services and highlighted the opportunity costs associated with their provision. These changes created significant budgetary pressures. As the economy slowed, tax revenues to federal, state, and local governments declined. The combination of increased outlays with decreased revenues led to considerable budget deficits. The federal budget deficit grew to $375 billion in 2003.[13] Effects on state budget deficits were also profound. State and local government deficits rose from $61 billion in 2001 to $82 billion in 2003.[14] Continuing deficits threatened to restrain economic growth, further constricting tax revenues and the possibility that the United States might "grow" its way out of government deficits. Not surprisingly, this environment encouraged renewed debate over governmental "efficiency," privatization techniques, and the need to "reinvent government" in ways that harnessed the cost savings typically associated with market competition.

EFFICIENCY BENEFITS FROM PRIVATIZATION

The desire to downsize government has been the subject of considerable debate. Proponents of outsourcing refer to Thoreau's dictum that "government is best which governs the least."[15] This idea is reflected in the Office of Management and Budget Circular A-76 and its Revised Supplemental Handbook: "In the process of governing, the Government should not compete with its citizens. The competitive enterprise system, characterized by individual freedom and initiative, is the primary source of national economic strength. In recognition of this principle, it has been and continues to be the general policy of the Government to rely on commercial sources to supply the products and services the Government needs."[16]

The concept of privatization is motivated, in part, by the presumption of private-sector efficiency. Government reliance upon commercial sources may reduce overall costs when market forces and profit motives act to discipline private firms. Fluctuating market pressures reward business executives who develop practices that stimulate innovation and flexibility—so-called best corporate practices (BCPs). Cost-cutting and efficiency improvements enhance a firm's competitive position by increasing profits. Increased profits flow from the ability of executives to experiment with new practices or adapt BCPs from other firms. The best firms adapt to what works, disregarding or foregoing outdated principles and excess capacity. The ability of firms to alter the structure of their work force and capital equipment quickly, integrating new technology or management techniques with their existing process, is key to success. Such improvements are expedited by systems of decentralized decision making that allow managers and workers to experiment with new processes and adopt those that work. The private sector possesses clear metrics for success—total cost, production levels, ratios of inputs to output, market share, and profitability. Importantly, private-sector executives are free to structure compensation packages that reward innovative and effective behavior. The use of "pay for performance" bonuses and profit sharing contribute to private-sector efficiency by instilling appropriate work-force incentives. Work-force management practices that allow firms to reward efficiency and terminate the employment of unproductive resources also contribute to the successful development and implementation of BCPs. The flexibility to change production techniques, quickly adopt new and innovative procedures in response to changing conditions, and create clear incentives that reward productivity and efficiency provide the private sector with a competitive ethos that is largely absent from the public sector.

Analysts have documented efficiency gains associated with privatization in several studies of the government's A-76 program. Circular A-76 requires government officials to contract out commercial activities that can be provided at lower cost by the private sector. While certain activities are exempt from A-76 review (including those vital to national defense or for which no commercial supplier is available), many are subject to cost-comparison studies. Contracts are awarded to the private sector when the total cost savings meet the minimum requirement of 10 percent. Cost-comparison studies require an estimate of the cost of providing the service "in-house" relative to the price of contracting out (which includes the contract bid, administration costs, adjustment for federal income tax benefits of the contract, and one-time conversion costs.) A Congressional Budget Office (CBO) study found that outsourcing saved approximately 35 percent for commercial-type government activities,[17] while an OMB analysis reported average savings of about 30 percent relative to original government costs.[18] Evidence also suggests that cost savings arise through the A-76 process even where the final contract is awarded in-house. Forcing government officials to compete with private-sector firms apparently instills competitive pressures that produce efficiency gains.

Officials in the U.S. Department of Defense (DoD) have acquired considerable experience with the A-76 process. Current initiatives include privatization of family housing, real property and vehicle maintenance, civilian personnel administration, food service, security and law enforcement, and other support services. According to a study produced by the Center for Naval Analyses, A-76 cost comparisons conducted by DoD between 1978 and 1994 yielded savings of 31 percent for the affected activities.[19] Although future competitions may be subject to diminishing returns, the apparent cost savings have bolstered support for A-76 competitions.

SHOULD EFFICIENCY BE THE PRIMARY GOAL?

Critics of privatization efforts argue that the emphasis on efficiency is misplaced. They argue a point, recognized in Circular A-76, to the effect that certain activities are inherently governmental and as such should not be subject to the competitive pressures of the marketplace. Adam Smith made a similar point in the *Wealth of Nations:*

> According to the system of natural liberty, the sovereign has only three duties to attend to . . . first, the duty of protecting the society from the violence and invasion of other independent societies; secondly, the duty of protecting, as far as possible, every member of society from the injustice or oppression of every other member of it . . . and, thirdly, the duty of erecting and maintaining certain public works and certain public institutions, which it can never be in the interest of any individual, or small number of individuals, to erect and maintain.[20]

As an example, few economists would argue that national defense should be fully privatized. Rather than having a military composed of "mercenaries" whose motivation depends on market forces, military service is better viewed as a civic obligation where personal gain is sacrificed for the public good and for which the government is not obligated to pay market rates. While the role of government envisioned by Smith was admittedly narrow, it reflects the belief that a free market may not be the best institutional mechanism for the provision of certain goods and services. In such cases, government officials willingly forego efficiency precisely because market pressures lead to outcomes incompatible with democratic ideals. As such, critics of outsourcing and privatization argue that providers of important public programs should be guided by a sense of civic responsibility rather than the pursuit of profit. They insist that the desire for equality of access, equal representation, or humanitarian or civic considerations outweighs efficiency concerns or cost-effectiveness. They worry that outsourcing reduces direct accountability and limits the government's ability to effectively respond to constituent concerns and democratic pressures.

Recruiting and maintaining a dedicated group of civil servants is difficult under modern conditions. During periods of economic expansion, as occurred during the 1990s, private-sector employers can highlight the opportunity for personal gain. Military leaders have long recognized the challenges associated with recruitment and retention during periods of economic prosperity. Periods of economic recession produce their own challenges. While increases in the unemployment rate ease recruiting concerns, difficulties in adjusting compensation and hiring practices limit the government's ability to respond to changing conditions. The use of purely economic recruitment incentives during hard times raises equity concerns. In the military, it tends to result in a situation where the poor bear a disproportionate burden for the broad public benefits of national defense.

In response to both situations, public officials seeking to effectively recruit public servants have turned increasingly to nonmonetary compensations that augment basic pay. The traditional practice of shielding government workers from competitive forces by providing greater job security is one such approach. Another is the more recent practice of utilizing social incentives such as those that preserve family life. Importantly, the latter has led the government to attract individuals who, in addition to being civic-minded, have other characteristics that affect overall productivity.

This is particularly apparent within the defense establishment. The DoD has difficulty offering wages that are competitive with private-sector earnings and so augments basic pay with other forms of compensation that are related to marital and dependents status. Military personnel policies provide an example of the challenges involved when government organizations compete in private labor markets, highlighting two important issues related to the "who should rule" debate. Social incentives affect the composition of the public-sector work force and, as a further consequence, affect the ability of military officers to adopt "best business practice" reforms.

MILITARY PERSONNEL POLICY: AN INTRODUCTION

Like many government agencies, the DoD is a large hierarchical organization, heavily dependent for the completion of its work upon skilled personnel. Military manpower requirements accounted for over 25 percent ($93.4 billion) of the fiscal year 2003 defense budget.[21] Prior to 1973, military leaders relied on a combination of volunteers and conscripts to meet work-force requirements. The creation of the all volunteer force (AVF) in 1973, largely viewed as a response to problems associated with the Vietnam-era draft, forced the military to compete with the private sector for its entire work force. While other government agencies face similar competition, several aspects of military service differentiate it from other forms of government work. These include the risks associated with combat, an emphasis on the rigid implementation of authoritarian relationships, and demanding physical training. In addition, because the skills required of military leaders are developed while they are serving within the military, "lateral entry" is not feasible. The U.S. military consequently utilizes an "up or out" promotion scheme, filling positions at the higher end of the hierarchy through the winnowing of a well-qualified pool of entry-level applicants, while training them over a long period of time.[22] As such, the military's involvement in the labor market is characterized by competition for a segment of highly skilled high school graduates.

To enhance its competitive position, defense department officials augment "basic pay" (the military equivalent of the wage rate) with a number of tax-free "allowances," including the basic subsistence allowance and the housing allowance. While basic pay is determined by pay tables designed to ensure that those of equal rank receive equal pay, the magnitude of allowances is influenced by an individual's marital and dependents status. These allowances reinforce the notion that the military "takes care of its own," creating a family-friendly atmosphere that is one of the principal benefits of a military career.

These policies affect the composition of the work force in ways that influence productivity. In the military, family-friendly policies lead to an active duty force that is disproportionately composed of individuals with family obligations. Yet the pressures associated with military service, such as combat and overseas assignments, are more easily borne by single soldiers without dependents. While several aspects of military service are unique, this particular case offers broad implications for the use of non-pay-related compensation as a means to attract persons to public service.

FAMILY STATUS OF MILITARY PERSONNEL

Military personnel are more likely to be married and have children than their civilian counterparts. This finding is supported by previous research and validated by econometric analysis that controls for demographic factors.[23]

Relative to workers in the civilian sector, military personnel tend to be younger, more likely to have only a high school diploma, and male. The difference in marriage rates and dependents status persists even when controlling for these and other demographic factors. Figure 8.1 compares the percentage of males in the military who are married for

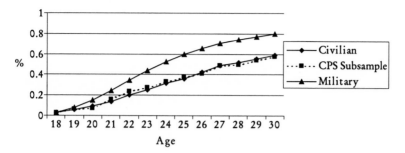

FIGURE 8.1 **Percentage Married in the Military
with Civilian Comparison Groups**

each age cohort, from eighteen to thirty years old, with two civilian groups. The first group consists of the entire pool of responses to the Current Population Survey (CPS; more than 22,000 observations for each year between 1995 and 1999). The second group, a subset of the supplement, consists of male high school graduates who were employed full time (more than 2,500 observations for each year).

As expected, the percentage married in each group increases with age. At age eighteen, the percentage married in each of the groups is nearly identical (2.6 percent for the military, 2.5 percent for the civilian group, and 2.8 percent for the subsample). For each year after age eighteen, however, the military group has the highest percentage of married individuals. This suggests that even after controlling for age (by comparing people of similar ages across groups), education, employment status, and sex (by comparing different groups), military members are more likely to be married than their civilian counterparts.

Analysis of the family status of military personnel is complicated by the definition of dependency. The number of dependents "sponsored" by a service member may include a spouse, children, or dependent parents. For this analysis, a member of the military was counted as having a child if that person was married and the sponsor of at least two dependents, or single and the sponsor of one or more dependents. Although this may introduce some bias into the results, it seemed the most reasonable way to deal with the limitations of the data set. Even so, the results must be interpreted cautiously. For each of three groups (the military, the CPS population as a whole, and a subset of the CPS consisting of male high school graduates employed full time), figure 8.2 presents the percentage of military personnel with children (dependents not having reached their eighteenth birthday) for the period from 1995 to 1999.

The military group had a higher percentage of individuals with children than the subsample for each age cohort between eighteen and

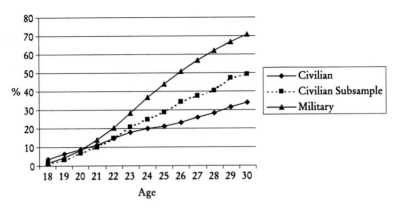

FIGURE 8.2 **Percentage with Children under 18, 1995–99**

thirty years old. Although differences at the lower end of the spectrum are small, this result suggests that military personnel are more likely to have children than are a similar group of civilians. Relative to the entire population surveyed for the CPS, military rates were slightly smaller at the low end of the age spectrum but much higher for each cohort after age twenty-three. The size of the differences at the middle and upper age ranges suggests that even if the results contain the bias noted earlier, the overall finding (military members are more likely to have children) would remain.

Econometric techniques, described in the appendix to this chapter, were utilized to gain insight into the magnitude of the effect of military service on family status. Specifically, predictions from the econometric model for a civilian high school graduate of mean age and income are compared with the predictions for a military member with the same demographic characteristics. The predicted probability of marriage estimated for a civilian is 16.4 percent, whereas the probability for a military member with the same characteristics is 33 percent. The predicted probability that a civilian would have a dependent is 11 percent, whereas the probability for a military member is 26 percent. These results should be interpreted cautiously. The actual proportion of twenty-three-year-old military males who were married in 1999 was approximately 49 percent, which is much higher than the probability predicted here. With respect to dependent status, the actual proportion of twenty-three-year-old military males who had a child in 1999 was approximately 36 percent, which is higher than the probability predicted here.

Taken as a whole, the results—in conjunction with the established findings of previous research—strongly suggest that members of the military are more likely to have family obligations than their civilian counterparts. Differences in family status cannot be explained solely on the basis of demographic factors.

Why is this so? There are at least two interpretations of this result. First, the military may be drawing more individuals with family obligations into service. If so, the percentage of new recruits (non–prior service, or NPS accessions) who were married or had children would be larger than the percentage of similar civilians. But that is not the case. For the period 1995 to 1999, the percentage of NPS accessions who were married was less than or equal to the married percentage in the civilian population. With regard to dependents status, the military rate is higher than the civilian rate for each age cohort after twenty years old—but at the lowest end of the age spectrum the civilian rate is equal to or slightly higher than the military rate. This is particularly important, as the majority of new recruits are under the age of twenty.

These data suggest a second interpretation, one with profound implications for the "who should rule" debate. Rather than drawing more married people into military service, aspects of that service make it more likely that those already in the military will marry and have children. The evidence is not conclusive (the military may be drawing a higher proportion of people who intend to take on family obligations but have not done so at the time of accession). Still, it does appear that military personnel policies contain incentives that favor the acquisition of dependents and influence the tendency of soldiers to marry.

This could occur in a number of ways. The structure of military compensation, with its focus on pay, allowances, and the provision of certain goods in kind, may make military service more attractive than jobs in the private sector for individuals with families. Also, policies for those already in the military may encourage those with families to stay. For example, military members with families are offered either family quarters or larger allowances than single members. Other benefits that differ according to dependents status (such as transportation and travel allowances and separation pay) may encourage family life.

EFFICIENCY EFFECTS: COST AND EFFECTS ON PERFORMANCE

In the process of creating incentives that attract volunteers to military service, government officials appear to have consciously or inadvertently created policies that emphasize a family-friendly work environment. The implications of these results depend critically on two factors.

First, it is important to understand the costs of supporting military members with families. In addition to the direct costs of the allowances, the military spends significant resources on other family support programs such as the Department of Defense Dependents Schools, commissary privileges, youth activity and family service centers, and morale, recreation, and welfare programs. In 1996, the Center on Family in America estimated that maintaining the dependent support structure consumed approximately 10 percent of the defense budget (a total of almost $25 billion).[24] In 1996, the Marine Corps allocated $156 million to family housing and $132 million for ammunition, while spending more on family service and child development centers than on spare parts.[25] The DoD's reliance on allowances that reward family status probably influences even more members to take on family obligations and exacerbates the costs of family support.

This allocation of resources may not be the most efficient way to help the military fight and win armed conflicts. Systematic research evaluating the costs and effectiveness of family support programs is difficult because military personnel costs are not consolidated into a single budgetary appropriation. The current process, which distributes personnel costs across several appropriation accounts, makes it difficult to track spending levels and compare military compensation policies with those in the civilian sector.[26] Without knowing the exact costs of personnel support, and how they are influenced by force composition, analysts cannot assess the opportunity costs of various programs. This limits the ability of public officials to make informed decisions and is inconsistent with BCPs in the private sector.

Second, it is important to understand the relationship between family status and job performance in the military. If military members with families perform better than those without, the allocation of funds to family support programs may be well spent. Alternatively, if single members are more able to handle the stresses of military life and outperform married soldiers, funds for family support may be better spent in other areas. Generally, existing studies of family status and military performance suggest that soldiers with families perform better in some areas and worse in others. A 1992 Rand study titled "Army Families and Soldier Readiness" found that relative to single soldiers, married soldiers in the army report fewer job-related problems, are more committed to the army, and expect to serve in the army longer. Similarly, a 1993 Office of the Assistant Secretary of Defense (OASD) (Personnel and Readiness) study, "Family Status and Initial Term of Service," reports that for the 1987 accession cohort, married soldiers had lower attrition rates and higher retention rates than single soldiers.

Also, according to that report, married soldiers had proportionally fewer indiscipline and substance abuse discharges.[27]

Yet other studies point in a different direction. To the extent that marital status can be linked to promotion-enhancing performance, the OASD study reports that promotion to the more competitive enlisted grades (E-5 to E-9) typically occurs at a faster rate for single soldiers. (Married soldiers and single ones get promoted to E-4 in a similar time frame.) Further, single soldiers report fewer problems responding to no-notice alerts and unit deployments. Finally, some studies have found that family status is not significantly related to individual readiness or performance on the skill qualification test.[28]

These studies demonstrate the difficulties associated with measuring differences in the performance of military members based on family status. While married members seem to be more stable than single members, single soldiers may be less encumbered by responsibilities detracting from the time and effort required to carry out the work. This view is supported by an analysis of survival and continuation rates. (This does not refer to survival in battle, but rather the proportion of given accession cohorts to remain in the military or complete their first term of service and reenlist.) Figures 8.3 and 8.4 show the percentage of accessions in the years 1990–94 who remained in the military for one to five years of service by marital and dependents' status.

As the figures suggest, single soldiers are more likely to remain in the military through the first few years of service, but married soldiers are more likely to remain thereafter. A similar result occurs for soldiers with dependents, although at a slower rate. The advantage to soldiers with dependents does not occur until the fifth year. A comparison of "conditional" survival rates, which show the percentage of

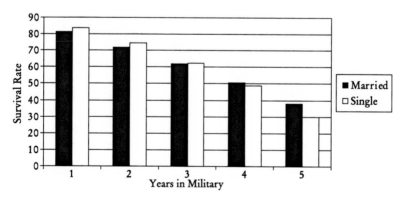

FIGURE 8.3 **Survival Rates by Marital Status, Averages, 1990–94**

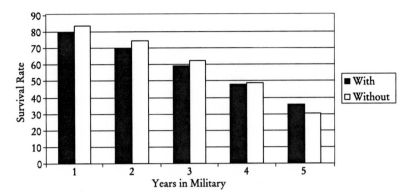

FIGURE 8.4 **Survival Rates by Dependents' Status, Averages, 1990–94**

the "surviving" cohort that makes it through each additional year rather than the percentage of the initial cohort that survives to a particular year, yields similar results. For cohorts entering between 1990 and 1995, continuation rates were higher for married members and for those with dependents. One interpretation of these results, consistent with previous research, suggests that the stresses of adjusting to military life are initially felt more strongly by soldiers with families, but that once the initial adjustment is made they tend to be more committed and stay longer than those without families.

Even a cursory examination of military personnel policies reveals the great challenges involved in creating the equivalent of BCPs for government service. While clear metrics exist for measuring success in the private sector (profits, costs, market share), few of those metrics are easily translated to military life. A clear understanding of what makes a good soldier and the different types of soldiers required for effective provision of defense might help to identify the optimal composition of the force and relevance of family obligations. Yet finding ways to define and track worker performance and develop sound pay practices that reward productivity is difficult. Private-sector firms are hierarchical organizations that typically use variation in pay to stimulate the most productive workers to seek advancement. The U.S. military, however, uses a relatively flat compensation scheme, with promotion to higher pay grades determined primarily by time in service (rather than by productivity). Large firms exploit the benefits associated with lateral entry from private-sector labor markets by adjusting the pay available to persons at the top of the hierarchy. The military uses "targeted reenlistment bonuses" to stimulate promotion from within the hierarchy and limits the use of flexible compensation packages that might permit lateral recruitment. Although pay policies in the military may reflect the long-standing military tradition that those with equal responsibility should receive equal pay, they are not consistent with the best business practices utilized in the private sector.

CONCLUSION

Waldo's insights regarding the impact of historical eras and events on the development of theories of administration remain as important today as when his book was written. Current events shape ideological perspectives. They influence the ways citizens view government, the demands placed on government, and views of "appropriate" administrative values and techniques. The terrorist attacks of September 11, 2001, had a profound impact on economic, political, and social forces in the United States that continue to influence the course of modern government.

Meeting these demands may strain the capacity of the administrative state. In reviewing the question of "who should rule," Waldo examined the prevailing view that "civilization as we hope to make it" required a special class of individuals prepared to carry out the work of the state. Without commenting immediately upon it, he summarized the doctrine advanced by early administrative reformers regarding the makeup of the civil service: "In general the claim is that the conditions of the modern world require a large and skillful body of bureaucrats, administrators, or experts; that the scientific method and the vast changes which it has brought about in the externals of life, the existence of the nation-state (or hope of a world-state) system, and the demand by all classes of society that government be used as an instrument for achieving the Good Life—that these stupendous facts compel us to recognize the necessity for a 'governing class.'"[29]

Unfortunately, economic conditions and current budgetary pressures make it difficult to ensure that "The Best shall serve the State."[30] While the competitive pressures associated with privatization and outsourcing may generate efficiency gains in many cases, government competition with private firms for labor may have adverse effects. Because government officials have difficulty competing with the private sector in terms of pay, they turn to other incentives to find a civic-minded governing class. The use of alternative incentive structures may affect the composition of the government work force in ways that are unplanned by their designers, or even limit the capacity of government officials to govern well and perform effectively. This line of reasoning can easily be applied to uniformed military personnel. Policies in the U.S. military, for example, lead to a force disproportionately composed of members with family obligations. This may or may not be consistent with the pressures of military life.

The use of alternative compensation schemes to create a family-friendly atmosphere in the military arose, in part, from the competitive pressures stemming from the implementation of the AVF. In many countries, military service is viewed as an obligation of citizenship. In the United States, however, significant difficulties with the use of government authority to compel service via the draft during the Vietnam era compelled a different policy. In a sense, current policies substitute a policy of "mutually beneficial exchange" (in the sense that joining the military is a labor market choice) for the use of government authority. While this may make participation in the military more "democratic" and less "authoritarian," such policies can discourage the recruitment of individuals concerned with public rather than private gain. As Waldo's discussion of how best to recruit a "governing class" demonstrates, this is an enduring problem with no easy solution.

It is interesting to note that military recruiting and retention problems, during the economic expansion of the 1990s, were least severe for the U.S. Marine Corps. In contrast to the advertising schemes used by other branches of the services (which focused on military service providing a useful set of technical skills highly valued in the private sector), the Marine Corps recruiting strategy focused on other values including personal challenge and growth, honor, tradition, discipline, hard work, and service of country. Perhaps governmental leaders are not well advised to compete for personnel using corporate labor market practices. In considering the most appropriate way to recruit a governing or administrative class devoted to public service, those leaders instead might stress the prestige of public employment, the opportunities for personal growth, and the moral or ethical rewards.

APPENDIX: RESEARCH METHODOLOGY

To establish the findings reported earlier in the chapter, data on marriage and dependents status in the military obtained from the Defense Manpower Data Center (DMDC) were compared with data from the March supplement to the CPS from 1995 to 1999.[31] Differences in marital and dependents status based on military service were evaluated using regression analysis. Because marriage and dependents status are binary variables, the logistic model was used. In the first model, the dependent variable was marital status (1 if married, 0 otherwise), and the independent variables were the constant, age in years, sex (1 if male, 0 otherwise), income in dollars per year, high school diploma (HSD; 1 if had a high school diploma, 0 otherwise), and civilian status (Civstat; 1 if not in the military, 0 otherwise). The regression output is as follows:

Model 1: Logistic Regression of Marital Status

ln P/(1 − P) = −6.3 + .27 Age − .54 Sex + (3.51E − 6) Income − .27 HSD − .92 Civstat

P-value: (.0001) (.0001) (.0001) (.0001) (.0001) (.0001)

P-value for Score statistic with 5 DF = .0001

Percentage of concordant predicted probabilities and observed responses = 77.8

The coefficient on civilian status is negative and significant well below the 1 percent level. The results suggest that even when controlling for a variety of factors, military service *is* associated with a higher probability of marriage. Each of the other variables contained in the regression is significant and has a sign consistent with expectations. Also, the Score statistic (which tests for the joint significance of the explanatory variables) and the high percentage of concordant predicted and observed responses (which assess the extent to which higher predicted probabilities are associated with more observances of marriage) suggest that the model fits the data well. Estimation of two other models, the Probit model and the linear probability model, both generate similar results.

Model 2 presents the results for dependents status, maintaining the independent variables developed previously.

Model 2: Logistic Regression of Dependents' Status

ln [P/(1 − P)] = −4.68 + .20 Age − .27 Sex − (2.1E − 7) Income − .76 HSD − 1.02 Civstat

P-value: (.0001) (.0001) (.0001) (.0001) (.0001) (.0001)

P-value for Score statistic with 5 DF = .0001

Percentage of concordant predicted probabilities and observed responses = 76.8

The coefficient on civilian status is negative and significant at well below the 1 percent level. This suggests that even after controlling for a variety of factors, being in the military *is* associated with a higher probability of having dependents. Each of the other variables contained in the regression is significant and has a sign consistent with expectations. As was the case for model 1, the Score statistic and the high percentage of concordant predicted probabilities and observed responses suggest that the model fits the data well. Results from a Probit model and the linear probability model generated similar results.

To generate specific predictions from the logistic model, the author had to specify a number of demographic characteristics and "create" an observation for which there is no clear analog in the actual data set. This is a limitation commonly associated with the analysis of binary data.

NOTES

1. Dwight Waldo, *The Administrative State: A Study of the Political Theory of American Public Administration*, 2nd ed. (New York: Holmes & Meier, 1984), 7.

2. Dwight Waldo, *Public Administration in a Time of Turbulence* (New York: Chandler, 1971), 284.

3. Ibid., 268.

4. The bailout signed into law on September 22, 2001, included $5 billion in direct federal aid and $10 billion in loan guarantees. In addition, the act helped the airline industry pay rising insurance costs in the wake of the terrorist strikes and limited liability in any federal lawsuit resulting from the hijackings. "Bush Signs Airline Bailout Package," *CNN.com*, September 23, 2001, www.cnn.com/2001/US/09/22/rec.airline.deal/index.html (accessed June 1, 2004).

5. Mickey D. Levy, "Healthy Economic Recovery and Rising Real Interest Rates," Shadow Open Market Committee, April 2002, www.somc.rochester.edu/Apr02/Levy402.pdf (accessed June 1, 2004).

6. Computations by author from data available from NASDAQ. Historical data can be accessed at http://dynamic.nasdaq.com/aspx/majorindices.aspx.

7. Alan Greenspan, Testimony before the Committee on the Budget, United States Senate, 107th Congress, 2nd sess. (Washington, DC: U.S. Government Printing Office, 2002).

8. George Bush, "Address before a Joint Session of the Congress on the United States Response to the Terrorist Attacks of September 11th," *Weekly Compilation of Presidential Documents* 37 (July–September 2001): 1349.

9. George Bush, "Address before a Joint Session of the Congress on the State of the Union," *Weekly Compilation of Presidential Documents* 37 (July–September 2001): 1349.

10. President of the United States, *The National Security Strategy of the United States of America*, September 17, 2002, 15, www.whitehouse.gov.nsc.nss5.html (accessed December 15, 2005).

11. Alan Fram, "War Cost Will Top $50 Billion, Pentagon Official Says," Associated Press Wire report, May 13, 2004.

12. *U.S.A. Patriot Act,* Public Law 107–56, *U.S. Statutes at Large* 115 (2001): 275.

13. Congressional Budget Office, "An Analysis of the President's Budgetary Proposals for Fiscal Year 2005," March 2004, 2.

14. Bureau of Economic Analysis, *National Income and Product Accounts,* U.S. Department of Commerce, May 27, 2004, table 3.3.

15. Henry David Thoreau, "Civil Disobedience," in *Walden and Other Writings,* ed. Joseph Wood Krutch (New York: Bantam Books, 1962), 85–86.

16. U.S. Office of Management and Budget, "Performance and Commercial Activities," Circular No. A-76 (rev.), August 4, 1983.

17. U.S. Congressional Budget Office, "Contracting Out: Potential for Reducing Federal Costs," Washington, DC, 1987, 27.

18. U.S. Office of Management and Budget, "Enhancing Governmental Productivity through Competition: A New Way of Doing Business within the Government to Provide Quality Government Services and Least Cost," Washington, DC, August 1988, 4.

19. Alan Marcus, "Analysis of the Navy's Commercial Activities Program," CNA Research Memorandum 92-226 (Alexandria, VA: Center for Naval Analyses, 1993).

20. Adam Smith, *The Wealth of Nations,* in *The Essential Adam Smith,* ed. Robert Heilbroner (New York: Norton, 1987), 687–88.

21. U.S. Department of Defense News Release, "Fiscal 2004 Department of Defense Budget Release," No. 004-03, February 3, 2003, www.defenselink.mil/news/Feb2003/b02032003_bt044-03.html (accessed June 1, 2004).

22. See, for example, Beth J. Asch and John T. Warner, *A Theory of Military Compensation and Personnel Policy* (Santa Monica, CA: Rand, 1994).

23. See, for example, P. A. Morrison, Georges Vernez, David Grissmer, and Kevin McCarthy, *Families in the Army: Looking Ahead* (Santa Monica, CA: Rand 1989).

24. David Evans, "More Families, Fewer Fighters: The Pentagon's New Welfare State," *San Diego Tribune,* March 5, 1995.

25. Jeffrey Burns, "Taking Care of Our People: At Any Price?" *Naval Institute Proceedings Magazine* 124, no. 1 (January 1988): 56–59.

26. For more on this topic, see U.S. Congressional Budget Office, "Consolidate Military Personnel Costs in a Single Appropriation," *Budget Options,* 050-16, March 2003.

27. M. Audrey Burnam, Lisa Meredith, Donald Sherbourne, Burciaga Valdez, and Georges Vernes, *Army Families and Soldier Readiness* (Santa Monica, CA: Rand, 1992); U.S. Department of Defense, Personnel and Readiness, *Family Status and Initial Term of Service,* 1993.

28. See Robert Sadacca and Ani DiFazio, *Analysis of Army Family Research Program Measures of Readiness* (Alexandria, VA: U.S. Army Research Institute for the Behavioral and Social Sciences, 1991), and references therein.

29. Waldo, *Administrative State,* 91.

30. Ibid., 93.

31. The March supplement to the CPS focuses on a variety of demographic factors including race, age, marital status, income, military service, educational attainment, and number of children. The family database maintained by DMDC combines information from the active-duty master database and the Defense Enrollment Eligibility Reporting System (DEERS) database to generate demographic information about military members and their families.

9

Business and Government

BARBARA S. ROMZEK

The administrative state that Dwight Waldo described and analyzed more than fifty years ago drew its motive force from the rapid expansion of government during the first half of the twentieth century. The growth in governmental responsibilities for providing public goods and services created the modern administrative state. That growth was closely allied with developments in the business sector. In characterizing the newly emerging administrative state, Waldo observed the importance of America's business civilization to public administration: "Despite increasing pressure of population on resources and continuing prodigality in the use of resources, America remained a uniquely wealthy country, and ours became characteristically a Business Civilization. This has influenced our methods of administration and our literature of public administration."[1]

Waldo's general observation is as true today as it was when he first wrote *The Administrative State*, but in a different manner. Waldo observed that the field of public administration derived its fundamental emphasis from the business background, notably the emphasis upon management and the use of organizational forms characteristic of business corporations, such as central direction, hierarchy, and specialization. During the first half of the twentieth century, however, as the administrative state emerged, government served as an important counterbalance to excesses of business practice and failures of the marketplace, including monopolistic practices, robber barons, and economic depression.[2] Government needed business practices, but it also needed to be strong in order to serve as a counterbalance to the shortcomings of business.

While some of the fundamental cultural principles remain, the business civilization of today manifests itself in mechanisms quite different from those that Waldo observed, reflecting recent history and the experiences of the past fifty years. A fundamental aspect of the American business culture includes the conviction that profit motive and competition are essential incentives for efficiency and quality. Political, economic, and administrative forces at the close of the twentieth century resulted in the application of this aspect to public administration. The last two decades of the twentieth century produced a general erosion of American public opinion regarding the capacity of government to provide public goods and services. Many politicians successfully campaigned on the slogan of "running government like a business." The watchwords of dominant political coalitions at all levels of the federal system included the desire to "make government more businesslike," but in this case by using nongovernmental organizations, especially private industry, to conduct the business of government. By late in the twentieth century, business practices came to be seen as the solution to government failures.[3] The George W. Bush administration expanded this thrust to include faith-based organizations providing government services.

This late twentieth-century phenomenon added new texture to the business civilization that Waldo observed. Not only was government to adopt as many business practices as possible, as was true in the mid-twentieth century, but government was now encouraged to offload as many of its functions to nongovernmental entities as was practical. This resulted in an explosion of interest in alternatives to traditional government operations; it fueled a significant transformation in administrative arrangements at the federal, state, and local levels of government.

This chapter focuses on one particular manifestation of the extension of "business civilization" into the administrative state—the use of privatization and contracting to pursue the business of government. Framed by the philosophic issues Waldo posed, this chapter examines the manner in which privatization and contracting have transformed public administration. It explores these developments as part of a larger cycle of reform, defines the practice of privatization, reviews supporting theories, summarizes the scope of contracting, and scrutinizes the manner in which the nature of public administration has changed in response. The impact of privatization and contracting on the work of government officials as they seek to manage contracts and third-party relationships has been revolutionary. Through a comprehensive review of the literature and issues associated with this development, the chapter shows how the commitment to one administrative ideology has reshaped basic assumptions about the nature of public administration in the modern state.

CYCLES OF REFORM: BEYOND GOVERNMENTAL BOUNDARIES

The history of U.S. government is one of cyclical reforms, with the cycles reflecting shifts in mood and competing philosophies regarding government operations. As noted in chapter 2, eleven major commissions sought to create different reforms of the federal administrative establishment during the twentieth century. Paul Light uses the metaphor of "tides" to capture the dynamic nature of administrative reform, noting that particular reform efforts often work at cross-purposes and appear to occur over increasingly shorter time frames.[4]

Such administrative reforms result from swings in public mood; when public events contribute to the perception that one publicly held value has been neglected at the expense of another, elected officials and the public call for reforms to address perceived shortfalls. As constraints on administrative discretion resulted in excessive rules and regulations, for example, reformers called for streamlined government and the liberation of managers from red tape. As excesses of discretion have occurred, often under entrepreneurial models emphasizing responsiveness to governmental "customers," reformers have pressed for changes that yield greater transparency and accountability. The inexorable cycles of reform arise from an American political ethos that embraces competing values such as individualism, efficiency, equality, responsiveness, and accountability. As a particular reform emphasizes one or two of these values, the others tend to be devalued or de-emphasized. In time, imbalance brings calls for yet another reform. Similar cycles occur in the business world.

The current cycle of reform touts the business practices of competition and responsiveness to customers as a model for government agencies to follow.[5] Government in the United States at the start of the twenty-first century was widely perceived to be inefficient, inflexible, and ineffective, while nongovernmental sectors were perceived to possess better management practices and responsiveness to clientele. The steady drumbeat of criticism about public bureaucracy overshadowed considerable problems with private-sector management.

Such rhetoric, while seemingly persuasive, contains significant cognitive dissonance, if not cultural confusion, about the contemporary state of American business enterprise. Viewed another way, the litany of cases concerning mismanagement, excessive profit taking, and even fraud in the nongovernmental sector could have raised greater concerns about business practices relative to governmental administration. Mismanagement in the nonprofit world affected the United Way of America, the Foundation for New Era Philanthropy, and the Catholic Church. Accountability failures have occurred within private companies performing government work under contract. Tenet Healthcare and HealthSouth faced Medicare fraud charges for treating patients who did not need government-financed care. An administrative law judge ruled that the El Paso Corporation, the largest supplier of natural gas in the nation, illegally helped to drive up prices for natural gas in California during the state's power crisis in 2000 and 2001. A senior trader at the Enron Corporation pleaded guilty to engaging in a conspiracy that illegally manipulated the California power market during the state's energy crisis, driving up prices and generating millions of dollars in excess profits for his employer.[6] The fact that the business paradigm continues to be wholeheartedly embraced despite accounting scandals and incidents of fraud, corruption, insider trading, and excessive corporate payoffs is evidence of the cultural strength of the widely held assumption that business is better at management than government.

Perceived governmental shortcomings provided the cornerstone for arguments supporting the widespread use of nongovernmental entities to carry out the business of government. An explosion of popular support for nongovernmental organizations providing traditional public services followed. Working "outside the box" of traditional government bureaucracies, public officials embraced contracting, public-private partnerships, and privatization. Such practices represented a search for greater economy, efficiency, flexibility, and responsiveness to clients in governmental affairs, in spite of Waldo's warning that such values could not be used as the prime criteria for measuring administrative performance. For the most part, other key values of the American political system, such as equity and legal accountability, have been overshadowed in the contemporary drive to transform the administrative state.

The new contracting regime encourages widespread use of nonprofit and for-profit corporations to provide public services *for* government and to supply goods and services *to* government. This new way of governing further embeds what Waldo called America's "business civilization" into the administrative practices of federal, state, and local governments. The range of alternatives designed to force public administrators to work "outside the box" of traditional government organizations has forced those managers to rethink many conventional administrative practices.

PRIVATIZATION: VARIATIONS ON A BUSINESS THEME

Privatization theories view reliance on the private sector as more likely to serve public interests than reliance on public agencies. Whereas government is widely perceived in classical economics to be best suited to solve problems that arise due to market failures, privatization is perceived in the current milieu as offering market solutions to nonmarket failures—that is, the shortcomings of government agencies.[7]

To say the term *privatization* is loosely used in the literature and popular discourse is an understatement. Salamon notes that while privatization has political appeal as a label, it is too general a euphemism to be useful in understanding government challenges in the twenty-first century. Salamon identifies at least ten different forms of privatization. In its broadest interpretation, privatization involves some form of engagement between government and nongovernmental entities in the pursuit of public purposes. Other phrases used to capture these phenomena include "third-party government," "indirect government," and "quasi government." Posner summarizes the supposed advantages of privatization in national affairs by noting that third-party arrangements "enhance the legitimacy of the federal presence, share the costs, provide critical skills and authorities not available in the federal government, and help adapt federal programs to unique local conditions and needs."[8]

Those who aspire to some level of conceptual precision generally restrict the privatization term to one of three different phenomena: off-loading of governmental responsibilities to the private sector, contracting, and public-private partnerships. To draw further distinction, privatization takes government completely out of a particular area of service delivery, as through the sale of community hospitals and clinics to for-profit firms or the sale of public utilities to private entities.[9] In such instances the government ceases to be responsible for delivery of the service.

Under *contracting*, government continues to be responsible for a public service, and most often continues to pay for the services produced, but the service itself is delivered through nongovernmental (nonprofit and for-profit) parties. A variant of the contracting model is *joint contracting*. This occurs when governments retain a portion of the contracted operation in-house, or when one government contracts with another for services or uses multiple contract arrangements that contain these features. Joint contracting enables agencies to retain in-house expertise, maximize competition among bidders by providing government employees with opportunities to bid on contract work against nongovernmental firms, and reverse the outsourcing decision if deemed desirable. An increasingly common technique permits government employees to hold onto their jobs through what is called managed competition, whereby public employees and public departments submit bids in response to requests for proposals (RFPs) along with private and nonprofit firms.[10]

Public officials may also engage business involvement in public purposes through public-private partnerships. These involve shared risk and competition, in which governmental and nongovernmental entities combine their efforts to achieve a particular public purpose. Public-private partnerships tend to be used in areas where full privatization seems less tractable. Such arrangements have been used extensively in areas beyond conventional service delivery, such as economic revitalization, where business leaders play prominent roles in local policy making.[11]

This shift of government work from internal production to some form of external production, either through contracting, joint contracting, privatization, or public-private partnerships, represents a significant transformation of government affairs. It also presents substantial challenges for governmental administrators. External production typically does not eliminate governmental responsibility for assuring citizens that they receive full access to public services. Yet it does change the tools available for that task. Don Kettl has articulated this challenge especially well, noting that the public management mechanisms needed to oversee external production differ significantly from the traditional command and control arrangements typically used in hierarchical relationships. To succeed at external production, Kettl says, government managers "must learn the points of leverage in networks; change their behavior to manage those points of leverage, develop the processes needed to make that work, and change the organizational culture from a traditional control perspective to one that accommodates indirect methods."[12] In essence, government managers are pressed to rely more on interpersonal and interorganizational skills that allow such officials to reach beyond agency boundaries and facilitate relationships within and between networks of contractors.

THEORIES ABOUT NONGOVERNMENTAL ENTITIES

Two independent theoretical streams help expert observers think about the role of nongovernmental entities in the production and delivery of public services. One is principal-agent theory and the other is network theory. Principal-agent theory views the relationship between nongovernmental entities and public officials as that of a person authorized to act on another's behalf, such as a lawyer or real estate agent. The value of this approach lies in its identification of the central paradox that arises in such relationships due to the inevitable information asymmetries between principals and agents. Agents frequently have an advantage in their dealings with clients because the agents have more information about the task at hand than principals do. To overcome the challenges of information asymmetries, principal-agent theorists suggest that public officials specify in detail the performance expectations, service goals, accountability mechanisms, and sanctions for shortfalls within the contractual relationship.[13]

Network theory has been used to illuminate the challenges of managing within the nonhierarchical situations that typically occur in complex contracting relationships. In the twentieth century, network arrangements became the primary organizational approach for designing and executing many social service policies.[14] The federal government contributed to the development of these networks through intergovernmental requirements that encouraged a "picket fence" approach to service delivery, thereby creating networks of program specialists and advocates. Such subsystems of policy specialists often matured into networks that acted as agents for enhanced federal spending. In some cases, elected officials sought to inspire such networks, as in the development of community action agencies and Head Start.[15] Contracting has expanded the development of such networks within which power tends to be shared among all participants, governmental and otherwise.

Advocates of contracting view the mechanism as a means to promote the efficiencies inherent in private markets within public services by shifting production from government bureaus to private producers.[16] Such efficiencies are thought to occur as a result of the incentives provided by competition and the profit motive. Advocates argue that contracting can correct excessive government size and service delivery problems attributable to the absence of market discipline in a monopolistic bureaucratic state.[17] These arguments apply regardless of whether the service in question is offered by local, state, or federal governments.

Critics of privatization question the viability of the market model. For many services—especially social services—true private markets do not exist, primarily because of inadequate provider supply. For these services, transferring production to a noncompetitive market offers limited, if any, economic benefits.[18] Because these services *cannot* take advantage of competitive market strengths, contracting often entails production or service by a nongovernment monopolist. Prager warns that "competition cannot be taken for granted; in its absence, the gains from contracting will be diminished, if not dissipated entirely."[19] Another important criticism was noted by Waldo and still holds true today. While the introduction of business standards (through contracting and privatization) can promote efficiency, it can also undermine important political values, such as equity, responsiveness, empowerment, and legitimacy. Such developments may de-emphasize the role and value of government itself.[20]

In a similar vein, others criticize contracting for the manner in which it transforms the social contract between government and its citizenry. Haque argues that the drive toward contracting and its market-driven modes of governance erode the public-private distinction, shrink government's socioeconomic role, narrow the composition of service recipients, worsen conditions of accountability, and result in declining levels of trust.[21] Such concerns highlight the need for critical studies on the use of private-sector values in public-service delivery and the resulting challenges to the public character of government.

TRANSFORMATION THROUGH CONTRACTING

Federal, state, and local officials have all embraced contracting with vigor. The trend owes much of its force to changing practices in the American federal system, especially contracting by the national government. Understanding the evolution of those practices illuminates the issues involved.

Federal Contracting

While federal contracting is as old as the republic, the scope of contemporary contracting by the federal government is enormous. As Kettl observes, "Every major policy initiative launched by the federal government since World War II—including Medicare and Medicaid, environmental cleanup and restoration, antipoverty programs and job training, interstate highways and sewage treatment plants—has been managed through public-private partnerships." The use of contract employees has been especially noteworthy in U.S. military operations. So many contract employees accompanied American troops to Iraq that enemy forces viewed them as legitimate targets for attack.[22]

Increased competition between public and private entities for federal government contracts was part of President George W. Bush's management agenda. The Office of Management and Budget emphasized the necessity for increased competition in its 2003 revision of Circular A-76, which provides guidance on the use of public-private competition and encourages development of customized plans by federal agencies to identify opportunities for public-private competition. The president's budget officers reported that officials at twenty-four different agencies identified 880,700 employees (out of a total of 1,636,000 full-time equivalent employees) doing work that could be put out for managed competition because the work was judged to be a commercial activity.[23]

Increased contracting raises important human resource issues. Federal contracts and grants generated more than 8 million jobs in 2002, up from less than 7 million in 1999. While federal civil service employment fell by almost 50,000 from 1999 to 2002, contract-generated jobs went up by more than 700,000, and grant-generated jobs grew by 333,000.[24] Not only is the federal government losing experienced staff and failing to replace them but the expansion in off-budget or contract work has increased the need for contract management expertise. Cutbacks in staff, combined with a federal work force that is rapidly approaching retirement age, present the federal civil service with a human resource challenge of significant proportions.[25] Remaining government employees face significant challenges in their effort to become "smart buyers." The lack of staff with specialized contract management expertise compromises the ability of federal officials to effectively monitor contracts.[26]

Government auditors recognize that downsizing government and increasing contract staff can be a risky business. A recent U.S. General Accounting Office (GAO) report included the National Aeronautics and Space Administration (NASA) on its "high risk" management list because of the difficulties faced by NASA employees in overseeing their contracts. The breadth of NASA contracting is extraordinary; in 2003 NASA officials sent $12.7 billion or about 90 percent of their annual budget to contractors. Yet those same officials encountered significant problems with their International Space Station development, resulting in $9 billion in largely contractor-generated cost overruns.[27]

NASA's complex mission presents significant management challenges to the agency. Increasingly, NASA officials turned to contract employees for help in managing risk.

> After the *Challenger* disaster [in 1986], NASA downsized its core staff of governmental employees, turned over more responsibility to contractors in exchange for stronger performance reporting, and transformed its procurement system to its famous "faster, better, cheaper" approach. The failure of several Mars missions caused critics to question the strategy, but it reflected an important underlying reality: NASA could not hope to manage its operations without expanding and strengthening its indirect tools, especially contracting.[28]

The highly visible *Challenger* explosion in 1986 and the loss of the space shuttle *Columbia* in 2003 raised serious questions about contractor management. The *Challenger* explosion occurred after contractors responsible for the shuttle's solid rocket boosters withdrew warnings about the effect of cold weather on booster performance. By 2003, most of the responsibility for shuttle flights had been transferred to a consortium of aerospace companies called United Space Alliance. Following the *Columbia* tragedy, besides the inevitable concerns about technological problems, investigators questioned whether the U.S. space agency had retained sufficient in-house expertise to effectively monitor contractor work.[29]

The politics and economics of contracting continue to present vexing issues for federal policymakers. Staffing questions and the uses of contracting were central issues in deliberations over the design of the new Transportation Security Administration (TSA), created in the wake of the terrorist attacks on September 11, 2001. Prior to the attacks, airlines contracted with private companies for passenger security. Individual airports commonly employed multiple companies for screening passengers and luggage. Competition among providers was vigorous, yet the companies employed screeners widely believed to be low skilled and lax in their enforcement efforts. The events of September 11, 2001, altered public and governmental expectations regarding airline security. After much debate, Congress decided that airport screeners in the United States would be federal employees of the TSA, part of the U.S. Department of Homeland Security. By the end of 2002, TSA had hired more than sixty thousand employees, including passenger and baggage screeners and federal air marshals.[30] In spite of the commitment to federal provision of airport security, officials at TSA experimented with privately provided screening at five U.S. airports.

The TSA example provides insight into the challenges of contracting out public services with public benefits. Public provision occurred
in the founding phase of TSA's organizational life cycle, when the federal presence in airport security was relatively new. The agency had little time to develop, promulgate, and implement performance standards
that might be used for monitoring contractors. The protocols for airport screening evolved slowly (as any number of shoeless travelers
padding through security checkpoints could attest), making the development of performance standards and contract expectations especially
difficult. TSA also faced considerable responsibility and pressure to
guard and ensure the public safety and welfare. The consequences
arising from a potential failure in security screening placed TSA in a
situation that necessitated close monitoring of employees. Yet close
monitoring of employees undercut the rationale for contracting in the
first place, namely the belief that private contractors possessed greater
flexibility and more incentives to seek out processes that are both efficient and effective for the task at hand.

The federal experience highlights issues concerning the capacity of
government employees to manage contracts under an intensive contracting regime.[31] In the state and local arenas, contracting challenges
manifest themselves along similar lines. The most significant change at
these levels has been the expansion of the scope of contracting into social service programs.

State and Local Government Contracting

Like the federal government, state and local governments have embraced smaller governments, reductions in force, restructuring, and alternative forms of delivering public services. As at the federal level,
state and local contracting has a long history, especially for publicly financed infrastructure such as bridges and highways. During the 1980s,
state governments expanded their use of privatization techniques.[32]
Policymakers restricted and removed government agencies from the
direct production of services and fundamentally reshaped the manner
in which those services were funded and delivered. The trend continued through the 1990s, when budgets were robust. The downturn in
the economy that occurred at the turn of the century put even more
pressure on state and local governments to find alternative ways to reduce costs. During that quarter century, political and economic trends
fueled an explosion in contracting at state and local levels.

The most significant transformation occurred in the type of service
areas subject to contracting. Across all fifty states, decentralization and

innovation transformed state personnel systems, with outsourcing of functions thought to be peripheral to core human resource management activities, such as health and benefits administration, employee assistance, drug testing, and human resource information systems operations. States embarked on social services contracting as part of the expanded discretion afforded under the Personal Responsibility and Welfare Reform Act.[33] In light of shrinking budgets for social services, state officials eagerly pursued contracting as a way to innovate, capture expertise, and hopefully control costs. By 1997 the U.S. General Accounting Office reported that 72 percent of social service programs in the states were contracted out.[34]

Local government contracting underwent similar changes. By the early 1980s, nonprofit and for-profit organizations delivered a majority of government-financed human services available at the local level. Although local governments still provided many services themselves, the level of contracting increased significantly between 1982 and 1992. One study found a significant increase in the level of contracting of all types in local government, from 12.6 percent to 28 percent, with suburban communities tending toward the most contracting. In larger urban areas, government-business partnerships played a significant role in altering traditional service delivery by local governments, especially in the area of economic revitalization. For more routine services, larger cities were less likely to contract than smaller cities. Among the 100 largest cities in the country, research indicates that 70 privatized fewer than ten services.[35] This pattern may be explained by the in-house efficiencies enjoyed by large urban governments due to economies of scale and the fact that this same large scale restricts the ability of city officials to locate contractors who can handle a large city's service demands.

Local governments continue to provide their own services through internal production where a great deal of uncertainty about service delivery operations exists and where the transaction costs involved in contracting are high. Council-manager governments show the most reluctance toward contracting, preferring almost all other production options (such as in-house, joint contracting, and intergovernmental partnerships) to private-firm contracting.[36]

CHALLENGES OF CONTRACTING

Some of the enthusiasm for contracting has been tempered by the experience of working with contractors and discovering that contracting does not necessarily reduce costs. Evidence that privatization and contracting will save money is at least a questionable, and perhaps a faulty, expectation. Cost calculations for comparing public and private provision are often problematic, due to the difficulty of identifying direct and indirect governmental subsidies. Research on state governments found cost savings of less than 5 percent due to contracting out. Research on child welfare service delivery found neither cost savings nor greater efficiency as a result of contracting. Aggressive efforts to produce cost savings can result in situations where contract bidding is so successful in reducing prices that contractors cannot complete the work without losing money, a situation found to exist in the case of foster care contracting in Kansas.[37]

Government officials occasionally employ contracting in arenas not suitable for the practice. Where service objectives are vague and where the governmental entity is unable to determine if quality measures have been met, contracting can create major headaches in implementation. This often occurs when public officials engage in contractor "creaming." In such instances, public officials break off "the easy and more profitable part to contract." This makes contracting appear more profitable than it actually is. The contractor produces the "creamed" services at less cost, but "the pieces left behind" cost more to deliver. The added cost or inefficiency of noncontracted elements is omitted from cost calculations.[38] Because government retains the least cost-efficient elements in-house, governmental efficiency declines further after contracts are let.

Values other than efficiency can be pursued through contracting, such as improved quality of service delivery. Rubin argues against the practice of evaluating contracts on the basis of whether they save money over hypothetical or actual municipal provision. She argues for quality measurement, where increased quality may justify increased spending. In some instances privatization can be more expensive and decrease quality. Oklahoma City's experience with its effort to privatize wastewater treatment resulted in contracts that were more costly in the long run due to complex performance issues, including health concerns, environmental regulation, and legal technicalities.[39] Sometimes contractor performance exceeds quality expectations, although this is rarely a cause for complaint. State officials in Kansas criticized foster care contractors who were experiencing financial difficulties for providing a level of care that was higher than the state thought warranted.[40]

Beyond issues of cost and quality, public officials have grappled with the management challenges that arise from contracting. Likewise, contractors continue to deal with the reality that although government work allows them to expand their businesses, the contracts often present serious administrative complications.

Effective contracting requires government managers to sustain cooperative relationships with individual vendors and work effectively within networks of contractors—while not losing sight of the ultimate performance goals guiding the contracting process. Success at these tasks requires public officials to master the skills of mutual goal setting, financial oversight, negotiation, communication, and bridge building.[41] Public servants accustomed to traditional command and control operations who turn to government contracting find themselves engaged in a variety of unfamiliar administrative processes—specifying roles, defining performance measures, managing competition, maintaining relationships, sustaining staff expertise, and managing accountability.

Specifying Roles. Contracting creates pressures to respecify the roles of top managers and service deliverers. This often requires a culture shift in basic assumptions about the work of governmental managers. No longer armed with the tools of direct hierarchy and formal authority, government contract managers inexorably turn to what Kettl calls "indirect methods" to elicit appropriate behavior from contractors. For example, to the extent that contracting creates complex networks, the role of the government agent as contract manager moves beyond that of contract monitor to include network facilitator. With such roles come different responsibilities that present managers seeking appropriate contract behavior with different leverage points. A clear specification of roles gives governmental officials and contracting entities an unambiguous understanding of their respective responsibilities. Role clarification, however, is not an easy task. Donahue notes that contracting is often overextended to cover duties that are difficult to specify in advance and inherently judgmental or political in nature.[42]

Federal welfare reform and state use of waivers are examples of the manner in which contracting transforms the roles of participants in the system. In Florida and Texas, many (if not most) welfare components were delivered through contracts with for-profit and nonprofit agencies. State administrators were deeply involved in the evaluation of that service delivery. In the case of Medicaid delivery, governmental roles shifted from that of bill payers for fee-for-service providers to evaluators of costly contracts with managed care organizations.[43]

Defining Performance. A key dimension of effective contracting is the government's ability to develop appropriate benchmarks and performance outcomes, as well as the ability to surmount the challenges of acquiring data on contractor performance. Through federal directives, the U.S. Office of Management and Budget has set a general goal that encourages the use of performance contracts for at least 20 percent of eligible federal contracting dollars.[44]

While performance contracting currently enjoys great popularity, it is difficult to do. The process presents significant political, managerial, and methodological challenges. Finding appropriate performance measures for federal contracts has been especially challenging. In 2003, the U.S. General Accounting Office criticized the Department of Energy for its inability to develop performance-based contract protocols. The department's own inspector general identified sites where performance-based measures were not used to improve contractor performance, where objective performance information on overall contractor performance was scarce, and where projects experienced significant cost growth and schedule delays.[45]

In Georgia and Virginia, contracting decisions were influenced by how easily officials could define objectives and monitor performance. State social service officers engaged in privatization initiatives have struggled to develop benchmarks and measure outcomes that allow assessment of actual performance. Contracts for service provision tend to lack performance baselines, performance targets, or clearly defined roles. Instead, contracts were lengthy, unduly complicated, overly focused on details, and ambiguous about goals. Riccucci found that the actual services delivered by frontline workers in welfare offices did not correspond with the policy directives issued by state officials. Recent research on contracting for ambulance services in the Kansas City metropolitan area found conflicts between the contract agency and the service provider over performance expectations and efficiency standards. In turn, these ambiguities led to doubts about the effectiveness of the ambulance service, ill will between parties, and an inability to ascertain which entity should be accountable for service shortcomings.[46]

When performance measures are difficult to specify, complementary measures have been used. For example, contracts may specify that a contractor adhere to industry standards or obtain accreditation from a relevant certifying body. The State of Kansas chose this strategy; it required contractors engaged in adoption and foster care to be accredited. While external accreditation provides some assurance regarding performance standards, it does not relieve the contracting agency of the responsibility to determine whether performance standards are met.[47]

Managing Competition. Advocates of contracting view competition, one of the cornerstones of the business model, as a principal mechanism for ensuring that contracting serves the public interest and that government gets fair value for its funds. Economists yearn for perfectly competitive markets but recognize that this ideal rarely exists.[48] Mechanisms other than competition can enhance the cost and quality goals of contracting, such as the use of appropriate economies of scale.[49] Even where competition exists, however, it can create problems for public officials. As Posner notes,

> Contractors' bids have a tendency to be deliberately undercosted and overpromised, contractors and grantees with sunk costs in a project have an inside track in obtaining follow-up assistance, and agencies sometimes are not good judges of quality.... The principal agent issues become correspondingly more consequential, as government principals must rely on agents who have exclusive knowledge of their own qualifications as well as price-quality tradeoffs, technical feasibility, and other key issues defining the contractual relationship.[50]

In some instances, competition adversely affects the quality of contracted services. "Competition can drive costs down too far," notes Irene Rubin. "A hungry company can promise more than it can deliver, and create problems during implementation."[51] In a case reported elsewhere, several foster care contractors in Kansas faced bankruptcy after taking on government contracts that had inadequate reimbursement rates.[52]

Sometimes competition is inadequate in areas where the government wants to write contracts. In the absence of a competitive marketplace, government officials resort to sole source contracts and accept the lack of competition as an unavoidable market condition. When competition is not naturally present, officials may try to elicit it through a managed competition model, wherein government employees bid on contracts open to the nongovernmental sector. Managed competition has been used successfully by cities and states to enlarge participation and provide government employees with an opportunity to innovate. State officials in Massachusetts, New York, and Virginia have used this approach, while local officials in Charlotte, Houston, Indianapolis, Phoenix, Portland, and Lee County, Florida, have all employed managed competition and reported positive results. Practices associated with joint contracting can also be used to adjust for shortcomings in competition. Scholars have paid minimal attention to informal and joint contracting, even though these practices may help public officials capture the advantages of economies of scale and pay marginal rather than full costs.[53]

As Domberger notes, provisions allowing in-house bids reaffirm the view that competition is the key to improved service delivery—not the transfer of public services to private providers. Managed competition is one way to legitimize privatization in the eyes of public employees. Employee resistance was noted as one of the biggest obstacles to Virginia privatization efforts because of the fear of lost jobs.[54] The solution is to let them compete.

Maintaining Relationships. The difficulty of specifying performance standards and encouraging competition redirects much of contract management into the realm of interpersonal relationships. Where formal standards or external incentives do not exist, personal intervention invariably rises. The need for personal intervention is especially apparent in contracts involving complex networks of contractors and subcontractors. For their internal workings, people in public agencies tend to operate hierarchically; in building and maintaining relationships with contractors, those people are obliged to work through complex horizontal interdependencies. Contracting with multiple actors and subcontractors is increasingly the norm; it is necessary when "public action can no longer be contained within vertical hierarchies but necessarily engages horizontal relationships across institutional and sectoral boundaries."[55] Yet such complexity can undermine the advantages of contracting when it exceeds the capacity of public managers to sustain their monitoring and facilitating roles.[56]

In an intergovernmental context, policy implementation is directly affected by the number of actors involved in the activity.[57] When contractors subcontract with other organizations, or interact with separate governmental contractors in the same program area, implementation complexity can increase exponentially. This dynamic is increasingly common in social services programs, which rely heavily on provider networks to deliver a complex range of services. Complex interdependencies are often the guiding characteristic when public agencies contract for social services with nongovernmental organizations, because the people who receive such services often require a multifaceted array, such as education, housing, health care, and individual psychological counseling services.

Successful contracting within networks forces participants to negotiate and collaborate, without regard to whether they are in principal or agent roles. Agranoff and McGuire note that the most complex contractor networks provide service flexibility, but they also require more managerial skill and time.[58] The tasks associated with "massaging" a service network—communication, mutual goal setting, altering incentives, and mending relationships—multiply as network size and diversity increase. The essentials remain the same regardless of size: attention to people and partner organizations and the creation of incentives that encourage cooperation.

Complex networks contain multiple actors with numerous agendas. Again, these tend to be systems with very high maintenance and management needs. Satisfying such administrative needs requires resources. In their study of mental health networks, Milward and Provan found that effective networks were more likely to exist in resource-rich environments.[59] The challenge of maintaining relationships that "encourage the formation and sustainability of positive interactions across the network" is substantial. As Posner notes, this includes the creation of situations "that make nonparticipation less attractive, limit interaction costs, promote transparency, and secure commitment to joint undertakings."[60]

The use of delivery mechanisms that go beyond the conventional agency-contractor relationship is a common feature in social service contracts delivered through networks. Many use the lead agency/multiple subcontractors model in which people in a single institution serve as facilitators for a broad network. Freundlich and Gerstenzang found working examples of the lead agency/multiple subcontractors model in Florida, Kansas, Maine, and Michigan. Sometimes a single contractor serves as the lead agency. In its welfare contracting, the state of Florida shifted the responsibility for direct service delivery in child welfare from the Department of Children and Families (DCF) to newly created lead nonprofit agencies for each county.[61]

Sustaining Staff Capacity. Cost reduction is a popular motive for government contracting, especially the reduction of staff costs associated with in-house administration. While program staff can be cut under contracting, the contract process requires the employment of contract managers. The implications of this shift are often overlooked in the enthusiasm for government contracting.

When contracting occurs, public executives typically move former program staff into contract management responsibilities. As governmental employees shift from service provision to contract management, they encounter the need for new skill sets and new mindsets to manage relationships with contractor organizations. Those skills are often qualitatively different from those needed to deliver social services.[62] At the same time, effective contract management requires government workers who possess the technical skills necessary to be smart buyers. Maintaining those technical skills is challenging when workers no longer involve themselves in direct program delivery. Effective contract management thus creates the need for human resources policies that provide the professional development opportunities, the training, and the salaries necessary to retain a capable staff. Research on Massachusetts human service programs confirmed the expected relationship between successful contract management and high levels of technical expertise and relationship skills. Contract management training increases the ability of the government workers to monitor contractor performance and provide technical assistance.[63] Without training, government employees quickly lose their ability to effectively manage contracts.

Contracting out thus requires investment across several dimensions of human resource management. Whether for social service contracts in Kansas or federal programs to control toxic waste, the capacity of government officials to assess the reasonableness of contract bids and the accuracy of performance reports depends heavily upon the ability of public executives to sustain a qualified staff.[64]

Managing Accountability. Increased accountability is part of the rhetoric of contracting. Advocates of contracting promise greater clarity and transparency regarding institutional performance and easy recourse when service delivery agents fail to meet expectations.[65] This is harder than it sounds. To maintain accountability, government officers must ascertain whether contractor performance meets expectations and be able to take action if expectations are not met. This requires good information regarding contractor performance and, once that information is in hand, appropriate mechanisms for accountability. Accountability is bolstered under government contracting to the extent that contracting promotes a review of current service levels and service specifications, introduces performance monitoring systems that otherwise would not have been put in place, and focuses attention on mechanisms for redress.[66]

The federal government tends to use ex ante accountability in its contracting, concentrating on oversight and control at the front end of the contract relationship. "Goals are negotiated interactively and federal expectations are documented in specific, often measurable terms."[67] Contract compliance is generally validated following the completion of contracts through ex post audits. The scale of federal contracting, however, often deters the completion of the latter activity. Federal employees are constrained by the "limited resources available to check on the thousands of providers often participating in public programs." Individual contractor officers in the Environmental Protection Agency and the U.S. Department of Labor, for example, are expected to oversee an average of 26,000 contract actions each year.[68]

While the scale of contracting activities is less for state and local governments, government employees face significant accountability challenges there as well. Accountability may be straightforward in a private market characterized by multiple providers, optimal levels of competition, and relatively uncomplicated services. But many state and local government contracts involve service delivery systems that are highly dependent on collaboration and cooperation among multiple providers. Research on multiple contracts in the state of Kansas found that more competitive, marketlike environments with multiple contractors and networks of service deliverers actually deterred opportunities for accountability, despite the expectations contained in conventional contracting theories suggesting that multiple providers will enhance accountability.[69]

Better monitoring of contractors who provide services to clients helps accountability, but the capacity for oversight is often an issue for state and local governments. As observers have noted, contracting tends to produce a "hollow state" in which remaining government employees find the process of maintaining accountability difficult. According to the U.S. General Accounting Office, performance monitoring is the weakest link in state and local privatization.[70]

Striking the right balance between contract oversight and contract flexibility can be difficult. Dicke and Ott identify audits, contracts, and monitoring as the most preferred methods for maintaining accountability over nonprofit contractors; other techniques often used include licensure, courts, codes of ethics, and markets. Freundlich and Gerstenzang found that monitoring tended to be either overdone or underdone in the programs they observed. The state of Kansas, for example, has been criticized by media, parents, and providers for what they view as excessive monitoring in the foster care program. Excessive monitoring, the critics say, leads to duplication, undue confusion, complexity, and expense. In response, the state of Kansas introduced a pilot program to test the impact of reducing the oversight of private agencies by state social workers, with the goal of reducing duplication and the time needed to place children in permanent foster care.[71]

When contract performance standards are not met, public officials face a significant and difficult issue in accountability. Should they impose sanctions as specified in the contract? When contractor performance falls short, public officials often choose to continue to contract. They may lack a viable alternative contractor or the political support necessary to invoke sanctions even when contractor performance warrants such action. Research indicates that government agencies encounter significant obstacles to the imposition of accountability standards on contractors. This is sometimes due to a lack of effective monitoring capacity. Other times it is due to a lack of political will.[72] A U.S. General Accounting Office study of the Department of Energy revealed that government officials often extended contracts noncompetitively even when contractors displayed performance shortcomings.[73]

CONCLUSION

Dwight Waldo had great respect for the influence of current events and situations on the choice of administrative methods. In the current political climate, the idea of contracting is likely to remain popular for some time. Support for contracting has an ideological as well as a financial basis. The values of efficiency, competition, and accountability serve as rallying points for proponents of contracting and are paramount in arguments for its use. Other motivations include the advantages of contracting for expertise, flexibility, quality, off-loading risk, and the interest of business firms in receiving public funds.[74]

The popular surge in governmental contracting has presented federal, state, and local officials with significant challenges as they pursue these strategies. Contracting requires governmental managers and contractors to develop skills for working within collaborative networks and cultivating interpersonal communication, trust, and mutual goal setting. Public administrators charged with the challenges of contract management find that they must also remain attentive to the public values of equity, responsiveness, legitimacy, and accountability. Critics of contracting argue that the "businesslike features" of contract management may render these traditional democratic values less relevant in an era of privatization. In a more practical sense, they warn that extensive contracting with business also introduces increased opportunities for patronage, kickbacks, illegal tactics, and corruption.[75]

At its core, contracting represents a further embedding of what Waldo called America's "Business Civilization" into the processes of government. The scale and pace of government contracting, in the words of Don Kettl, have been "truly revolutionary."[76] Contracting out government services is widespread throughout federal, state, and local levels of government; even greater levels of contracting may be expected in the future. The use of contractors to support American engagement in Afghanistan and Iraq has been broad and deep; similar patterns are emerging in the domestic arena of social services. Contracting has become so pervasive that some observers have characterized nonprofit, faith-based, and for-profit contractors as the new street-level bureaucrats.[77] These trends underscore the importance of deepening the understanding of contracting on public affairs and the political theories that guide it.

Despite differences in the use of particular methods and variations among levels of government, the overall contracting patterns are remarkably similar. Public administrators have been placed on a steep learning curve as they attempt to adapt to working "outside the box" of traditional, in-house service delivery. They have sought to adapt to new administrative roles, to the need for clarity in defining contractor performance, and to the acquisition of new skills for the management of competition, enhancement of staff capacity, and the maintenance of accountability.

The long-standing practice of contracting in the United States, dating back to the earliest days of the nation, has taken on a new look in the twenty-first century. The scale of contemporary contracting is unprecedented, ranging from ambulance services to trash collection, weapons manufacturing, welfare services, and space shuttles. The broader range of contractor involvement introduces extraordinary complexity into the process of governance, presenting public administrators with considerable challenges as they attempt to transform key components of governmental operations. Successfully meeting these challenges requires new philosophies and integrative thinking on a scale that is not often associated with conventional governmental reform. Such changes cannot be accomplished in a strictly mechanistic way, simply by focusing on the techniques involved. Rather, the changes require increased attention to the relationships between administrative practices and the political theories of governance that Waldo sought to explain in *The Administrative State*.

NOTES

1. Dwight Waldo, *The Administrative State: A Study of the Political Theory of American Public Administration*, 2nd ed. (New York: Holmes & Meier, 1984), 9.

2. Elliot Sclar, *You Don't Always Get What You Pay For: The Economics of Privatization* (Ithaca, NY: Cornell University Press, 2000).

3. David Osborne and Ted Gaebler, *Reinventing Government: How the Entrepreneurial Spirit Is Transforming the Public Sector* (Reading, MA: Addison-Wesley, 1992); Fred Thompson and Hugh T. Miller, "New Public Management and Bureaucracy versus Business Values and Bureaucracy," *Review of Public Personnel Administration* 23, no. 4 (2003): 328–43.

4. Paul Light, *The Tides of Reform: Making Government Work, 1945–1995* (New Haven, CT: Yale University Press, 1997).

5. Osborne and Gaebler, *Reinventing Government;* Al Gore, *Common Sense Government: Works Better and Costs Less* (New York: Random House, 1995).

6. John Murawski, "Former United Way Chief Gets 7 Years in Jail: Sentence Praised by Charities," *Chronicle of Philanthropy,* July 12, 1995; Steven Steklow, "New Era's Bennett Gets 12 Years in Prison for Defrauding Charities," *Wall Street Journal,* September 23, 1997; Laurie Goodstein, "Catholics in Survey Seek Accountability by Church," *New York Times,* July 7, 2003; Kurt Eichenwald, "How One Hospital Benefited on Questionable Operations," *New York Times,* August 12, 2003; Milt Freudenheim, "Troubled HealthSouth Faces Medicare Fraud Investigation," *New York Times,* September 11, 2003; Richard Oppel and Lowell Bergman, "Judge Concludes Energy Company Drove Up Prices," *New York Times,* September 24, 2002; Kurt Eichenwald and Matt Richtel, "Enron Trader Pleads Guilty to Conspiracy," *New York Times,* October 18, 2002.

7. Sclar, *You Don't Always Get What You Pay For.*

8. Donald F. Kettl, "Managing Indirect Government," in *Tools of Government,* ed. Lester Salamon (New York: Oxford University Press, 2002); Paul L. Posner, "Accountability Challenges of Third-Party Government," in *Tools of Government,* ed. Salamon, 524; Lester M. Salamon, "The New Governance and the Tools of Public Action: An Introduction," in *Tools of Government,* ed. Salamon, 1–47; Jonathan Koppell, *The Politics of Quasi Government: Hybrid Organizations and the Dynamics of Bureaucratic Control* (Cambridge, UK: Cambridge University Press, 2003).

9. Phillip J. Cooper, *Governing by Contract: Challenges and Opportunities for Public Managers* (Washington, DC: CQ Press, 2003).

10. Sclar, *You Don't Always Get What You Pay For;* Jocelyn Johnston, Barbara Romzek, and Curtis Wood, "The Challenges of Contracting and Accountability across the Federal System: From Ambulances to Space Shuttles" (paper presented at the 7th National Public Management Research Conference at Georgetown University, Washington, D.C., October 11, 2003), forthcoming in *Publius;* Simon Domberger, *The Contracting Organization* (New York: Oxford University Press, 1998); Irene Rubin, "Municipal Contracts: Alike in All Unimportant Respects" (paper presented at Association for Budgeting and Financial Management [ABFM] Conference, Washington, D.C., September 18, 2003); U.S. Office of Management and Budget, "Competitive Sourcing: Reasoned and Responsible Public-Private Competition," September 2003.

11. Stephen H. Linder, "Coming to Terms with Public-Private Partnership: A Grammar of Multiple Meanings," in *Public-Private Policy Partnerships,* ed. Pauline V. Rosenau (Cambridge, MA: MIT Press, 2002); Alan DiGaetano and Elizabeth Strom, "Comparative Urban Governance: An Integrated Approach," *Urban Affairs Review* 38, no. 3 (2003): 356–95.

12. Kettl, "Managing Indirect Government," 493.

13. Sclar, *You Don't Always Get What You Pay For.*

14. Robert Agranoff and Michael McGuire, "Multinetwork Management: Collaboration and the Hollow State in Local Economic Policy," *Journal of Public Administration Research and Theory* 8 (January 1998): 67–91; Kettl, "Managing Indirect Government"; H. Briton Milward and Keith Provan, "Governing the Hollow State," *Journal of Public Administration Research and Theory* 10, no. 2 (2000): 359–79; Madelyn Freundlich and Sarah Gerstenzang, "Privatization of Child Welfare Services: Challenges and Successes" (report by Children's Rights, Inc., New York, 2003); Barbara S. Romzek and Jocelyn M. Johnston, "Contracting Implementation and Management Effectiveness: A Preliminary Model," *Journal of Public Management Research and Theory* 12, no. 3 (2002): 423–53.

15. Posner, "Accountability Challenges of Third-Party Government."

16. E. S. Savas, *Privatization: The Key to Better Government* (Chatham, NJ: Chatham House Publishers, 1987); John E. Chubb and Terry Moe, *Politics, Markets, and America's Schools* (Washington, DC: Brookings Institution, 1990).

17. William Niskanen, *Bureaucracy and Representative Government* (Chicago: Aldine/Atherton, 1971); Gordon Tullock, *The Politics of Bureaucracy* (Washington, DC: Public Affairs Press, 1965).

18. Donald Kettl, *Sharing Power: Public Governance and Private Markets* (Washington, DC: Brookings Institution, 1993); John Donahue, *The Privatization Decision* (New York: Basic Books, 1989); Janet Rotherberg Pack, "Privatization of Public-Sector Services in Theory and Practice," *Journal of Policy Analysis and Management* 6, no. 4 (1987): 523–40; Mark Schlesigner, Robert Dowart, and Richard Pulice, "Competitive Bidding and States' Purchases of Services: The Case of Mental Health in Massachusetts," *Journal of Policy Analysis and Management* 5, no. 2 (1986): 245–63.

19. Jonas Prager, "Contracting Out Government Services: Lessons from the Private Sector," *Public Administration Review* 54, no. 2 (1994): 183.

20. H. George Frederickson, *The Spirit of Public Administration* (San Francisco: Jossey-Bass, 1997); William T. Gormley, "Privatization Revisited," *Policy Studies Review* 13 (1994–95): 215–34; Thompson and Miller, "New Public Management and Bureaucracy."

21. M. Shamsul Haque, "The Diminishing Publicness of Public Service under the Current Mode of Governance," *Public Administration Review* 61, no. 1 (2001): 65–78.

22. Kettl, *Sharing Power,* 4; Renae Merle, "Contracts for U.S. Military More Often Seen as Targets," *Kansas City Star,* October 19, 2003.

23. U.S. Office of Management and Budget, "Competitive Sourcing."

24. Paul Light, "Fact Sheet on the True Size of Government," Center for Public Service, Brookings Institution, September 5, 2003.

25. Patricia Ingraham, Sally Coleman Selden, and Donald Moynihan, "People and Performance: Challenges for the Future Service: A Report from the

Wye River Conference," *Public Administration Review* 60, no. 1 (2000): 54–60.

26. Posner, "Accountability Challenges of Third-Party Government."

27. U.S. General Accounting Office, *Major Management Challenges and Program Risks: NASA,* GAO-03-114, January 2003.

28. Kettl, "Managing Indirect Government," 505; see also Barbara S. Romzek and Melvin J. Dubnick, "Accountability in the Public Sector: Lessons from the *Challenger* Tragedy," *Public Administration Review* 47, no. 3 (1987): 227–38.

29. Columbia Accident Investigation Board, *Report of the Columbia Accident Investigation Board,* August 26, 2003.

30. Statement of Gerald L. Dillingham, in U.S. General Accounting Office, *Transportation Security: Post September 11th Initiatives and Long-Term Challenges,* GAO-03-616T, March 31, 2003.

31. David C. Wyld, *Seaport: Charting a New Course for Professional Services Acquisition for America's Navy* (Washington, DC: IBM Endowment for the Business of Government, 2003).

32. Keon S. Chi and Cindy Jasper, *Private Practices: A Review of Privatization in State Government* (Lexington, KY: Council of State Governments, 1998).

33. Sally Coleman Selden, Patricia Wallace Ingraham, and Willow Jacobson, "Human Resource Practices in State Government: Findings from a National Survey," *Public Administration Review* 61, no. 5 (2001): 598–607; Gilbert B. Siegel, "Outsourcing Personnel Functions," *Public Personnel Management* 29, no. 2 (2000): 225–36; James W. Fossett, Malcolm Goggin, John Hall, Jocelyn Johnston, Richard Roper, L. Christopher Plein, and Carol Weissert, "Managing Medicaid Managed Care: Are States Becoming Prudent Purchasers?" *Health Affairs,* July/August 2000, 39–49; Freundlich and Gerstenzang, "Privatization of Child Welfare Services"; R. I. Paulson and Mary Armstrong, "Evaluation of the Florida Department of Children and Families Community-Based Care Initiative" (research report conducted under contract to the University of South Florida, funded by the Florida Department of Children and Families, 2003); Norma Riccucci, "Implementing Welfare Reform in Michigan: The Role of Street-Level Bureaucrats," *International Journal of Public Administration* 25, no. 7 (2002): 902–21; Romzek and Johnston, "Contract Implementation and Management Effectiveness."

34. U.S. General Accounting Office, "Privatization: Lessons Learned by State and Local Governments," GAO-97-48, March 1997.

35. Lester M. Salamon, *Partners in Public Service: Government-Nonprofit Relations in the Modern Welfare State* (Baltimore: Johns Hopkins University Press, 1995); Salamon, "New Governance and the Tools of Public Action"; Jeffrey D. Greene, "Cities and Privatization: Examining the Effects of Fiscal Stress, Location, and Wealth in Medium-Sized Cities," *Policy Studies Journal* 24, no. 1 (1996): 135–44; DiGaetano and Strom, "Comparative Urban Governance"; Robert Jay Dilger, Randolph R. Moffett, and Linda Struyk,

"Privatization of Municipal Services in America's Largest Cities," *Public Administration Review* 57, no. 1 (1997): 21–26.

36. Trevor L. Brown and Matthew Potoski, "Contract-Management Capacity in Municipal and County Governments," *Public Administration Review* 63, no. 2 (2003): 153–64.

37. George A. Boyne, "Bureaucratic Theory Meets Reality: Public Choice and Service Contracting in U.S. Local Government," *Public Administration Review* 58, no. 6 (2003): 474–84; State of Kansas, Legislative Post Audit, "Reviewing State Contracting for Consultants and Other Professional and Technical Services," 96-38, 1996; Rubin, "Municipal Contracts"; Chi and Jasper, *Private Practices;* Freundlich and Gerstenzang, "Privatization of Child Welfare Services"; Romzek and Johnston, "State Contracting, Social Service Networks, and Effective Accountability: An Explanatory Model," *Public Administration Review* 65, no. 4 (2005): 436–49.

38. Rubin, "Municipal Contracts," 16.

39. Ibid.; David Morgan, "The Pitfalls of Privatization: Contracting without Competition," *American Review of Public Administration* 22, no. 4 (1992): 251–69.

40. Jocelyn Johnston and Barbara S. Romzek., "Examining the Stability Hypothesis: Comparing Stable and Dynamic Systems in Social Service Contracts" (paper presented at the 6th National Public Management Research Conference, Bloomington, Indiana, October 2001).

41. Kettl, "Managing Indirect Government."

42. Ibid.; Donahue, *Privatization Decision.*

43. Paulson and Armstrong, "Evaluation of the Florida Department of Children and Families Community-Based Care Initiative"; Fossett, Goggin, Hall, Johnston, Roper, Plein, and Weissert, "Managing Medicaid Managed Care."

44. U.S. Office of Management and Budget, "Competitive Sourcing."

45. Robert D. Behn and Peter A. Kant, "Strategies for Avoiding the Pitfalls of Performance Contracting," *Public Productivity and Management Review* 22, no. 4 (1999): 470–89; U.S. General Accounting Office, "Major Management Challenges and Program Risks: Department of Energy," GAO-03-100, January 2003.

46. U.S. General Accounting Office, "Privatization"; Freundlich and Gerstenzang, "Privatization of Child Welfare Services"; Romzek and Johnston, "Contract Implementation and Management Effectiveness"; Riccucci, "Implementing Welfare Reform in Michigan"; Johnston, Romzek, and Wood, "Challenges of Contracting."

47. Domberger, *Contracting Organization.*

48. Sclar, *You Don't Always Get What You Pay For.*

49. Rubin, "Municipal Contracts."

50. Posner, "Accountability Challenges of Third-Party Government," 537.

51. Rubin, "Municipal Contracts," 5.

52. Donald Klingner, John Nalbandian, and Barbara S. Romzek, "Politics, Administration and Markets: Conflicting Expectations and Accountability," *American Review of Public Administration* 32, no. 2 (2002): 117–44.

53. Jocelyn M. Johnston and Barbara S. Romzek, "Contracting and Accountability in State Medicaid Reform: Rhetoric, Theories, and Reality," *Public Administration Review* 59, no. 5 (1999): 383–99; U.S. General Accounting Office, "Privatization"; Kansas City, Missouri, City Auditor's Office, "Special Report: A Model for Public/Private Competition, Public/Private Competitive Contracting Model," August 1996; Sclar, *You Don't Always Get What You Pay For;* Carole L. Jurkiewicz and James S. Bowman, "Charlotte: A Model for Market-Driven in Public-Sector Management," *State and Local Government Review* 34, no. 3 (2002): 205–13; Rubin, "Municipal Contracts."

54. Domberger, *Contracting Organization;* U.S. General Accounting Office, "Privatization."

55. Posner, "Accountability Challenges of Third-Party Government," 547.

56. Romzek and Johnston, "Contract Implementation and Management Effectiveness."

57. Agranoff and McGuire, "Multinetwork Management"; Donald Van Meter and Carl Van Horn, "The Policy Implementation Process: A Conceptual Framework," *Administration and Society* 5, no. 4 (1975): 445–88.

58. Agranoff and McGuire, "Multinetwork Management."

59. Laurence J. O'Toole and Kenneth J. Meier, "Modeling the Impact of Public Management: Implications of Structural Context," *Journal of Public Administration Research and Theory* 9, no. 4 (1999): 505–26; Laurence E. Lynn, Carolyn J. Heinrich, and Carolyn J. Hill, "Studying Governance and Public Management: Challenges and Prospects," *Journal of Public Administration Research and Theory* 10 (April 2001); Kenneth Meier and Laurence J. O'Toole, "Managerial Strategies and Behavior in Networks: A Model with Evidence from U.S. Public Education," *Journal of Public Administration Research and Theory* 11, no. 3 (2001): 271–93; Milward and Provan, "Governing the Hollow State."

60. Posner, "Accountability Challenges of Third-Party Government," 546.

61. Freundlich and Gerstenzang, "Privatization of Child Welfare Services"; Paulson and Armstrong, "Evaluation of the Florida Department of Children and Families Community-Based Care Initiative."

62. Ralph M. Kramer, "Voluntary Agencies and the Contract Culture: Dream or Nightmare?" *Social Service Review,* March 1994, 33–60; Frederickson, *Spirit of Public Administration;* Johnston and Romzek, "Contracting and Accountability in State Medicaid Reform"; Kettl, "Managing Indirect Government."

63. Vincent Gooden, "Contracting and Negotiation: Effective Practices of Successful Human Service Contract Managers," *Public Administration Review* 58, no. 6 (1998): 499–509; Martha Derthick, *The Influence of Federal Grants: Public Assistance in Massachusetts* (Washington, DC: Brookings Institution,

1970); Walter Williams, *The Implementation Perspective: A Guide for Managing Social Service Delivery Programs* (Berkeley: University of California Press, 1980); Paul Peterson, Barry Rabe, and Kenneth Wond, *When Federalism Works* (Washington, DC: Brookings Institution, 1986); Van Meter and Van Horn, "Policy Implementation Process."

64. Romzek and Johnston, "Contract Implementation and Management Effectiveness"; Posner, "Accountability Challenges of Third-Party Government," 540.

65. Sclar, *You Don't Always Get What You Pay For.*

66. Domberger, *Contracting Organization;* Romzek and Johnston, "State Contracting, Social Service Networks, and Effective Accountability."

67. Posner, "Accountability Challenges of Third-Party Government," 538.

68. Ibid., 539–40.

69. Romzek and Johnston, "State Contracting, Social Service Networks, and Effective Accountability."

70. Milward and Provan, "Governing the Hollow State"; U.S. General Accounting Office, "Privatization."

71. Lisa A. Dicke and J. Steven Ott, "Public Agency Accountability in Human Services Contracting," *Public Productivity and Management Review* 22 (June 1999): 502–16; Freundlich and Gerstenzang, "Privatization of Child Welfare"; Ruth Santner interview, Program Manager, Kansas Foster Care Program, Kansas Department of Social and Rehabilitation Services, 2003; "Memorandum of Agreement between the Kansas Department of Social and Rehabilitation Services Topeka Area Office and the Kansas Children's Service League," July 1, 2003.

72. Posner, "Accountability Challenges of Third-Party Government"; Johnston and Romzek, "Contracting and Accountability in State Medicaid Reform."

73. U.S. General Accounting Office, "Major Management Challenges and Program Risks: Department of Energy."

74. Rubin, "Municipal Contracts."

75. Haque, "Diminishing Publicness of Public Service"; Rubin, "Municipal Contracts"; Thompson and Miller, "New Public Management."

76. Kettl, "Managing Indirect Government," 508.

77. Wendell Lawther, "Contracting for the 21st Century: A Partnership Model," in *The Procurement Revolution,* ed. Mark A. Abramson and Roland S. Harris (New York: Rowman and Littlefield, 2003); David Van Slyke, "Agents or Stewards: How Government Manages Its Contracting Relationships with Nonprofit Social Service Providers" (paper presented at the 7th National Public Management Research Conference, Georgetown University, Washington, D.C., October 10, 2003).

10

Institutional Values and the Future Administrative State

ROBERT F. DURANT

After the cold war began in the late 1940s, a number of public ad-ministration scholars worried that democratic values such as responsiveness, equity, equality, due process, and constitutional rights would become marginalized if not displaced entirely by specialists intent on making government work effectively at the lowest possible cost. Building on earlier scholarly work contrasting narrow conceptualizations of economy and efficiency with the broader vision of "social economy" and "social efficiency," Dwight Waldo argued famously in *The Administrative State* that the real question confronting scholars and practitioners was "efficiency for what?" Explained Waldo, the "descriptive or objective notion of efficiency is valid and useful, but only within a framework of consciously held values."[1]

Waldo further noted the difficulty of assessing efficiency when disagreements over values occurred. As a person's "frame of reference" widens and "disagreement about ends" deepens, calculation of "science" and "objectivity" becomes more difficult, and statements about the relative efficiency of different arrangements become "less accurate, more controversial." To meet this challenge, Waldo called for "complete administrators" or "philosophers of administration." Such persons, he proposed, would possess "a knowledge of the place of the public service in its relationship with basic economic and social forces and some realization of the potentialities of government as a means for meeting human needs."[2] Waldo concluded *The Administrative State* by discussing the institutional values motivating governmental administration in the mid-twentieth century; this chapter extends the discussion into the twenty-first century.

WICKED POLICY PROBLEMS IN THE NEOADMINISTRATIVE STATE

Today, no more apt advice regarding the limits of specialists, the virtues of generalists, and the importance of embedding efficiency within a broader context of values could be given to public administrators worldwide than that issued by Dwight Waldo. The cold war has ended, and with it the refracting of global policy problems through the crabbed lens of bipolar politics. Ascendant in salience in the post–cold war era is a host of what scholars call "wicked" policy problems.[3] These are policy issues (e.g., drug abuse, teenage pregnancy reduction, terrorism, urban runoff, and global warming) where no accepted definition of the problem exists. Moreover, one problem is interrelated with others, cross-sectoral (public-private-nonprofit) collaboration is essential for success, and the solutions proffered are precarious, controversial, and difficult to implement. Wicked problems are also "multiattribute" in nature; solutions to them require the balancing of a variety of values rather than the predominance of any one value. For such problems, technocratic expertise and efficiency are (as Waldo might put it) necessary but insufficient ingredients. Needed, as well, is the synthesizing, public interest–oriented, multiattribute thinking that Waldo promoted as vital to democratic governance.

Globalization, the context of twenty-first-century public administration, exacerbates the challenges created by wicked policy problems.[4] As Thorsten Benner and his associates at the Global Public Policy Institute in Berlin, Germany, cogently summarize, globalization brings four major types of challenges for public administrators: the need for administrative strategies that cross national boundaries (geographic challenges), the need for rapid decision making in a world of twenty-four-hour markets and media (temporal challenges), the need for different types of knowledge (multidisciplinary challenges), and the need for institutional credibility (legitimacy challenges).[5]

The rub is that the attributes of the classic administrative state as it evolved in the twentieth century seem decidedly unsuited to the challenges posed by wicked policy problems in the twenty-first century.[6] Wicked problems beg cross-functional and cross-jurisdictional solutions, procedural flexibility and discretion wielded by administrators closest to the situation, outcomes-based measures of success, and stakeholders involved in defining both problems and solutions. As such, agencies must be empowered to reconceptualize their purpose, reconnect with citizens, and redefine administrative orthodoxy. Yet the administrative state's emphasis was on centralizing decision-making power in the nation's capital, on pursuing federal goals through the disbursement of federal largesse to state and local governments, and on limiting subnational discretion in the pursuit of those goals. Federal agencies, in turn, were predisposed toward functional departmentalization, subsystem politics, hierarchical processes, and procedural controls.

Moreover, this incongruity aside, the administrative approaches embodied in movements such as the American New Deal and the Great Society will not return soon. The realpolitik of fiscal stress, downward pressures on the size of governments due to market globalization, and political advantage suggests that presidents and congress members will continue to face perverse credit-claiming incentives to take on new obligations, but without increasing the visible size of the government's work force in Washington, D.C.[7] Reigning instead will be a "neoadministrative state."[8] As it has evolved thus far, the neoadministrative state consists of pushing federal governmental responsibilities and the authority to act on behalf of national societies upward to international bodies, downward to state and local governments, and outward to private and nonprofit actors.

One thing has not changed, however, as the administrative state has morphed into the neoadministrative state. Whether global, regional, national, or subnational in origin, the wicked policy problems confronting public administrators in the United States and abroad make Waldo's advice about embedding efficiency within a broader context of values as compelling today as when it was first written. Nevertheless, a narrow "one-size-fits-all" market-oriented prescription for administrative reform now animates governance discussions worldwide (albeit with somewhat less luster than in the early 1990s).

As embraced typically by minimal state proponents, the new public management (NPM) is an administrative theory that accords no special role for either the public service (in Washington or elsewhere) or the public interest, aside from what market forces allow or dictate. In contrast, the so-called new governance model attractive to positive state proponents (especially in the United States and Canada) affords an administrative theory that better links "the essential unity of politics and administration and recognizes the importance of the state in balancing market forces."[9] Both sets of administrative theories, however, embrace to varying degrees the following concepts as central animating principles of administrative reform in the twenty-first century: down-sizing, contracting, competition, decentralization, de-funding, deregu-lation, partnerships, and economism (i.e., economic, human resource, and technical efficiency).[10]

What is more, a disturbing naiveté exists among reformers in both camps, a naiveté reminiscent of that informing the "associationalist" movement of the early twentieth century.[11] In that so-called "forgot-ten progressive" movement, federal government agencies were to serve largely as sources of information, coordination, and national guidance for subnational associations. Experts in the federal bureaucracy were to stimulate cooperative efforts by public, private, and civic partic-ipants in these associations but were to stay out of the actual pro-duction and distribution of services. Unfortunately, the assumptions of the associationalist movement proved terribly misguided, and the movement failed miserably, to the detriment of citizens who depended upon government to buffer them from impersonal market forces.

Might a similar fate await contemporary "neoassociationalist" ad-ministrative theories (such as the NPM and new governance) as they confront wicked policy problems in the twenty-first century? This chapter argues that to avoid this fate administrative agencies at all levels and in all sectors of the neoadministrative state must acquire, nurture, or support three institutional features geared toward trust building as they reconceptualize purpose, reconnect with stakeholders, and re-define administrative rationality. Those features are governmental ca-pacity building, transparency of processes (not just outcomes), and cultural sensitivity. Yet these are features that proponents (especially minimal statists) of today's neoassociationalist models de-emphasize, overlook, or dismiss altogether. Without them, however, neither the remnants of the classic administrative state nor today's evolving neo-administrative state will be able to address effectively the challenges posed by wicked policy problems in the twenty-first century.

In making this argument, the chapter examines the manner in which these trust-building features are needed and can help to embed today's administrative reform emphases within Waldo's larger context of dem-ocratic values. Stressing the contemporary movement's continuities and discontinuities with earlier reform initiatives, it begins by further elabo-rating the logic and realpolitik of administrative reform in the United States. The chapter next examines the manner in which three sets of wicked policy problems create pressures to reconceptualize public pur-pose, reconnect with stakeholders, and redefine administrative rational-ity. These three policy problems are global aging, global security, and global ecological threats. The chapter concludes with a discussion of the future of the neoadministrative state. Highlighted are the manner in which the prescriptions associated with today's neoassociationalism may cripple society's ability to confront wicked policy problems unless its proponents (and especially, its minimal state devotees) embrace capacity building, transparency, and cultural sensitivity.

MARKETS, MANAGERIALISM, AND THE NEOADMINISTRATIVE STATE

In *The Administrative State,* Waldo wrote that public administration "is a response on the part of its creators to the modern world." Among a litany of factors to which administrative reformers responded in the Progressive Era, Waldo observed, were the "tremendous wealth" of the United States, the appearance of elaborate business corporations during the latter phases of the Industrial Revolution, the increase in specialization, and the growth of professions.[12] Neither can one understand the transition from the administrative state to the neoadministrative state in the United States without appreciating the continuing role each of these factors has played. Significantly, however, the management principles informing these factors are the opposite of those influencing the rise of the administrative state.

As Waldo described, the administrative theory regnant in the Progressive and the New Deal eras coupled the "Great Society" vision of Graham Wallas, the Progressive "gospel" of government activism articulated by Herbert Croly in his *Promise of American Life,* and the corporate model as a means for planning, administering, and regulating societies for the public good.[13] Married, in the process, were business principles such as corporate planning, corporate structuring, and the administrative orthodoxy (e.g., hierarchy, division of labor, and rules and regulations) to a decidedly "positive state" philosophy.

In contrast, today's reform agenda is infused with a political philosophy that is largely the antithesis of Wallas's and Croly's progressivism. Unlike Progressives and New Dealers who saw government regulation as the solution to market failures, today's reformers see markets as the solution to government failures. Whereas the Progressives and New Dealers saw the virtues of centralizing power in Washington agencies, many reformers today speak of the virtues of decentralizing power to states, localities, frontline workers, contractors, and nonprofit organizations. They speak, too, of deregulating business and financial capital to let markets flourish, of "busting bureaucracy," and of greater accountability through the transparency that markets, benchmarking, competitive sourcing, and citizen surveys convey.

As described in chapter 2 of this book, the seeds of this reform movement were sown in the late 1970s and 1980s. During those decades, elected leaders faced calls to take on new obligations while cutting taxes, and to do so without increasing the visible size of government. They responded by crafting an administrative apparatus in which an ever-growing proportion of the federal bureaucracy no longer directly made or implemented policy.[14] Rather, people in these agencies arranged, coordinated, and monitored networks of public, private, and nonprofit organizations that pursued public actions with or on behalf of them. In turn, these complex, nonhierarchical, and loosely coupled networks operated with ever-expanding discretion. Then, as cutbacks in intergovernmental funding occurred, federal agencies were less and less able to affect their "partners'" structures, budgets, personnel decisions, priorities, and decision rules. In the process, the authority to exercise policy discretion on behalf of society diffused from public agencies to institutions in the private and civic spheres.

This dynamic accelerated further during the 1990s in the United States as a Baptist-Bootlegger coalition of minimal and positive state proponents pushed a "D^5" government reform agenda: downsizing, devolving, de-funding, deregulating, and de-centering government's role in addressing society's ills. In the contemporary equivalent of a politics-administration dichotomy, proponents of a minimal state philosophy pushed a neomanagerialist theory of administration. Elected officials were to decide policy ends, and administrators were to determine ways to realize them in consort with or monitoring private or nonprofit actors. Emphasized in these judgments is a "complex mixture of public choice theory, agency theory, and transaction-cost economics."[15] Implicit is a decision-making paradigm featuring market, technocratic, and objective rationality.

Meanwhile, with a Republican majority in the U.S. Congress for the first time in forty years, neoliberal progressives in the William J. Clinton administration tried to preserve an activist role for government in the face of minimalist demands. To this end, they promoted and embraced the new governance agenda of the National Performance Review. Moreover, they did so partially to substitute discussions about methods for more fundamental debates about governmental roles, debates they might easily lose because of conservative Republican majorities in Congress.

Despite these differences in public philosophy, however, politically pragmatic positive and minimal state proponents found common rhetorical ground in the "best business practices" movement noted in earlier chapters. Popular perceptions of government overload, fiscal stress, and maladministration had, after all, helped Ross Perot garner 19 percent of the 1992 U.S. presidential vote. Thus, in the boom-boom economy of the mid to late 1990s, corporate executives such as the now-discredited Jack Welch and corporate giants such as the not-yet-scandalized Enron Corporation provided the catchwords of private-sector practice (e.g., core competencies, flattened hierarchies, and partnering) that became the rhetorical glue holding the minimalist-positivist reform coalition together.

Many positive state proponents truly believed that government could "do more with less" by setting clear priorities, reducing bureaucratic layers, and eliminating inefficiencies. In the process, positive state agenda could be preserved, many thought, by applying private-sector techniques (such as strategic planning, activity-based cost accounting, and total quality management) and treating government agencies as if they were businesses (identifying "core" activities, encouraging a sense of "ownership," and managing for results). They further hoped to stretch scarce resources by transferring responsibility for "periphery" activities to third-sector actors and creating partnerships (public, private, and nonprofit) for service delivery.

Moreover, the suitability of the bureaucratic model for a post-industrial society was also challenged in business, academic, and journalistic circles. Many observers embraced what Jan Kooiman calls the concept of communicative governance for addressing "the growing complexity, dynamics, and diversity" of problems facing societies.[16] Proponents argued that the bureaucratic, hierarchical, state-centered approach to governing was anachronistic in the face of these problems. They called for sharing responsibility with state and private actors, for horizontal cooperation (rather than adversarial and vertical relationships), for flexibility and adaptation to local circumstances, and for adaptive learning approaches to institutional change. Kooiman was joined in America by, among others, Hugh Heclo, who famously portrayed policy making as "collective puzzlement on behalf of society."[17]

Finally, and as noted earlier in this chapter, the attributes associated with the neoadministrative state seemed decidedly better suited to the challenges posed by wicked problems than did the attributes of the traditional administrative state. Operations within the traditional administrative state were perceived widely as lacking boundary-spanning capabilities (across programs, agencies, jurisdictions, and disciplines), quick decision making, and trust among citizens. Yet wicked problems such as HIV/AIDS, assaults on the global commons (viz., atmospheric, oceanic, and biodiversity), nonpoint source pollution, international terrorism, and world hunger demanded "creative institutional innovations . . . that connect governments, international organizations, civil society, and the corporate sector."[18] Regimes that exhibit a capability to address problems like these are typically characterized by "flexibility and a capacity to adapt institutions, rules and procedures . . . without losing sight of the overall objective."[19] Yet these attributes of what Joseph Nye and Robert Keohane call "networked minimalism" are hardly ones associated with the classic administrative state.[20]

For all the theoretical promise of the neoadministrative state, however, it also poses profound challenges. Stemming from the logic of the D^5 agenda that has informed it, these challenges can render the neoadministrative state just as impotent in dealing with wicked policy problems as was the classic administrative state. As implemented during the 1990s, the D^5 agenda privileged managerialism, efficiency, cost cutting, and cost-effectiveness as criteria for judging state intervention. De-privileged in the discussion have been Waldo's "efficiency for what" concerns, most notably those of equity, constitutional rights, equality, and distributive justice. These problems are compounded, as noted in earlier chapters, by the tendency of many reformers to incorporate fact-value dichotomies in their governing philosophies. Moreover, in "thinning" the capacity of government agencies to perform their work, the D^5 agenda has clouded democratic accountability. Who is responsible, for instance, when government programs fail if government agencies lack the capacity to oversee their agents?

These concerns notwithstanding, pressures will continue to expand the obligations of the federal government, but without increasing the visible size of federal budgets and work forces.[21] Consider the following demographic and budget realities confronting the United States. Presently, seven programs account for three-fourths of all federal spending: Social Security, Medicare, Medicaid, interest on the national debt, civil service pensions, military pensions, and national defense. With 76 million baby boomers beginning to retire around 2010, and without commensurately significant steps before then to alter benefits, raise taxes, or reduce debt, the Social Security and Medicare needs of baby boomers will absorb most government resources by 2030.[22]

In the interim, federal policymakers will also continue facing strong pressures to expand both entitlement benefits (e.g., for closing the "doughnut hole" in the recently enacted and expensive prescription drug benefit for seniors) and defense spending (in the wake of the war on terror). As interest payments on the national debt continue to drain resources from the government treasury, the proportion of funds devoted to the discretionary budget (presently only one out of six federal dollars collected) will stagnate and decrease (witness President Bush's FY 2006 budget proposals). Yet discretionary dollars provide the fuel that fund, among other activities, the operating costs of agencies and the intergovernmental grants they disperse for domestic programs. In turn, pressures on state and local governments will grow to either raise taxes, cut programs, or some combination of both. Nor will even rolling back President George W. Bush's tax cuts in their entirety reverse the entitlement-related funding pressures cascading through each level of government, as significant structural deficits will remain.[23]

Moreover, even an unlikely return to the attributes of the classic administrative state does nothing to alleviate inherent characteristics of bureaucracies that are ill suited to addressing wicked policy problems. Thus, progress in addressing the wicked policy challenges of the twenty-first century requires those studying and practicing public administration to learn how to make the neoadministrative state run effectively. Moreover, definitions of effectiveness naturally move beyond efficiency when collective puzzlement on behalf of society is the task; it means also incorporating values such as responsiveness, representativeness, accountability, and equity.

Such a joint problem in administrative theory and political philosophy is as profound as that ever confronted by any nation. Nevertheless, harnessing the dynamism of markets, the passion and commitment of nongovernmental organizations (NGOs), and the public service ethos of career civil servants is a challenge that will endure. To see why, the next four sections of this chapter review three sets of wicked policy problems—global aging, global security, and global ecological challenges—that will require collective puzzlement on behalf of society within the neoadministrative state in the twenty-first century.

SYNOPSIS OF THREE WICKED
PROBLEM CHALLENGES

Dwight Waldo steadfastly believed in the close relationship between administrative practices and the societal context in which those methods prevailed. One of the most significant aspects of what might be called the modern ecology of public administration is the progression of a demographic bulge that Peter Peterson has characterized as "the Gray Dawn."[24] These trends are real, worrisome, and offer both challenges to and constraints on public administrators in the United States as they try to cope with them in domestic and international settings.

Demographers estimate that by 2020 adults over age sixty-five will comprise a larger proportion of the world's population than children under age five.[25] This so-called generational crossover stems from a confluence of positive developments. These include a reduction in population growth, longer life spans, and a narrowing of the longevity gap between the developed and developing worlds. Thus, demographers project that countries in the *developed* world will experience an unprecedented growth in their elderly populations and an unparalleled decline in the number of their youth. Today, 20 percent of Italy's population is over age sixty-five; Japan hit that mark in 2005, as will Germany in 2006. They will be followed by Britain and France in 2016, and the United States and Canada in 2021 and 2023, respectively. In contrast, many nations in the *developing* world will experience the opposite trend: a youth boom.[26]

As is typical of wicked policy problems, however, this otherwise positive news brings myriad challenges in its wake. For example, those nations identified as graying presently face $35 trillion in unfunded pension liabilities, with the United States alone saddled with $10 trillion in unfunded liability for old-age Medicare health benefits. Standard & Poor's, the credit rating agency, says that if fiscal trends continue, the cost of programs for aging populations will fuel downgrades in the borrowing instruments of France, the United States, Germany, and the United Kingdom from investment grade to the speculative, or junk bond, category. This could happen in France by the early 2020s, the United States and Germany before 2030, and the United Kingdom before 2035. Each is presently in the top Triple A category, ensuring they can borrow at low rates.[27]

Likewise, U.S. Pentagon and State Department planners routinely worry about disruptive "youth bulges" in the world's urban centers, with demographers expecting these populations to rise from 1 billion in 1985 to 4 billion by 2025. Meanwhile, health professionals already are witnessing the rise of chronic diseases associated with older populations (e.g., obesity, diabetes, cardiovascular diseases, hypertension, and cancer). Indeed, the World Health Organization calculates that death rates from noncommunicable diseases have overtaken those from communicable diseases (infectious and parasitic diseases) in all parts of the world except Africa. Meanwhile, death rates from noncommunicable diseases among middle-aged workers (those in so-called prime labor force ages) are seven times higher in developing nations than in the developed world. Lost in the process are the most productive economic years of these citizens, which further promotes poverty and diminishes the tax revenues needed for capital investments in health systems and research.

A second set of wicked problems facing public administrationists involves global security. Two brief examples are illustrative: food security and terrorism. Demographers expect the world's population to soar to 8 billion persons by 2025 and to 9.3 billion by 2050, before leveling off in the late twenty-first century. This poses a significant conundrum for the developing world, as well as for food donors such as the United States and Europe in the developed world. While agricultural yields must soar to meet these demographic pressures, arable land, agricultural labor, and water supplies are diminishing. Predicted by 2020 is an increasingly large population of wealthy, urban consumers combining with 2 billion new poor citizens worldwide to demand 40 percent more food than currently produced.

As demand grows, so will the side effects of increased supply. Recent research suggests that meeting projected food needs with conventional production methods (e.g., heavy pesticide use) will triple the rate of environmentally noxious nitrogen and phosphorous dumped into terrestrial ecosystems. Some scientists also argue that meeting demand in these ways could require the conversion to farming of natural ecosystems covering an area larger than the size of the United States. Thus, the environmental consequences of harvesting these lands would rival the effect that greenhouse gases currently produce on the global ecosystem.[28]

A second conundrum emerges with terrorist threats. Even before the September 11, 2001, terrorist attacks on the World Trade Center and the Pentagon, U.S. defense intellectuals were discussing the "new threat paradigm" (NTP) facing national security planners. Biological, chemical, and radiological attacks and other weapons of mass destruction, financed by rogue nations and delivered by terrorists, became the most likely war-fighting scenarios in the twenty-first century.[29] Moreover, in the wake of this so-called asymmetrical warfare, defense planners expected theatres of battle to shift to volatile and perilous urban areas as the developing world's poverty-stricken, underemployed, and youth-dominated urban populations increase. Becoming reality all too soon in places such as Baghdad, Gaza, Karachi, Mogadishu, and Tuzla, these scenarios require fundamental and difficult shifts in U.S. strategic, operational, and tactical doctrine.[30]

A third global security challenge facing public administration arises from economic activities that threaten ecosystem integrity. The ecological systems on which societies depend (e.g., clean air and water) are being damaged as a result of large-scale transformations of the Earth's landscapes.[31] Carbon emissions from human activities are contributing to global warming. Because of agricultural runoff from factory farms, the amount of fixed nitrogen in global ecosystems has doubled since 1992, leaving among other impacts approximately fifty "dead zones" of algae blooms that have stifled other life forms. Humanity's consumption of freshwater is now approaching 50 percent of available supplies, with agriculture accounting for nearly 70 percent of consumption. Habitat degradation from activities such as logging, farming, dam building, and urban growth is resulting in a loss of biodiversity. Finally, two-thirds of the world's fisheries are categorized as depleted, overexploited, or fully exploited. Such events energize national and international bodies and NGOs to pressure governments for redress. Helping determine how far, fast, and equitably this occurs begs the acumen of public administrators worldwide.[32]

In Dwight Waldo's day, challenges like these called for "complete public administrators" possessing an awareness of the relationship between government and basic economic and social forces and an appreciation for the power of government to meet basic human needs.[33] No less can be expected today if the collective puzzlement on behalf of society that these problems require is to proceed profitably. But as the next three sections illustrate, doing so requires that public administrators have the will, wherewithal, and flexibility to *reconceptualize* purpose, *reconnect* with stakeholders, and *redefine* administrative rationality in the twenty-first century.

RECONCEPTUALIZING PURPOSE

For Waldo, a sound and principled sense of purpose was crucial for public administrators. The wicked problem challenges just discussed, however, require agencies with the institutional capacity to reconceptualize their purposes, many of which were encoded in the DNA of Waldo's administrative state. Moreover, doing so requires skills going well beyond knowledge of the management techniques that animated the classic administrative state. Global aging, for example, creates the pressures noted earlier to reconceptualize the long-standing focus of health organizations on eliminating communicable diseases.

Such a reconceptualization, however, will not be easy. Presently, for example, two-thirds of all U.S. foreign assistance for health care programs in the developing world is targeted for children's diseases and population control. Moreover, the political economy surrounding those programs is formidable, resilient, and ill disposed toward change. As Susan Raymond notes, targeting "huge resources on narrow problems over long periods of time has created both tunnel vision and significant vested interests in [children's] problems among those who disburse the funds and those who win the contracts to implement the programs."[34] In spite of such interests, however, public officials addressing the health care needs of "citizens as individuals" will be hard pressed to avoid reconceptualizing purpose.

The trends noted earlier regarding global security also suggest a need to reconceptualize purpose. Moreover, by necessity, such a reconceptualization needs to contain a sense of moral imperative and democratic administration. The issue of food security is illustrative. For a variety of public health, ideological, cultural, technoscientific, and economic reasons, the "precautionary principle" is now routinely applied to genetic engineering research, testing, and development.[35] Turning traditional regulatory logic on its head, the precautionary principle shifts the burden of proof away from opponents of biotechnology to prove that the harms they allege will occur. Rather, proponents of biotechnology must prove that speculative harms will not occur.

The application of this principle has had profound implications for research and commercialization of genetically modified foods. Centered in Europe in the wake of food regulation scandals such as the spread of "mad cow disease," and disseminated globally by international NGOs such as Greenpeace, opposition to genetically modified foods based on the precautionary principle prompted the European Union (EU) to enact in 1998 a de facto five-year moratorium on new food approvals. Then, in 2003, officials within the EU adopted a rigorous regulatory regime predicated on the precautionary principle.

As Robert Paarlberg argues, the U.S. position in favor of genetically modified foods has not been helped by its failure to sign international agreements such as the Convention on Biological Diversity.[36] Rather than sitting as a negotiator able to help shape the Cartagena Protocols on Biosafety, for instance, the United States participated only in an "observer" status. In related developments, U.S. agricultural assistance to developing nations fell by 50 percent between 1992 and 1999, while European contributions to international organizations now double those of the United States.

The results were predictable. European nations ensconced the precautionary principle in international biosafety regimes such as the Cartagena Protocols. NGO opponents of genetically modified foods also began pressing developing nations to adopt a European-style regulatory regime predicated on the precautionary principle. Simultaneously, funding from the Global Environmental Facility (GEF) helped recipient nations build regulatory systems incorporating the precautionary principle.[37] Consequently, administrators within U.S. regulatory and trade agencies (e.g., the Environmental Protection Agency [EPA], Department of Agriculture, the Food and Drug Administration [FDA], and the Commerce Department) face pressures to reconceptualize their approach in light of the precautionary principle. However, they cannot do so by risking their ability to explore biotechnological discoveries that might yet alleviate food security challenges worldwide.

By the same token, terrorist attacks on the United States, its assets, and allies led the Bush administration to declare the nation's cold war policy of containment anachronistic. With the advent of asymmetrical warfare, the Bush administration argued, a doctrine of preemptive military strikes was imperative. This, in turn, required a reconceptualization of military doctrine, force sizing, and training. Moreover, it came atop an effort in the 1990s to transform the military into a faster, more mobile, stealthier, and more lethal force to meet the NTP of the post–cold war era.[38]

In a related issue, the global threat of terrorism required new approaches toward international cooperation. Such cooperation is required to interdict terrorist weapons and plans, the drug sales from rogue states that fund terrorists, the international money transfers among cells that finance terrorist activities, and the movements of terrorists themselves. As Jonathan Stevenson points out, "America's security is organically linked to Europe's vulnerability to infiltration by terrorists."[39] Meanwhile, at home, public administrators are challenged to balance civil liberties with security needs.

The wicked policy problems associated with global environmental threats also have prompted some to advocate a reconceptualization of U.S. foreign assistance programs. They argue that a primary principle informing these programs should be a "triple bottom line" of economic, social, and environmental values that promotes sustainable development.[40] But sustainable development is a controversial concept, open to various interpretations, and readily reframed in debates as a redistributive policy that merely shifts money from wealthy nations to poorer ones.[41]

The United Nations Educational, Scientific, and Cultural Organization, for example, defines sustainable development as the imperative for every generation to leave air, water, and soil resources "as pure and as unpolluted as when [they] came on earth."[42] Others, such as economist Robert Solow, find leaving the world as each generation finds it unwise. Why should one generation close off the option to a future generation to be better off, just because that potential growth requires resource depletion? Still others, such as Dan Esty, argue that sustainable development is merely a buzzword that "slides over the difficult tradeoffs between environment and development in the real world."[43] Whichever view prevails, however, Waldo's philosophers of administration have a vital role to play in informing these debates and in reconceptualizing the purpose of government.

RECONNECTING WITH STAKEHOLDERS

For Waldo, effective administrative leadership required an ability to connect with the persons affected by administrative action. If anything, the need for such connections has grown more critical in the twenty-first century. In terms of global aging, for example, the need to connect administrators with citizens and stakeholders is evident in the area of corporate pharmaceutical development. Analysis reveals a decidedly market-driven disconnect between medicinal supply and health needs in developing nations.[44]

In the seventeen poorest nations in the world, for example, less than ten dollars per person was spent in 1998 on all health care, including pharmaceuticals. Indeed, less than 2 percent of spending for drugs dealing with cardiovascular disease occurred in six nations (China, Egypt, India, Indonesia, Pakistan, and the Philippines), while less than 1 percent (only 8 of 1,233) of drugs licensed worldwide between 1975 and 1997 were developed for tropical diseases. The irony is that while these nations are financially poor, many are biologically rich and perhaps house tomorrow's miracle drugs for these and other diseases. Thus, administrators must also reconnect with citizens in developing nations who fear the "bioprospecting" of their ecosystems without fair compensation.

Similarly illustrative of the normative and pragmatic need to reconnect with stakeholders is the set of wicked problems associated with global security. Much of the homeland security program under way in the United States (as well as the protection of civil liberties) depends on citizens spotting and reporting suspicious behavior in their neighborhoods, workplaces, and travels. Protecting U.S. water supplies, foiling terrorist attacks on power and chemical plants, and avoiding thefts of hazardous materials during transport also require the vigilance and cooperation of private actors. Meanwhile, training troops for asymmetric warfare has involuntarily "reconnected" the military with citizens affected by those exercises.[45] Required training maneuvers create environmental detritus that falls squarely within the regulatory

purview of statutes such as the U.S. Endangered Species Act, the Clean
Air Act, the Clean Water Act, the Safe Drinking Water Act, and the
Marine Mammals Protection Act. These challenges mount as weapons
with greater maneuverability, speed, and range typically are louder, require more space for maneuvering, and emit more pollutants. The Pentagon thus faces a burgeoning coalition of aggrieved "neighbors" that
routinely challenge military operations in court.

Wicked food security problems also cry out for public administrators who can reconnect with citizens and stakeholders. As Jack Hollander notes, 60 percent of tropical forest losses worldwide are related
directly to the ecologically harmful activities of impoverished small-
scale subsistence farmers. Because of their economic situation, these
farmers cultivate "erosion-prone hillsides, semiarid areas where soil
degradation is rapid, and cleared tropical forests where crop yields can
drop sharply after just a few years."[46] Finding ways to make these individuals act in more ecologically friendly ways is a major development
challenge for public administrators worldwide. Likewise, effective environmental and natural resources management often depends on the
joining of technical competence found in administrative agencies with
the promotion of deliberative democracy. Indeed, reconnecting with
stakeholders is the predicate for such initiatives as regulatory negotia-
tions, environmental dispute resolution, effective risk communication,
and cooperative rangeland conservation agreements for critical habitat
preservation.

Finally, regardless of the deliberative model used, environmental
justice in the governmental realm requires administrators to include
those previously marginalized in decision making. By virtue of their
respect for individual rights and equal protection, environmental regu-
lators are obliged to redress inequalities in the health benefits and burdens inflicted by polluters on racially, ethnically, and economically
diverse citizens. Absent these efforts, public administrators may routinely find themselves in court. Nor is environmental justice advanced
without considering the well-being of future generations.

REDEFINING ADMINISTRATIVE RATIONALITY

To achieve his vision of democratic administration, Waldo understood
that public administrators needed to exhibit skills that went beyond
those conventionally possessed by business managers. In his mind,
public administrators had to develop what Paul Appleby called "an ingrained disposition to put the public interest first and, thus, to recog-

nize the great, essential, and pervasive difference that distinguishes public administration from the management of private enterprise."[47] But, as each of the three sets of challenges discussed in this chapter illustrates, today's wicked policy problems typically exceed the jurisdiction and expertise of single agencies. They also require partnering with private and nonprofit organizations, as well as flexibility and adaptability as collective puzzlement unfolds. As such, prior conceptualizations of what constitutes administrative rationality must be rethought. Moreover, this must happen not only within public agencies but also among their partners in the neoadministrative state.

Again, Thorsten Benner and his colleagues describe best why this rethinking of administrative rationality is necessary in the twenty-first century:

> States, international organizations, companies, and NGOs now find themselves on the same playing field—and are gradually recognizing their interdependence in shaping the environment in which they operate. New cross-sectoral public policy networks are responding to that interdependence to confront issues that no single sector, public or private, could successfully tackle alone. . . . Unlike traditional hierarchical organizations, these networks are evolutionary in character and flexible in structure. They bring together disparate groups with oftentimes considerably varying perspectives, combining knowledge from different sources in new ways to result in new knowledge.[48]

Within this context, administrators are needed who are skilled "catalysts" building, nurturing, informing, and brokering multisided bargaining processes. This, in turn, requires a rethinking of administrative rationality (by legislators and administrators alike), a rethinking that values and rewards a constant commitment to "learning what to prefer," resetting priorities in that light, and shifting resources accordingly.[49]

Rethinking administrative rationality also means reducing the historical wariness within public agencies about cooperation with other organizations and stakeholders.[50] With wicked problems, constrained resources, and results-based accountability so prominent today, partnering with other organizations theoretically becomes more administratively rational for public administrators. In the process, however, accountability for actions can grow more difficult to discern in the "disarticulated" state.[51] All this, in turn, makes salient a major unresolved moral and ethical issue that neither minimal nor positive state proponents seem to know how to solve: how, using what tools, and under what conditions can public administrators make it administratively rational for private and civic sector actors to assume Waldo's "ingrained predisposition to put the public interest first"? Arguably, the opaqueness of networks raises the importance of complementing Herman Finer's "outer checks" with Carl Friedrich's "inner checks" of democratic administration.[52] Based on recent corporate scandals and on illustrations presented in previous chapters in this book, however, progress in this endeavor will not come easily.

VALUES, WICKED PROBLEMS, AND THE NEOADMINISTRATIVE STATE: A SUMMARY AND RX FOR ADMINISTRATIVE REFORM

This book began with a reaffirmation of Dwight Waldo's original insight that administrative issues ultimately are matters of political philosophy. Most salient are questions concerning "who should rule" and the distribution of power among governmental branches. The resolution of these issues depends considerably on the preferences of the people addressing them. Their preferences, in turn, are influenced by dominant views of the purposes of the state, the political and social climate, and instances of reforms leading to excesses that create new demands for reform.

During its history, the United States has moved through four distinct eras of administrative reform. The security and economic development needs of the new nation encouraged reforms that brought energy to the executive. The process of territorial expansion and extended suffrage prompted more decentralized methods of administration, including patronage. The demands of industrialization produced the classic administrative state, which in turn is giving way to market and networked (i.e., neoassociationalist) arrangements, partially in reaction to bureaucratic shortcomings.

As the three sets of wicked problems discussed in this chapter illustrate, the evolution of the neoadministrative state is not fully complete as yet. It will continue to evolve, made necessary yet challenged by wicked policy problems and the inherent deficiencies of a hollow state. As noted, however, many of the wicked problems confronted by public officials in the neoadministrative state require a high level of discretion exercised by public, private, and nonprofit actors. As a consequence, what Waldo propounded for the *administrative state* bears restating today for the *neoadministrative state*. To maintain popular and legislative support, those conducting the public's business must be perceived as committed to and capable of attaining efficiency, but within the broader context of democratic values that culturally diverse citizens cherish.

Yet the contemporary D[5] agenda that informs the neoadministrative state slights Waldo's advice. In particular, minimal state reformers marginalize the importance of building the capacity of public agencies, of ensuring transparency in all institutions, and of nurturing cultural sensitivity in ethnically diverse nations and in a globalized world. The needed attention given chronic diseases that global aging heralds, for example, requires large-scale capital investments in diagnostic, treatment, and monitoring services.[53] Nor does anyone overestimate the need for federal aid to develop the capacity of state and local "first responders" to perform vital homeland security tasks.

Likewise, not only do the people who regulate environmental and natural resources activities, as well as the institutions they regulate, have to get the science right. They also must ensure that citizens *believe* they do. Establishing transparency while simultaneously considering the scientific, socioeconomic, cultural, and ethical consequences of proposed actions is hard to do. But as recent scholarship on attitudes toward the acceptance of genetically modified foods in the EU reveals, perceptions of the technique's morality and trust in government's capacity to protect citizens from harm were the two most powerful predictors of citizens' support for these foods.[54] Thus, the more difficulty that public officials encounter in explaining the complex, competing, and confusing claims surrounding wicked policy problems, the more important transparency and credibility become for otherwise policy-challenged, skeptical, and litigious stakeholders.

Cultural sensitivity is yet another factor affecting the ability of administrative officials to help create effective solutions to wicked policy problems in the neoadministrative state. Slighted in Waldo's classic, cultural sensitivity means attentiveness to the cultural prisms through which people perceive risk, economic development, security, good health, and corporate actions. Domestically, for example, administrators in both the public and private sectors encounter the cultural prisms through which low-income and minority citizens view economic development, the war on terror, and environmental protection. Worldwide, a large collection of politically savvy, vocal, and internationally networked citizens perceives as threatening their livelihoods and cultures a host of factors that most Americans take for granted. These include globalization, capitalism, economic and scientific development, and Western models of scientific discovery. Respect for cultural diversity is not just a politically correct value in the twenty-first century, it is an attribute that directly affects how well governmental officials can address the era's most challenging wicked problems.

Failure to address these three components of trust building may or may not eventually cause the downfall of the neoadministrative state. Still, proponents of the neoadministrative state do well to note the aforementioned fate of the associationalist movement of the 1920s. Like today's D⁵ reform movement, associationalism appeared at a time of fundamental socioeconomic transformation. With Herbert Hoover's book *American Individualism*, the literary "bible" of this movement, associationalists offered an administrative theory for reconciling America's individualist values with a sense of collective responsibility for others. Indeed, so prominent was this theory that the *New York Times* claimed that Hoover's book would join the Federalist Papers as a classic of American political philosophy.[55]

In envisioning the associative state, these "forgotten progressives" wanted federal agencies to encourage and assist community-based, self-help projects. In today's parlance, the federal government's role was one of building civic capital through education, encouragement, and assistance to citizens, businesses, and nonprofit organizations in a highly decentralized and fragmented state. Minimally resourced experts in the federal government would do this by serving as sources of information, coordination, and national guidance; they also would stay out of the actual production and distribution of services. Proponents of the associative state fervently believed that what today's complexity theorists call "self-emergent" organizations would arise to combat that era's problems. Properly educated associations of business, state and local governments, voluntary associations, and citizens would willingly assume social and economic responsibilities and recognize that their self-interests depended on cooperation.

Ultimately, however, the associationalist bubble burst, most ironically as Herbert Hoover prepared to assume the presidency. Absent federal government pressures to form associations, these presumably self-emergent partnerships floundered. Major industries refused to partner with one another, the trust necessary between business and labor began to wane amid a worsening economy and scandals, and associations quickly turned into oligopolies. Educating, empowering, and enabling cross-sectoral partnerships to develop on their own with minimal federal government intervention simply did not meet the challenges of Hoover's time. They are just as unlikely to do so in the twenty-first century. As such, those who promote the D⁵ agenda should beware. They may be putting their agenda decidedly at risk by ignoring the fate of the associationalist movement and by dismissing advice to embed efficiency within a broader "framework of consciously held values." That fate might surprise them, but it would not have surprised Dwight Waldo.

NOTES

1. Dwight Waldo, *The Administrative State: A Study of the Political Theory of American Public Administration,* 2nd ed. (New York: Holmes & Meier, 1984), 193–94.

2. Ibid., 97, 196.

3. See, for example, Horst J. W. Rittel and Melvin Webber, "Dilemmas in a General Theory of Planning," *Policy Sciences* 4 (1973): 155–69.

4. For an insightful discussion of the impact of international factors on public administration within nations, see Laurence J. O'Toole Jr. and Kenneth Hanf, "American Public Administration and Impacts of International Governance," *Public Administration Review* 62, Special Issue (September 2002): 158–67.

5. Thorsten Benner, Wolfgang H. Reinicke, and Jan Martin Witte, "Global Public Policy Networks: Lessons Learned and Challenges Ahead," *Brookings Review* (Spring 2003): 18–21.

6. As in the chapter on "Who Should Rule?" the term "administrative state" in this essay refers to a state managed by public administrators according to public administrative theories and principles.

7. Paul C. Light, *The True Size of Government* (Washington, DC: Brookings Institution, 1999); Robert F. Durant, "Whither the Neoadministrative State: Toward a Polity-Centered Theory of Administrative Reform," *Journal of Public Administration Research and Theory* 10, no. 1 (2000): 79–109; Donald F. Kettl, *The Transformation of Governance* (Baltimore: Johns Hopkins University Press, 2002).

8. Durant, "Whither the Neoadministrative State."

9. For a thorough discussion of the differences in philosophy and approach offered by new governance and new public management proponents, see Robert Wettenhall, "The Rhetoric and Reality of Public-Private Partnerships," *Public Organization Review* 3, no. 1 (2003): 77–107, 80.

10. For an excellent discussion of economism, see Robert C. Paehlke, *Democracy's Dilemma: Environment, Social Equity, and the Global Economy* (Cambridge, MA: MIT Press, 2003).

11. Joan Hoff Wilson, *Herbert Hoover: Forgotten Progressive* (Prospect Heights, IL: Waveland Press, 1992).

12. Waldo, *Administrative State,* 7, 9.

13. Herbert Croly, *The Promise of American Life* (New York: Macmillan, 1909).

14. Durant, "Whither the Neoadministrative State"; Light, *True Size of Government.*

15. Larry D. Terry, "Administrative Leadership, New-Managerialism, and the Public Management Movement," *Public Administration Review* 58, no. 3 (1998): 194.

16. An excellent resource on this literature is the collection in Jan Kooiman, ed., *Modern Governance: New Government-Society Interactions* (London: Sage, 1993).

17. Hugh Heclo, *Modern Social Politics in Britain and Sweden: From Relief to Income Maintenance* (New Haven, CT: Yale University Press, 1994), 305.

18. Charlotte Streck, "The Clean Development Mechanism: A Playing Field for New Partnerships," in *Proceedings of the 2001 Berlin Conference on the Human Dimensions of Global Environmental Change*, ed., Frank Biermann, Rainer Brohm, and Klaus Dingwerth (Potsdam: Potsdam Institute for Climate Impact Research, 2002), 266–73.

19. Ibid.

20. Joseph S. Nye Jr. and Robert O. Keohane, "Power and Interdependence in the Information Age," *Foreign Affairs* 77 (September/October 1998): 81–95.

21. Durant, "Whither the Neoadministrative State"; Kettl, *Transformation of Governance;* Light, *True Size of Government.*

22. Matthew Miller, *The 2% Solution: Fixing America's Problems in Ways Liberals and Conservatives Can Love* (New York: Public Affairs, 2003).

23. David S. Broder, "Stealthy Budget Cuts," *Washington Post,* February 27, 2005, B7.

24. Peter G. Peterson, "Gray Dawn: The Global Aging Crisis," *Foreign Affairs* 78, no. 1 (1999): 42–55.

25. See Susan Raymond, "Foreign Assistance in an Aging World," *Foreign Affairs* 82 (March/April 2003): 91–105.

26. Peterson, "Gray Dawn."

27. Paivi Munter, "US, Germany, France, UK Face Junk Debt Status," *The Financial Times,* March 20, 2005, http://news.ft.com/cms/s/3460ab64-9982-11d9-ae69-00000e2511c8.html (accessed March 21, 2005).

28. David Tillman, Kenneth G. Cassman, Pamela A. Matson, Rosamond Naylor, and Stephen Polasky, "Agricultural Sustainability and Intensive Production Practices," *Nature* 8 (August 2002): 671–77.

29. Jonathan B. Tucker, "Asymmetric Warfare," *Forum* (Summer 1999): 32–38, http://forum.ra.utk.edu/specialreport.html (accessed March 26, 2002).

30. Colonel Thomas X. Hammes, *The Sling and the Stone: On War in the 21st Century* (St. Paul, MN: Zenith Press, 2004).

31. Jane Lubchenco, "State of the Planet 2002: Science and Sustainability" (paper presented at the Earth Institute, Columbia University, May 13, 2002, www.earth.columbia.edu/sop2002/sopagenda.html [accessed July 10, 2002]).

32. For an excellent set of diverse perspectives on this issue, see Karen T. Litfin, ed., *The Greening of Sovereignty in World Politics* (Cambridge, MA: MIT Press, 1998).

33. Waldo, *Administrative State,* 97.

34. Raymond, "Foreign Assistance in an Aging World," 102.

35. For a summary of these issues and their consequences, see Robert F. Durant with Thanit Boodphetcharat, "The Precautionary Principle," in *Environmental Governance Reconsidered: Challenges, Choices, and Opportunities,* ed. Robert F. Durant, Daniel Fiorino, and Rosemary O'Leary (Cambridge, MA: MIT Press, 2004), 105–43.

36. This discussion borrows heavily from Robert L. Paarlberg, "Reinvigorating Genetically Modified Crops," *Issues in Science & Technology,* U.S. National Academy of Science (Spring 2003). Reprinted on List Serve of agbioreview@yahoo.com (accessed April 24, 2003).

37. The GEF is a funding mechanism established in 1991 in which business and civil societies work to implement international agreements on issues such biodiversity and global climate change.

38. See, for example, Robert F. Durant, "Whither Environmental Security in the Post-9/11 Era: Assessing the Legal, Organizational, and Policy Challenges," *Public Administration Review* 62 (September 2002): 115–23.

39. Jonathan Stevenson, "How Europe and America Defend Themselves," *Foreign Affairs* 82, no. 2 (2003): 75–90, 79. The argument in this section relies heavily on this article.

40. For a discussion of how this "triple bottom line" might be operationalized, see Paehlke, *Democracy's Dilemma.*

41. See, for example, Robert Paehlke, "Sustainability," in *Environmental Governance Reconsidered,* ed. Durant, Fiorino, and O'Leary, 35–67.

42. Vijay Vaitheeswaran, "Survey: The Global Environment," *The Economist* 4 (July 2002), www.economist.com/science/displayStory.cfm?storyid= 1199867 (accessed July 9, 2002).

43. Ibid.

44. This discussion relies heavily on statistics afforded in Jean Olson Lanjouw, "Opening Doors to Research: A New Global Patent Regime for Pharmaceuticals," *Brookings Review* (Spring 2003): 13–17.

45. See, for example, Durant, "Whither Environmental Security."

46. Jack M. Hollander, *The Real Environmental Crisis: Why Poverty, Not Affluence, Is the Environment's Number One Enemy* (Berkeley: University of California Press, 2003), 40.

47. Paul H. Appleby, *Big Democracy* (New York: Russell & Russell, 1945), 43.

48. Benner, Reinicke, and Witte, "Global Public Policy Networks," 18.

49. The concept of "learning what to prefer" is associated with perceptions of implementation as mutual adaptation, evolution, and hypothesis testing. See, for example, the essays in Jeffrey Pressman and Aaron Wildavsky, *Implementation* (Berkeley: University of California Press, 1984).

50. See James Q. Wilson, *Bureaucracy* (New York: Basic Books, 1991).

51. H. George Frederickson, "The Repositioning of American Public Administration," John Gaus Lecture, American Political Science Association Annual Meeting, Atlanta, Georgia, September 3, 1999.

52. Carl J. Friedrich, "Public Policy and the Nature of Administrative Responsibility," *Public Policy* (1940): 3–24; Herman Finer, "Administrative Responsibility in Democratic Government," *Public Administration Review* 1 (Summer 1941): 335–50.

53. Raymond, "Foreign Assistance in an Aging World," 103.

54. Robert F. Durant and Jerome S. Legge Jr., "'Wicked' Problems, Public Policy, and Administrative Theory: Lessons from the GM Food Regulatory Arena," *Administration & Society* (in press).

55. Wilson, *Herbert Hoover.*

I I

Conclusion:
Additional Notes on the Present Tendencies

HOWARD E. McCURDY
and DAVID H. ROSENBLOOM

Dwight Waldo was fond of posing administration issues in the form of dichotomies. In contemplating the future direction of the field, he frequently presented conflicting tendencies. Thus the locus of administrative power in the modern state, to cite one illustration, would be determined in part by the apparent conflict between centralization and decentralization.[1] The outcome would not be exactly centralization or decentralization, but some combination of the two. In this Hegelian notion, an abstract concept (thesis) encourages the development of a contradiction (antithesis), which produces pressures for a reconciliation (synthesis).[2]

Waldo did not anticipate that such reconciliations would be determined strictly on the basis of the administrative issues involved. Rather, he saw that the resolution of administrative concepts would be determined by broader forces in society. Those forces also took the form of conflicting tendencies. Thus a reconciliation of the advantages of centralization with the virtues of decentralization could be influenced by the synthesis emerging from social movements such as the competition between industrialization and postindustrialism.

Social movements constantly change. New syntheses emerge. From Waldo's point of view, the balance among various administrative practices changes as well, reflecting the impermanent nature of social movements as a whole. In this theory of organizational relativity, the particular administrative arrangements existing at any one time arise from the struggle between conflicting social movements. Waldo believed that those outcomes depended considerably on the preferences of the people engaged in the struggle. Administrative arrangements ultimately stood as an expression of values, he believed, and were temporary. Administrative arrangements, social movements, values and preferences—in Waldo's universe, they revolved around and influenced one another.

This final chapter summarizes the concluding comments from the two editions of Waldo's *Administrative State* and amplifies them with observations contained in the current book. The observations are summarized in the form of dichotomies, as Waldo liked to view them. Waldo believed that the direction of administrative thought would be determined by fluctuations taking place within many dichotomies. Out of respect for the constant state of change this would present, he titled his conclusion "Notes on the Present Tendencies." Many of the tendencies he observed in 1948 and 1984 still remain, presented here in contemporary terms.

THE NATURE OF PUBLIC ADMINISTRATION

Waldo wrote *The Administrative State* to create an antithesis to the dominant—and at that time, somewhat weakened—approach to public administration. He characterized public administration as a field of study dominated by "orthodox ideology," words carefully chosen to suggest the presence of both conventional perspectives and personal values. The prevailing ideology provided a resolution to conflicting tendencies of enormous significance. "At the heart of 'orthodox' ideology," he wrote, "is the postulate that true democracy and true efficiency are synonymous, or at least reconcilable."[3] True democracy represents the will of the people; true efficiency represents the selection of methods that are correct with respect to an unbiased standard, irrespective of what people desire.

The reconciliation of democracy and efficiency, from the orthodox point of view, required the resolution of other dichotomies. Orthodox theorists produced the politics-administration dichotomy and resolved it by stating that organizational work could be divided into decision and execution. Decision (or politics, in the case of government) remained an expression of values, allowing execution (or administration) to become a science. Orthodox theorists suggested that a value-free science of administration could discover universally applicable principles, empirically verifiable without reference to ethics or political philosophy, in all forms of administrative life, including governmental and business activity. This allowed the reconciliation of facts and values.

The emerging administrative practices were as applicable to business management as to public administration, permitting a reconciliation of business and government.

These were neat reconciliations, but ones that rapidly broke down in the presence of other dichotomies. No dichotomy was as damaging in this respect as the simultaneous desire to root public administration in science and the desire that it reflect common experience. The former led to objective analysis, the latter to pragmatism. At the time of the first edition, the orthodox approach was under attack from people who wanted to make public administration more scientific. Although it enjoyed considerable support, especially among practitioners of public affairs, the smug pragmatism embodied in the orthodox approach engendered "a considerable measure of doubt and even iconoclasm." Scientific approaches to public administration would exert great influence over the field, Waldo predicted. In 1948, he called them "the most important of the theoretical movements now influencing American administrative study." By 1984, he felt obliged to modify this statement.[4] The pursuit of science created its own dichotomies. Considerable doubt existed about the doctrine of efficiency, thought by orthodox theorists to provide an objective guide to the scientific search for administrative principles. Efforts to make public administration more scientific in the postorthodox period produced the facts-values dichotomy, which Waldo consistently disparaged as an unrealistic division.

Waldo hoped that the "disintegration of the old outlook" might produce "the synthesis of a new."[5] Waldo discounted the idea that political science, the field in which the study of public administration emerged in the early twentieth century, could provide much help in creating this synthesis. Lured by the same impulse sweeping public administration, political scientists had moved away from matters administrative into scientific studies of voting and public opinion. Political theorists, who might have shown some interest in the fact-versus-value issue, had in Waldo's view likewise abandoned what he called the Roman view of government (a concern for administrative affairs as part of the governance process), exhibiting instead the disinterest in administrative arrangements shown by Greek philosophers. Perhaps a new synthesis would emerge in the future, but for the upcoming decades it appeared that people studying public administration would need to find "some manner of institutional embodiment in other places."[6] Searching for the resolution of issues before them, people thinking about public administration would turn increasingly to social psychology, sociology, economics, and business administration, as well as traditional political concerns. Waldo concluded the pages of The Administrative State with the observation that "administrative thought must establish a working relationship with every major province in the realm of human learning" in order to be effective, a statement he reiterated in the second edition.[7]

THE PRESENT DICHOTOMIES

Waldo wrote *The Administrative State* during a period marked by particular administrative demands. The Western world was engaged in a period of extensive industrialization. As a consequence of its role in World War II, the United States had emerged as a military superpower with extensive military and foreign responsibilities. Governmental leaders in the United States had created a huge administrative apparatus, as a result of both the social welfare programs enacted during the Great Depression and the war effort. Waldo began *The Administrative State* by recounting what he termed "the material background" to American public administration: the expansion of governmental responsibilities, the closing of the frontier, the importance of business and the modern corporation, urbanization, the second phase of the Industrial Revolution, the advance of specialization, the Great Depression and the recent world war, and the constitutional system that framed governmental action.[8]

Waldo recounted these developments because he believed they motivated the dominant ideological framework supporting the study of administration. He followed his presentation on "the material background" with a discussion of "the ideological framework." The events of the early twentieth century, especially in America, had encouraged a number of ideological beliefs: faith in democracy and the mission of America to spread it, the concept of fundamental laws (such as the natural rights to life, liberty, and private property), a widespread acceptance of the inherent value of progress, faith in science as a means of discovery, and most important, the "gospel of efficiency."[9]

Both the material background and the ideological framework produced, in Waldo's view, a particular type of public administration. That version of public administration had been developing since the late nineteenth century within the movement for progressive reform, a political ideology with its own set of beliefs and values. Progressive reform encouraged scientific approaches to administrative practice, the establishment of a neutral civil service made up of specialists and experts, the rise of bureaucracy as the dominant form of governmental organization, and a widespread acceptance of economy and efficiency as the dominant motivating values of administration.

All this is recounted as a means of reinforcing Waldo's central idea, the reason he believed that the doctrines of public administration constituted a political philosophy. Administrative practices, thought to be universal by their promoters, were in Waldo's eyes the product of a particular set of material and ideological circumstances. In earlier times, he noted, the value of efficiency had been supplanted by other concerns. In the European Middle Ages, when churches dominated societal affairs, faith was far more important than efficiency. In the Age of Enlightenment, rationality prevailed. The "high development and wide acceptance" of efficiency, Waldo adroitly observed, was "due to the fact that ours has been, *par excellence,* a machine civilization."[10] Efficiency for administration was a machine concept, a means of measuring the loss of energy due to friction or drag.

Waldo revisited *The Administrative State* in 1984, thirty-six years after the first edition, and here it is revisited yet again. The material and ideological conditions affecting American public administration at the beginning of the twenty-first century are not the same as those that existed when Waldo wrote the first edition, and they have changed since the second edition as well. Consequently, many of the administrative beliefs that dominated mid-twentieth-century America have been replaced with new concerns.

The Administrative State and the Postadministrative State

The administrative state, as Waldo defined it, grew out of a particular set of circumstances associated with the Industrial Revolution. These included the rise of bureaucracy as a dominant form of organization and the growth of the governmental administrative establishment. None of these circumstances are permanent. As any student of administration knows, organizational features such as bureaucracy have both strengths and weaknesses and are subject to adjustment as the excessive features associated with their weaknesses prevail.

In his chapter on the transformation of the administrative state, Donald Kettl summarizes the material and ideological changes that have affected the conduct of government since the second edition of Waldo's book. The progressive belief in the ability of government to create positive social change has dimmed in favor of general skepticism about the capability of old-line bureaucracies to adjust to modern circumstances. Growing distrust has motivated an important shift in attitudes toward governmental administration. Progressive reformers believed in administration through government. Modern administrative reformers believe in administration outside of government. As

Kettl points out, this has affected both the tools that administrators wield and the strategies employed. Public officials have shied away from direct provision of services by civil servants to provision by contractors and moved away from public programs set up to directly influence national challenges in favor of economic incentives that encourage people to alter their behavior.

The indirect nature of government in the post–administrative state has had a profound effect on the prescriptions offered by reformers. Experts associated with the administrative science movement when Waldo wrote his book believed in reform through structural change. They reorganized administrative relationships, established civil service systems, and revised budgetary processes. Modern reformers have moved away from structural change, preferring instead the indirect advantages established through networks of public, for-profit, and nonprofit providers and the empowerment of managers. In such networks, issues of accountability arise more frequently than problems of efficiency. Reformers in the first half of the twentieth century who believed that efficiency would provide a universal administrative standard for all time have been replaced by people preoccupied with other concerns.

To Waldo, this shifting nature of public administration was perfectly natural. It was a consequence of alternations in the material and ideological background and the realization that American public administration ultimately constituted a political philosophy whose premises could never be frozen for all time.

Efficiency and Other Administrative Values

To orthodox administrative theorists, economy and efficiency defined the nature of administrative reform. "They have often been held to be the ultimate administrative values," Waldo observed in the next to last chapter of his book, "serving to unify and direct all inquiry."[11] Waldo attacked this premise, but was never sure how to replace efficiency.[12] How can one possibly endorse inefficiency, its antonym? Developments in the postindustrial state have helped to resolve this conundrum.

No dichotomy received more attention in Waldo's works than the one arising between the search for "facts" and the expression of "values." It dominated his discussion of economy and efficiency on the pages of The Administrative State. It produced a famous exchange with the administrative scientist Herbert A. Simon on the pages of the American Political Science Review.[13] Simon argued that facts could be

separated from values and studied scientifically, helping him to produce a theory of administrative decision making for which he received
the Nobel Prize.

Drawing heavily on his understanding of efficiency, Waldo took the
opposite point of view. To him, efficiency was not an absolute value
but rather a relative one, reshaping its meaning in response to shifting
preferences. "'Efficiency for what'?" was his common concern. Efficiency in his mind was always "measured in terms of other values."[14] A
particular administrative arrangement need not always produce the
same efficiency effect, as in a natural science experiment, because the
meaning of efficiency moved as new values appeared. (For his part, Simon also found the discussion of efficiency and administrative arrangements unacceptably vague, preferring to concentrate on other
concerns such as the quality of decisions in organizations.)

Governmental expectations during the latter stages of the Industrial
Revolution produced a demand for efficient bureaucracies. Yet other
values and purposes produced their own administrative requirements.
The rapid territorial and demographic expansion of the United States
during the nineteenth century elevated the desire for expanded suffrage and added representation, encouraging arrangements such as the
principle of rotation that from the standpoint of later reformers
seemed patently inefficient. As the authors of this book have endeav-
ored to show, pure efficiency conflicts with many values. These include transparency, accountability, individual rights, liberty, due
process, public participation, and constitutional principles such as the
separation of powers, equality, equity, distributive justice, trust, cultural sensitivity, and maintenance of governmental capacity.

Waldo understood that the relationship between administrative values and institutional arrangements was much more dynamic than
afforded by a simple "facts" and "values" dichotomy. Drawing on
Waldo's interest in dichotomies, McCurdy suggests that new values
and arrangements emerge from excesses and weaknesses inherent in
the forms dominant at any one time. This places administrative arrangements in a constant state of change, one in which the quest for efficiency provides an incomplete guide.

Positivism and Pragmatism

One of the most perplexing issues affecting public administration
concerns the choice of methods. Appropriate methodology is a continuing issue as yet unresolved, and the subject of an entire chapter in this
book. Waldo dealt with the issue in two chapters of *The Administra-*

tive State, one titled "The Criteria of Action" and the second treating the search for principles of administration.

Advocates of the orthodox ideology clearly aspired to the use of scientific methods. Devotion to scientific methods appears in the nomenclature of orthodoxy. Its advocates characterized their movements with terms such as "scientific management," "administrative science," and the "science of administration." Curiously, the principles that emerged from these movements possessed a distinctly unscientific flavor. As Waldo observed in his chapter on administrative principles and the scientific method, they drew more on the traditions of higher law and American pragmatism than empirical investigation. Higher laws such as moral codes are not derived through scientific study. Rather, they are revealed often through insight, experience, and common sense, methods of knowing quite compatible with the pragmatic doctrine that common people can discover truth by observing the practical consequences of their beliefs. As such, the "principles" of public administration resemble general codes of behavior more than the principles of natural science found in such fields as physics.

Critics of the principles, notably Herbert Simon, argued that their derivation suffered from methods not sufficiently scientific. As Waldo anticipated, publication of *The Administrative State* was followed by a period in which scientific methodology became even more pronounced in the study of administrative affairs. The behavioral revolution, with its strong positivistic bent, swept the social sciences. Later scholars used empirically derived economic principles and statistically based analysis to fathom public policies.

For all the emphasis placed upon scientific methods as a means of administrative verification, actual efforts at administrative reform remained distinctly pragmatic. Positivism is a philosophy of inquiry that excludes everything but the properties of knowable things. Administrative reforms, particularly those advanced in the late twentieth century under the "reinvention" heading, prescribed a number of actions such as privatization for which the effects were at best uncertain, and at worse unknowable. Waldo observed in the 1984 edition of *The Administrative State* that "logical positivism has become less fashionable," a trend not broken by present tendencies.[15]

Public administration as a field of study continues to waver between positivism and pragmatism. The emphasis at any one time seems to depend on personal preferences rather than outright superiority. Shifts in emphasis often occur in response to the weaknesses inherent in each approach. Positivism has been used to demolish beliefs rising out of common sense, and pragmatism has been used to advance doctrines that seem knowable on the basis of personal experience. Waldo hoped that people studying public administration would use both, allowing the nature of the material being studied to define the method of inquiry. He remained deeply suspicious of "all philosophies and methods that offered Truth," hoping that the search for knowledge would be guided by the quest rather than any particular doctrine.[16]

Separate Powers and Executive Control

"Generally speaking," Waldo observed in the chapter devoted to an analysis of the issue, "students of administration have been hostile to the tripartite separation of powers." Early reformers favored an executive-centered public administration. This was clearly a matter of political philosophy, traceable to the preferences of people more comfortable with unbroken lines of authority and unity in the executive. Waldo saw no reason to retract his observation in the second edition of his book and termed the intervening scholarship on the subject to be "comparatively unproductive."[17]

Recent tendencies have not favored a clear resolution of this issue. Administrative reforms in the "reinvention" mold clearly favor a reduced role for legislative oversight, with executive officials "empowered" to achieve public goals while exercising maximum discretion. As one of its effects, the modern trend toward privatization further weakened legislative and judicial oversight by lodging administrative responsibility in nongovernmental organizations not universally obliged to respect all of the procedures imposed on public employees.

Even as pragmatic reformers failed to pursue a balance of powers, practical events favored an increased judicial and legislative role in administration. Wielding their constitutional authority, judges and legislators intervened in administrative affairs with increasing frequency as the twentieth century progressed. Curiously, Waldo did not observe these trends as they occurred. The basis for U.S. legislative control of modern public administration began in 1946, as David Rosenbloom points out in his chapter on the subject. That was two years before Waldo published the first edition of his book and well before the subsequent revision.

In theory and practice, people involved in public administration remain much divided on the issue of separated powers versus executive control. Modern tendencies simultaneously favor both approaches to the oversight of public administration. The issue remains one of constitutional theory, reinforcing Waldo's overall thesis that the most important administrative issues ultimately resolve themselves into matters of political philosophy.

Expert and Outside Rule

"Any political philosophy necessarily must answer the question 'Who should rule?'" Waldo forcefully stated in the first edition of *The Administrative State*.[18] The answer offered by progressive reformers of administrative affairs was unequivocal. Experts should rule, or what Waldo later characterized in his revised remarks as professional civil servants. The preference for a politically neutral civil service staffed by experts or members of professions drove early administrative reform. It sought to replace the values of representativeness exemplified by the spoils system or alternative concepts such as governments led by able elites.

Belief in the virtues of a professional civil service was widespread among early reformers. It is hard to imagine an agent of reform advocating a system of administration staffed by civil servants not experts in their fields. Yet as Patricia Ingraham observes in her chapter on the subject, the most recent administrative reforms have not favored the power of professional civil servants. In fact, reformers have sought to reduce it. They have done so by attempts to export administrative responsibility for public programs to persons outside of the governmental sphere. This follows the reform philosophy favoring a system of administration in which public officials "steer" but do not "row."

Recent tendencies clearly add a new dimension to the old conflict over who should rule. Reformers in the orthodox tradition framed the issue as a matter of expert versus inexpert rule. Presented that way, it is hard for people to vote against professional expertise. While not denying the virtues of expertise, modern reformers insist that people outside the government are better positioned to innovate and act in the public interest than persons caught within the web of bureaucratic routine.

The people who created the permanent civil service sought to isolate public employees from the forces of the marketplace, through techniques such as job security. As the provision of public services moved into the marketplace, the nature of public employment changed. This has occurred in functions absolutely central to governmental responsibilities, such as national security, where military leaders compete in the marketplace for troops that go to war. Public services in the post–administrative state are provided by a broad mix of civil servants, private contractors, and employees of not-for-profit organizations. The result is a rethinking of the incentives necessary to motivate effective public service, mixing traditional appeals to the common good with incentives directed at personal and economic needs. John Cadigan's chapter titled "Competition for Human Capital" explores these trends.

Thick and Thin Governmental Institutions

Waldo wrote very little about the size of government in the first edition of *The Administrative State*. The United States had undergone a tremendous expansion of governmental girth during the first half of the twentieth century, guided by and helping to inspire the doctrines of public administration. Waldo simply repeated Pendleton Herring's observation that a modern democratic state seemed to require a "great administrative machine" and a "huge bureaucracy."[19] He found little reason to retract those comments thirty-six years later.

His comments on the size of government appeared in a chapter dealing broadly with "the good life." All political ideologies contain a vision of the world properly run. Public administration, which Waldo characterized as political philosophy, was no exception. People proclaiming the doctrines of administrative reform tended to favor planned societies, the mastery of nature, materialism, urbanism, and use of governmental resources to secure social purpose. In one of his most insightful observations, Waldo noted that the literature of American public administration—in spite of its clear abandonment of laissez-faire philosophy—did not envision the substitution of governmental bureaucracies for business enterprise. "There is not a hint of doctrinaire socialism in all the literature of public administration," he correctly observed, explaining in a footnote that he meant the American version.[20]

In many other parts of the world, administrative reform of the early variety became closely associated with state-run enterprise. Unlike the United States, where business firms and public agencies expanded their administrative apparatuses in tandem, government expansion in other countries supplanted business activities through techniques such as nationalization. The dominant thrust of American administrative reform contained no such impulse. "Far from thinking in terms of a conflict between government and business," Waldo observed with reference to early twentieth-century reformers, "they thought of their work as the extension of business to government."[21]

Herein, the influence of American administrative theory has been profound. Worldwide public administration theory owes much to

American thought. The theory of socialism and the social welfare state do not. In the conflict between the two, the American approach has prevailed. With few exceptions, state bureaucracies no longer supplant business enterprise. In fact, current administrative reforms worldwide favor business growth through techniques such as privatization.

To people schooled in traditional public administration, the triumph of American ideologies has reached the level of excess. The worldwide reaction to governmental largess threatens the balance between corporate growth and public administration. As Larry Terry explains in chapter 7, the dismantling of public administration could lead to a hollow state with thin administrative institutions and a loss of the capacity to govern. This could threaten what Waldo characterized as the "symbiotic relationship" between the administrative state and modern civilization. "By civilization is meant a comparatively dense population with one or more urban concentrations," he said. Such arrangements, he believed, led inexorably to a level of social complexity that required "the development of administration-bureaucracy."[22]

Business and Government

Through the circumstances of its development, Waldo explained, the United States became a preeminent "Business Civilization." By historical standards, the United States is an extremely wealthy nation. The source of that wealth is business activity taking place largely through corporations. This history, according to Waldo, intensely affected "our methods of administration and our literature of public administration."[23] Much of the content of public administration is businesslike, dealing with the processes utilized to make modern corporations run.

These circumstances have created a situation in which business leaders are well situated to influence the practice and philosophy of public administration. As a phenomenon, this has occurred worldwide, even in countries not possessing great wealth. Under the reform doctrines of the new public management, public officials are taught how to think and act like business entrepreneurs. An increasingly large number of public responsibilities are delivered through business firms and nonprofit organizations run along business lines. The administrative state, as Waldo described it, is in decline. The chapters by Larry Terry and Barbara Romzek explore the relationship between business approaches and public administration.

CONCLUSION

Waldo wrote *The Administrative State* to demonstrate that early doctrines of public administration consisted of more than universally applicable prescriptions about good management. The doctrines, he insisted, contained a political theory well rooted in the particular ideologies and cultures they served. The doctrines proffered answers to classical issues of political philosophy, such as the nature of the good life, the criteria for action, the proper separation of powers, and the question of who should rule.

This volume has sought to update Waldo's insights, particularly with reference to the latest round of administrative reforms—what is known generally as the new public management. Based on his experience with orthodox administrative ideology, Waldo understood that all new reforms contained political philosophies of their own. They prescribe more than good management, incorporating as well preferences about the purpose of civilized life and how it should be organized.

Waldo also recognized that no administrative philosophy could be separated from what he called the "material and ideological background" that it served. He spent much of *The Administrative State* discussing the setting from which American public administration emerged.

Many of the chapters in the current volume do the same. Chapter 10 in particular, written by Robert Durant, discusses the broad challenges likely to shape public administration in the twenty-first century. He is particularly concerned with what he terms "wicked" policy issues, much different in form than the activities that promoted the rise of the early administrative state a century ago. Durant and others fear that the doctrines of modern public administration, growing out of early orthodoxy and transformed by the new emphasis upon a weaker administrative state, will prove incompatible with the new material and ideological background.

Through his work, Waldo sought to demonstrate that administrative choices were ultimately philosophic preferences. The principles used to express those choices were not set at the moment of creation for all time like laws in the natural world. He was willing to go anywhere, to "every major province in the realm of human learning," to understand how those preferences arose and the manner in which administrative thought might meet "the demands of present world civilization."[24] He ended his book with that commitment, and there is no better way to close the present one.

NOTES

1. Dwight Waldo, *The Administrative State: A Study of the Political Theory of American Public Administration*, 2nd ed. (New York: Holmes & Meier, 1984), 128; see also Waldo, *The Enterprise of Public Administration* (Novato, CA: Chandler & Sharp, 1980), 139–42.

2. Frank Thilly and Ledger Wood, *A History of Philosophy* (New York: Henry Holt, 1951), 480–82.

3. Waldo, *Administrative State*, 199.

4. Ibid., liii–liv, 199, 201.

5. Ibid., liii–liv, 202.

6. Ibid., liv.

7. Ibid., 203.

8. Ibid., 7–14,

9. Ibid., 14–21.

10. Ibid., 19.

11. Ibid., 186.

12. At times, he contrasted efficiency with social equity—or the "equity state"—and organizational humanism. See, for example, Waldo, *Enterprise of Public Administration*, 41.

13. Dwight Waldo, "Development of Theory of Democratic Administration," *American Political Science Review* 46, no. 1 (1952): 81–103; Herbert Simon reply to Waldo and Waldo reply in *American Political Science Review* 46, no. 2 (1952): 494–96, 501–3.

14. Waldo, *Administrative State*, 193.

15. Ibid., xxxviii.

16. Ibid., xlix, 178.

17. Ibid., 104, xliii.

18. Ibid., 90.

19. Ibid., 71.

20. Ibid.

21. Ibid.

22. Ibid, xxiv.

23. Ibid., 9.

24. Ibid., 203.

Contributors

John Cadigan holds the position of assistant professor at American University. His research focuses on topics involving public choice, game theory, experimental methods, defense policy, and the analysis of electoral institutions. Cadigan's published works have appeared in the *Journal of Theoretical Politics, Public Choice, Economics of Governance, Topics in Economic Analysis and Policy, Review of Public Personnel Administration,* and the *Journal of Public Economic Theory.* He recently received the American University Department of Public Administration 2002 Excellence in Teaching Award.

Robert F. Durant is a professor in the Department of Public Administration at American University in Washington, D.C. His research focuses on executive branch politics, policy implementation, environmental policy, and administrative reform. He most recently published *Environmental Governance Reconsidered: Challenges, Choices, and Opportunities* (with Daniel J. Fiorino and Rosemary O'Leary). In 2003 he received the Charles H. Levine Award for excellence in research, teaching, and service to the public administration community. He has received several awards for his research, including the 1993 Gladys M. Kammerer Award from the American Political Science Association for the best book published on U.S. policy for *The Administrative Presidency Revisited: Public Lands, the BLM, and the Reagan Revolution.*

Patricia Ingraham is Distinguished Professor of Public Administration at the Maxwell School of Citizenship and Public Affairs, Syracuse University. Her research interests include public organizational change and reform, organizational capacity and accountability, and leadership in public organizations. The author or editor of eleven books, Ingraham's record includes *The Art of Governance: Analyzing Management and Administration; Governmental Performance: Why Management Matters;* and *The Foundation of Merit: Public*

217

Service in American Democracy. She is the recipient of numerous awards, including the 2001 Dwight Waldo Award, the 2004 John Gaus Award, and the 2005 Paul Van Riper Award for distinguished scholarship and service.

Donald F. Kettl is Stanley I. Sheerr Endowed Term Professor in the Social Sciences at the University of Pennsylvania, where he is director of the Fels Institute of Government and professor of political science. His research focuses broadly on issues of public management. In his current work, he examines efforts of state and local governments to strengthen homeland defense preparedness. Kettl has recently published *System under Stress: Homeland Security and American Politics; The Transformation of Governance: Public Administration for the 21st Century;* and *The Global Public Management Revolution,* second edition.

Howard E. McCurdy is professor of public administration and policy at American University. His teaching and research focus on public management, organization theory, public policy, and public financial management. His research has appeared in journals such as *Public Administration Review* and *Space Policy.* A specialist in the management of science policy, he has published six books on the American space program, including *Space and the American Imagination.* He is the recipient of the 2001 Distinguished Research Award from the American Society for Public Administration/National Association of Schools of Public Affairs and Administration and the 1999 Eugene M. Emme Astronautical Literature Award.

Norma M. Riccucci is professor of public administration at Rutgers University, Newark. She has published extensively in the areas of public management, affirmative action, human resources, and public sector labor relations. Her recent publications include *How Management Matters: Street-Level Bureaucrats and Welfare Reform* and *Managing Diversity in Public Sector Workforces.* She is the recipient of the American Society for Public Administration/National Association of Schools of Public Affairs and Administration 2002 Distinguished Research Award and is a Fellow in the National Academy of Public Administration.

Barbara S. Romzek is interim dean of the College of Liberal Arts and Sciences and professor of public administration at the University of Kansas. Romzek's research focuses on the implementation of public policy, particularly at the state and local levels, and the use of government contracting. Among her published books are *New Governance for Rural America: Creating Intergovernmental Partnerships* and *New Paradigms for Government: Issues for the Changing Public Service.* Romzek is a fellow of the National Academy of Public Administration and has received the William E. and Frederick C. Mosher Award from the American Society for Public Administration and the Kauffman Award from the American Political Science Association.

David H. Rosenbloom, distinguished professor at American University, focuses his scholarship on public administration and democratic constitutionalism. He joined the National Academy of Public Administration in 1986 and is the recipient of numerous awards, including the 2001 American Political Science Association John Gaus Award for Exemplary Scholarship in the Joint Tradition of Political Science and Public Administration and the 1999 American Society for Public Administration Dwight Waldo Award for Outstanding Contributions to the Literature and Leadership of Public Administration. His book, *Building a Legislative-Centered Public Administration: Congress and the Administrative State, 1946-1999*, received the National Academy of Public Administration's 2001 Louis Brownlow Book Award.

Larry D. Terry is vice president for business affairs and professor of public administration at the University of Texas at Dallas. He is a fellow of the National Academy of Public Administration and the recipient of the 1996–97 William E. and Frederick C. Mosher Award from the American Society for Public Administration. Terry is widely known for his book *The Leadership of Public Bureaucracies: The Administrator as Conservator* and is currently completing a book titled *Administrative Interpretation of Law: How Public Administrators Create Meaning*. He served as editor-in-chief of *Public Administration Review*, 2000–2005.

Index

The letter t following a page number denotes a table. The letter n following a page number denotes an endnote.